X-O MANOWAR

BY THE
SWORD

ROBERT VENDITTI | CARY NORD | STEFANO GAUDIANO | MOOSE BAUMANN

CONTENTS

Collection Cover Art: David Aja

Assistant Editor: Josh Johns (#1-4)
Associate Editor: Jody LeHeup (#2-4)
Editor: Warren Simons

X-O Manowar®: By the Sword. Published by Valiant Entertainment
LLC. Office of Publication: 424 West 33rd Street, New York, NY
10001. Compilation copyright ©2012 Valiant Entertainment LLC.
All rights reserved. Contains materials originally published in
single magazine form as X-O Manowar #1-4. Copyright ©2012
Valiant Entertainment LLC. All rights reserved. All characters, their
distinctive likeness and related indicia featured in this publication
are trademarks of Valiant Entertainment LLC. The stories,
characters, and incidents featured in this publication are entirely
fictional. Valiant Entertainment does not read or accept unsolicited
submissions of ideas, stories, or artwork. Printed in the U.S.A.
Fourth Printing.
ISBN: 9780979640940.

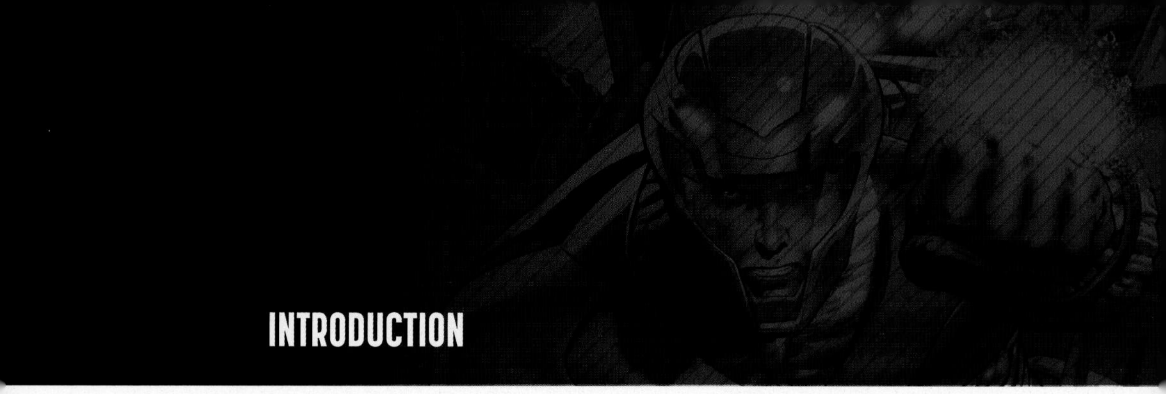

INTRODUCTION

What you are holding in your hands is a true piece of history.

The relaunch of X-O MANOWAR didn't just signal the return of Valiant Comics; it signaled the return of one of the all-time greatest comic book characters ever realized. A generation ago, Valiant Comics captured the hearts and minds of comic readers worldwide, and with good reason. Valiant Comics has always prided itself on putting storytelling above all else – and has always delivered the goods. This was a company that, originally, represented the future of what comics could be. And, finally, with Robert Venditti and Cary Nord's all-new take on Valiant's flagship hero, X-O Manowar, the future has arrived.

As you begin reading the tale related on the next few pages, you might find yourself becoming any one of a few things. Immersed. Amazed. Astounded. Why, you may ask, had no one done X-O Manowar like this before? Why not sooner? Behind the scenes, a great many men and women have worked to make this book a reality, but the true thanks belongs to a character that should never have disappeared from the printed page.

In just the first few issues of their new series, Rob and Cary pinpointed exactly what makes X-O Manowar such a resonant and beloved hero. In their hands, he is not just a barbarian in a suit of armor. Here, the most primitive of men wields the universe's most powerful weapon. It's a concept rooted in the collision of many great genres – superheroes, sci-fi, historical fiction, action-adventure – with, most importantly, many big ideas. Here, in X-O MANOWAR, we are introduced to a character that can lay the foundation for an entire universe to follow.

That single fact alone is a testament to just how strong a character Jim Shooter, Bob Layton, Barry Windsor-Smith, and Jon Hartz forged when they dreamed Aric of Dacia into existence two decades ago. And now, Robert and Cary have expanded the mythos they created and taken it to previously unimaginable heights. Here, you will begin a journey unlike any you have taken before. This journey is not Aric's alone, but one that belongs to all of us who join him. It is in these very pages that a bold, new universe begins; and X-O Manowar – a man out of time, trapped in a strange new world – is our guide to a place where warring alien factions, telekinetic teenagers, and immortal adventurers all walk among us. Here, history is rewritten in a new and exciting way. Count yourself lucky that now you can join us from the very first page.

Because X-O MANOWAR is more than just a comic book. X-O MANOWAR is more than just another story. X-O MANOWAR is an epic.

And sometimes history is worth waiting for.

Ryan McLelland
Writer/entertainment reporter who has written for *Ain't It Cool News*, *Newsarama*, *Latino Review*, and *Comic Shop News*.

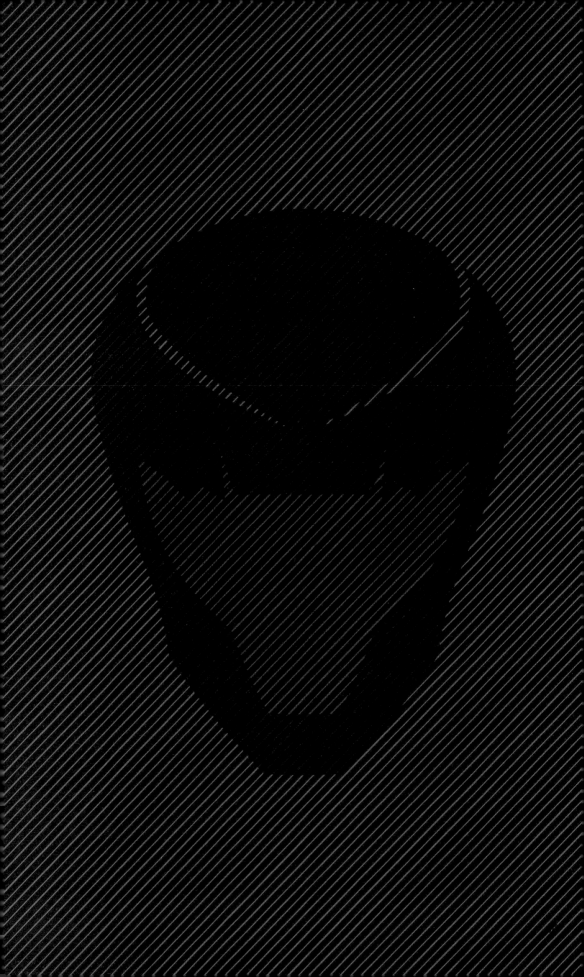

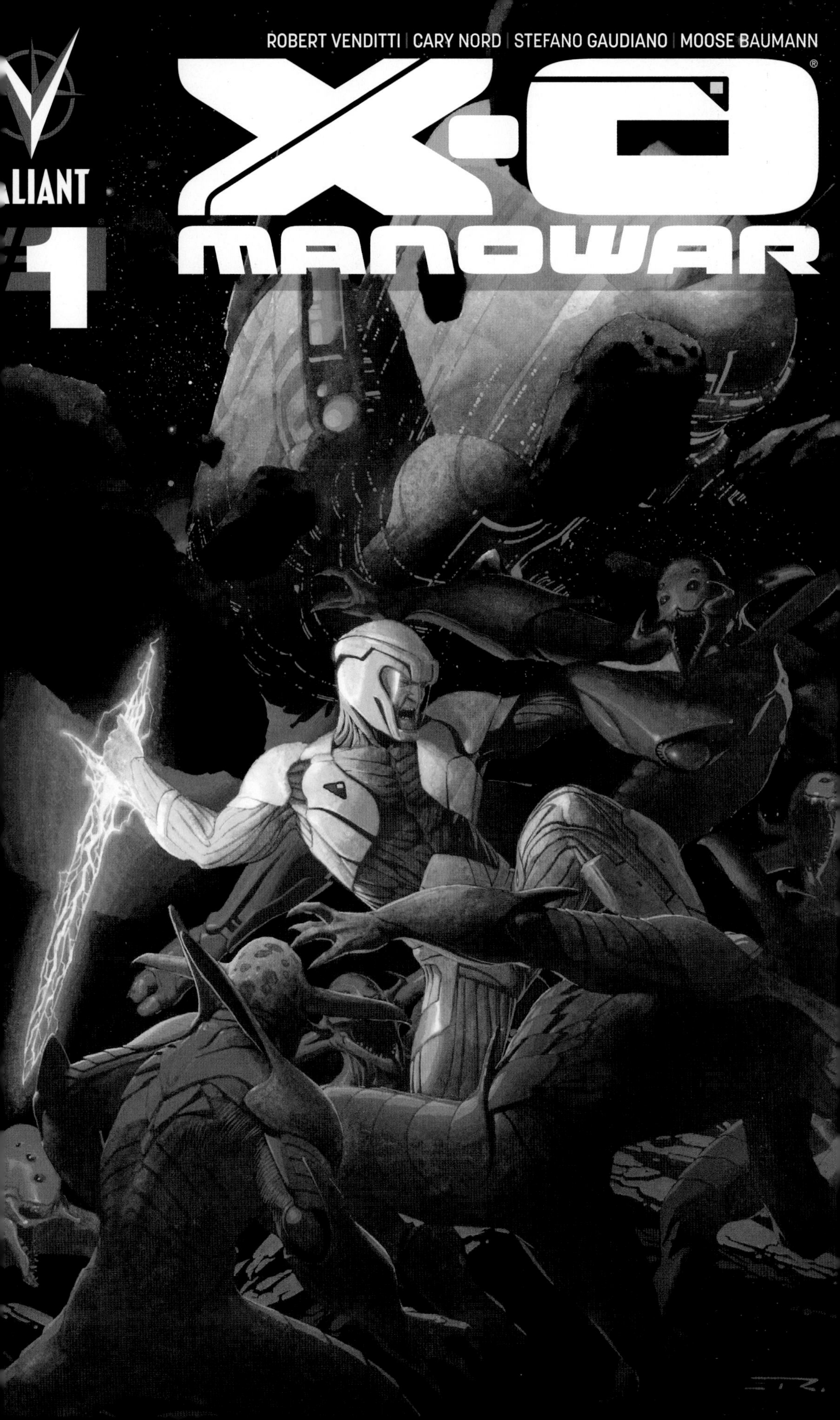
ROBERT VENDITTI | CARY NORD | STEFANO GAUDIANO | MOOSE BAUMANN
X-O MANOWAR
#1

EXTENT OF ROMAN EMPIRE **400 AD**

WELCOME TO X-O MANOWAR #1. WELCOME TO 402 AD.

TIMELINE

375 AD Aric of Dacia is born

376 AD The Huns invade Dacia. The Visigoths migrate south.

395 AD Alaric I becomes King of the Visigoths

▼ YOU ARE HERE

402 AD *The Battle of Pollentia:* The Visigoths vs The Romans. King Alaric I vs Flavius Stilicho

370 AD — 380 AD — 390 AD — 400 AD — 410 AD

VISIGOTHS

Traditionally nomadic, Visigoths lived in unwalled farming settlements positioned along major rivers on the Roman border.

Visigoth Wealth
Measured by the number of cattle owned.

=$$$

Visigoth Idiom
"Happiness is a good horse."

=:)

Horses were revered in Visigoth culture.
Visigoth warriors were often buried with the bodies of their horses.

Visigoth Warrior and Arms
1 Sahs (Knife)
2 Agja (Short Sword)
3 Gaizis (Wood Spear)
4 Skildus (Round Shield)

1
2
3
4

ROMANS

The most powerful ancient civilization on Earth, dominating Western Europe to Asia Minor. The sole superpower of the ancient world.

Roman Wealth
A wealthy man might own as many as 500 slaves.
An emperor might have more than 20,000.

=500 =20,000

Life Expectancy
Average Life Expectancy for Roman at Birth: 28 years old
Average Life Expectancy for Roman at Age 15: 52 years old

=28
=52

Roman Legionnaire and Arms
1 Pugio (Dagger)
2 Spatha (Long Sword)
3 Hasta (Thrusting Spear)
4 Plumbata (Throwing Dart)

1
2
3
4

Design: Rian Hughe

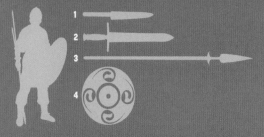

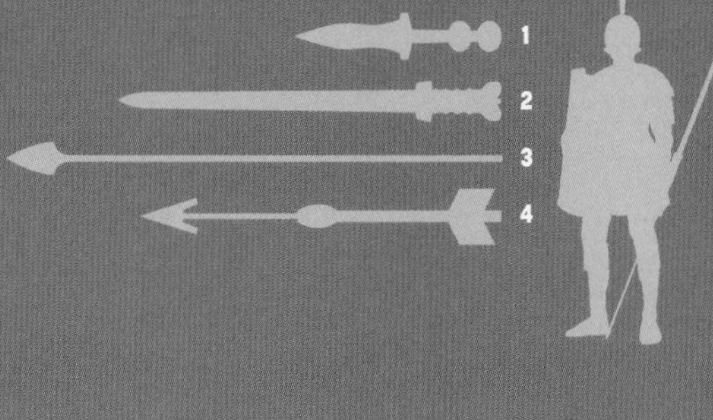

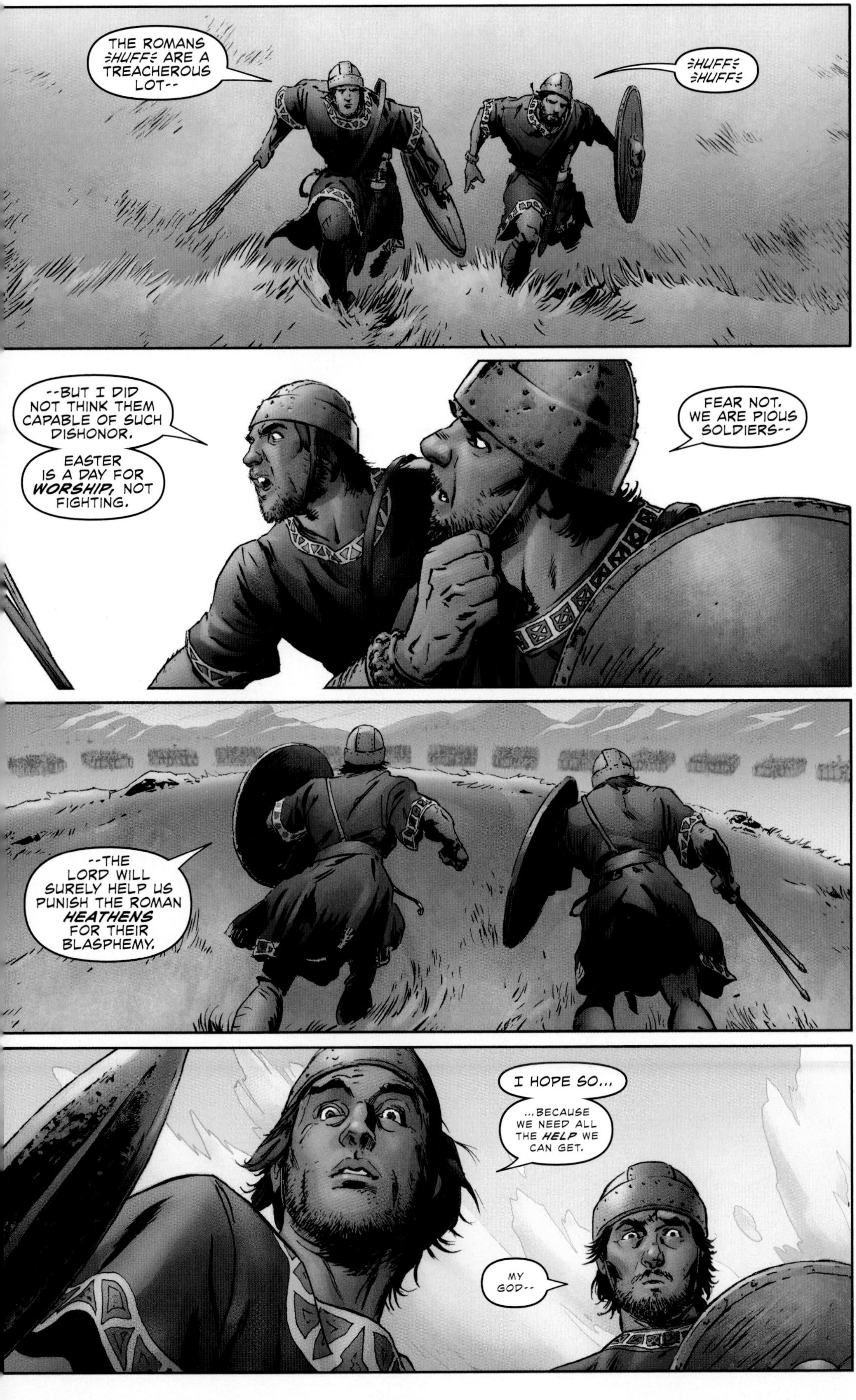
THE ROMANS *HUFF* ARE A TREACHEROUS LOT--
HUFF *HUFF*
--BUT I DID NOT THINK THEM CAPABLE OF SUCH DISHONOR.
EASTER IS A DAY FOR WORSHIP, NOT FIGHTING.
FEAR NOT. WE ARE PIOUS SOLDIERS--
--THE LORD WILL SURELY HELP US PUNISH THE ROMAN HEATHENS FOR THEIR BLASPHEMY.
I HOPE SO...
...BECAUSE WE NEED ALL THE HELP WE CAN GET.
MY GOD--

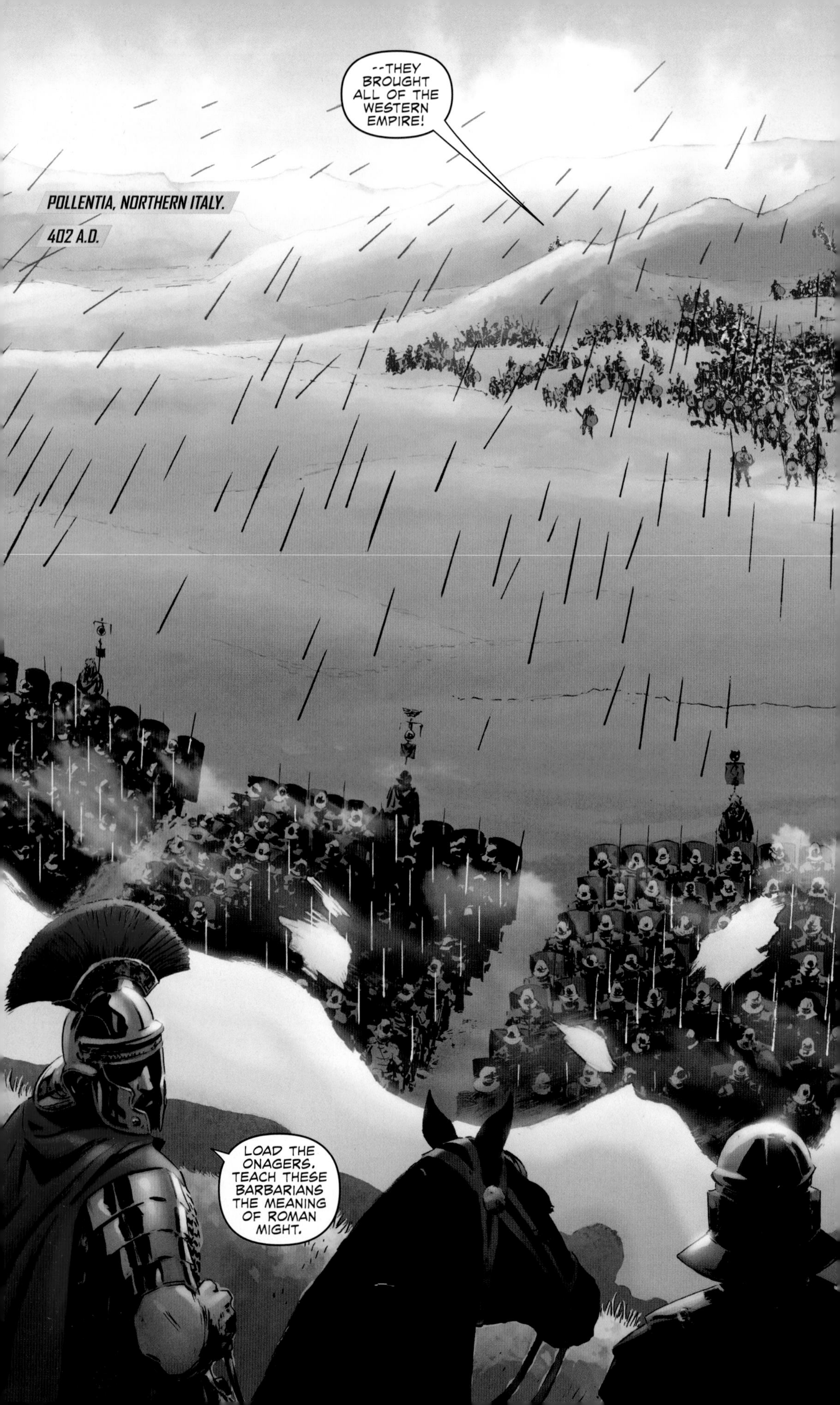
POLLENTIA, NORTHERN ITALY.
402 A.D.
--THEY BROUGHT ALL OF THE WESTERN EMPIRE!
LOAD THE ONAGERS. TEACH THESE BARBARIANS THE MEANING OF ROMAN MIGHT.

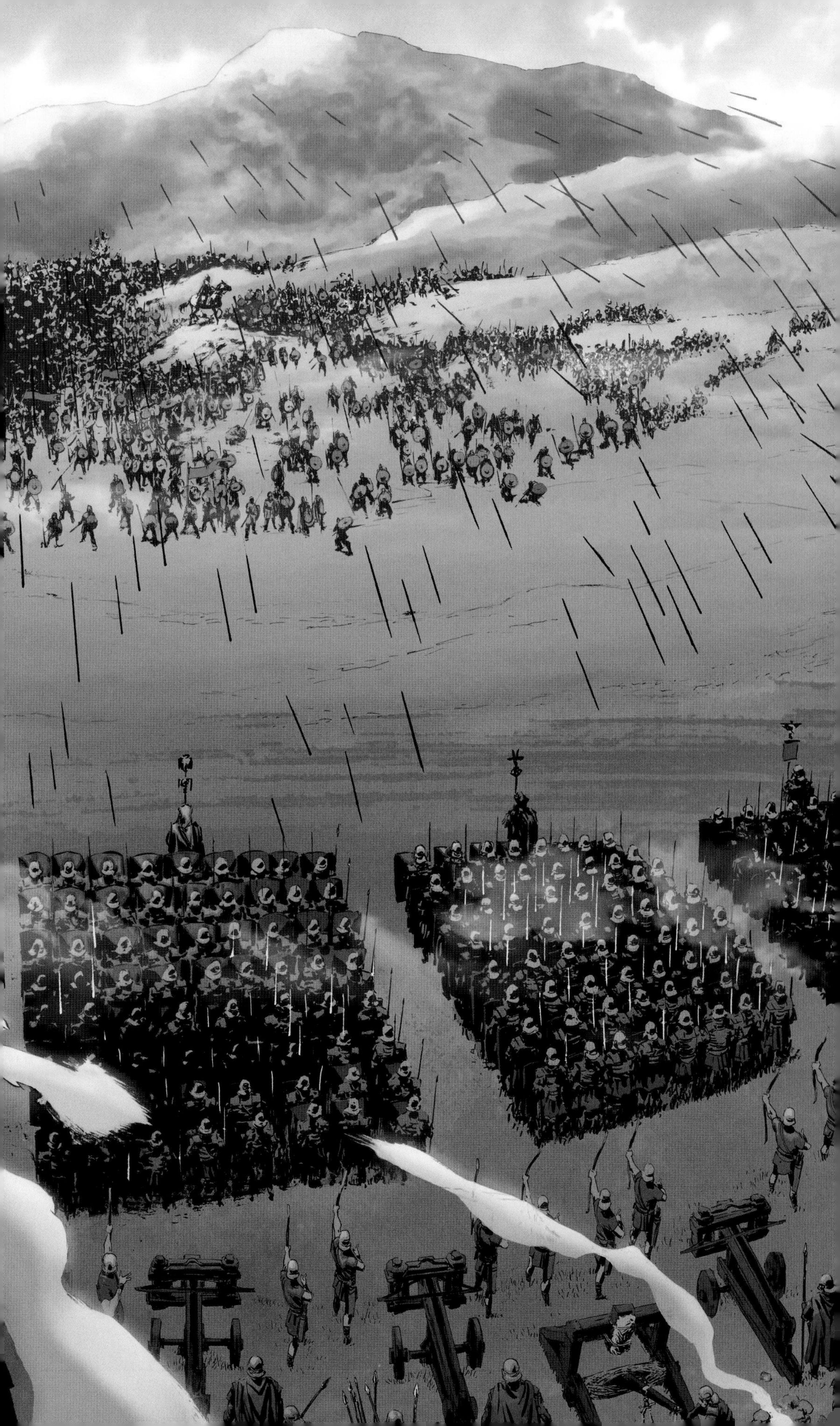

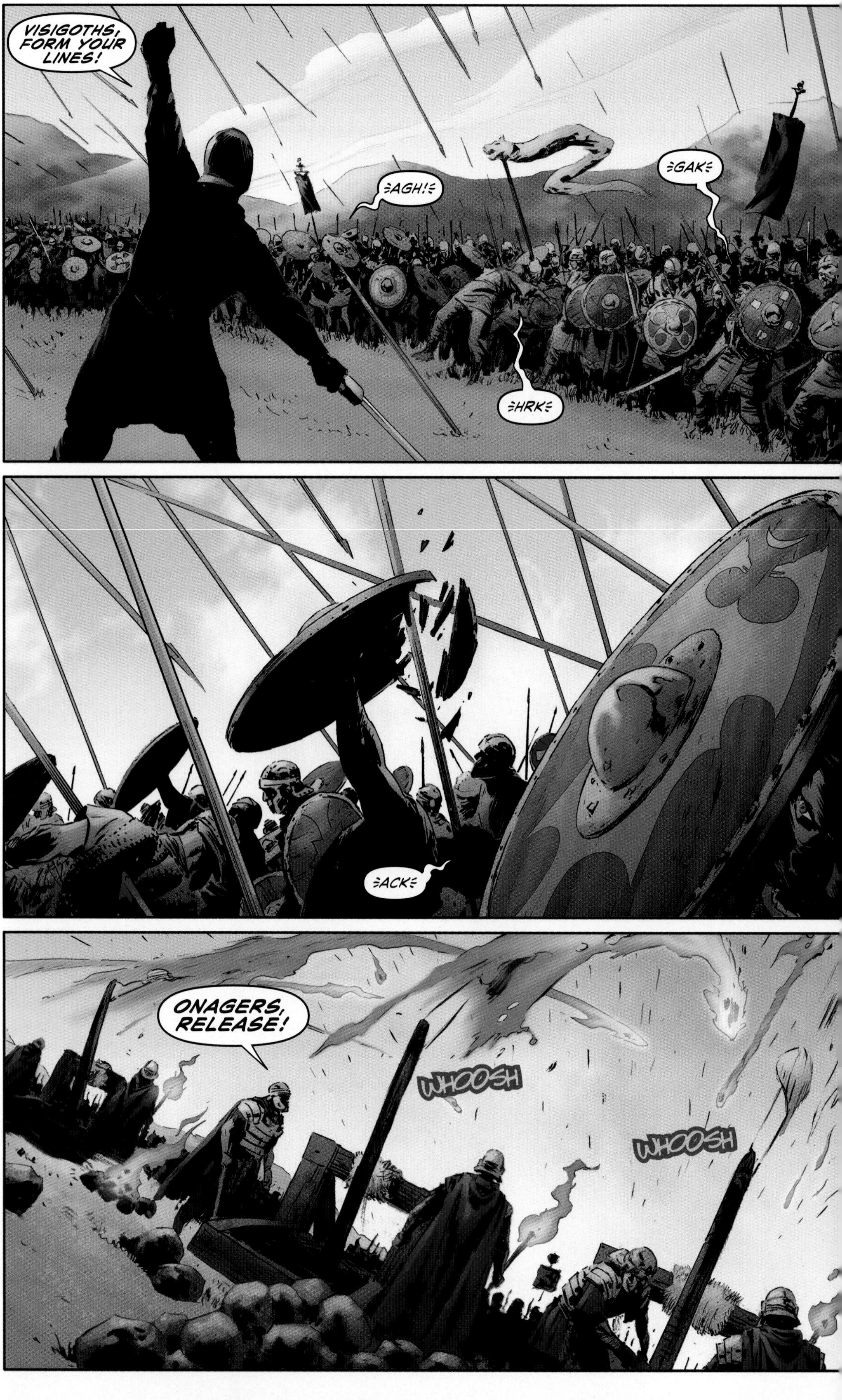
VISIGOTHS, FORM YOUR LINES!
AGH!
GAK
HRK
ACK
ONAGERS, RELEASE!
WHOOSH
WHOOSH

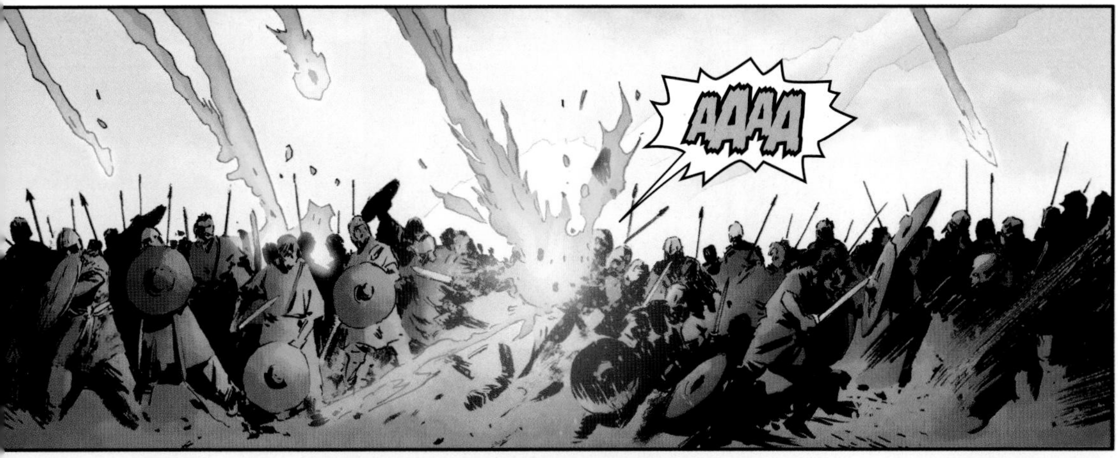
AAAA

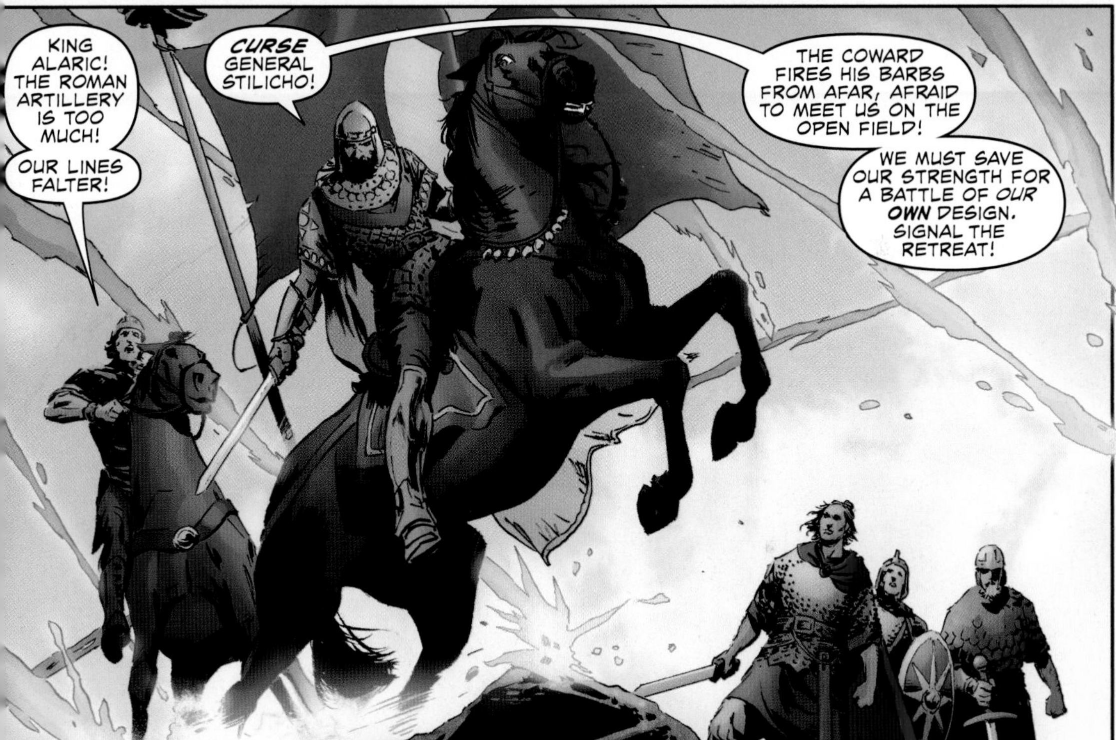
KING ALARIC! THE ROMAN ARTILLERY IS TOO MUCH!
OUR LINES FALTER!
CURSE GENERAL STILICHO!
THE COWARD FIRES HIS BARBS FROM AFAR, AFRAID TO MEET US ON THE OPEN FIELD!
WE MUST SAVE OUR STRENGTH FOR A BATTLE OF OUR OWN DESIGN. SIGNAL THE RETREAT!

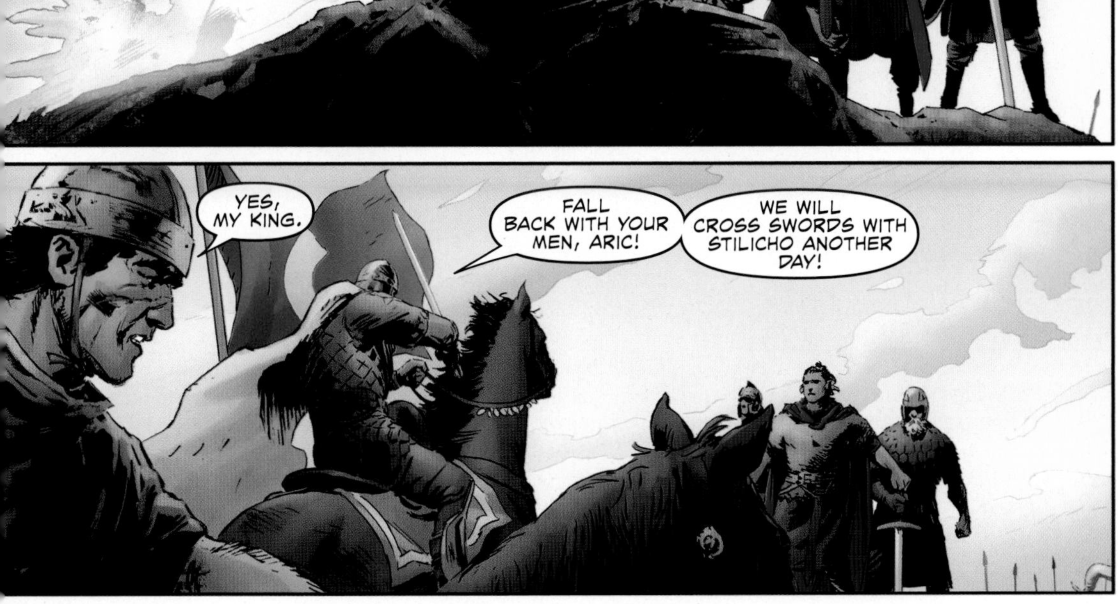
FALL BACK WITH YOUR MEN, ARIC!
WE WILL CROSS SWORDS WITH STILICHO ANOTHER DAY!
YES, MY KING.

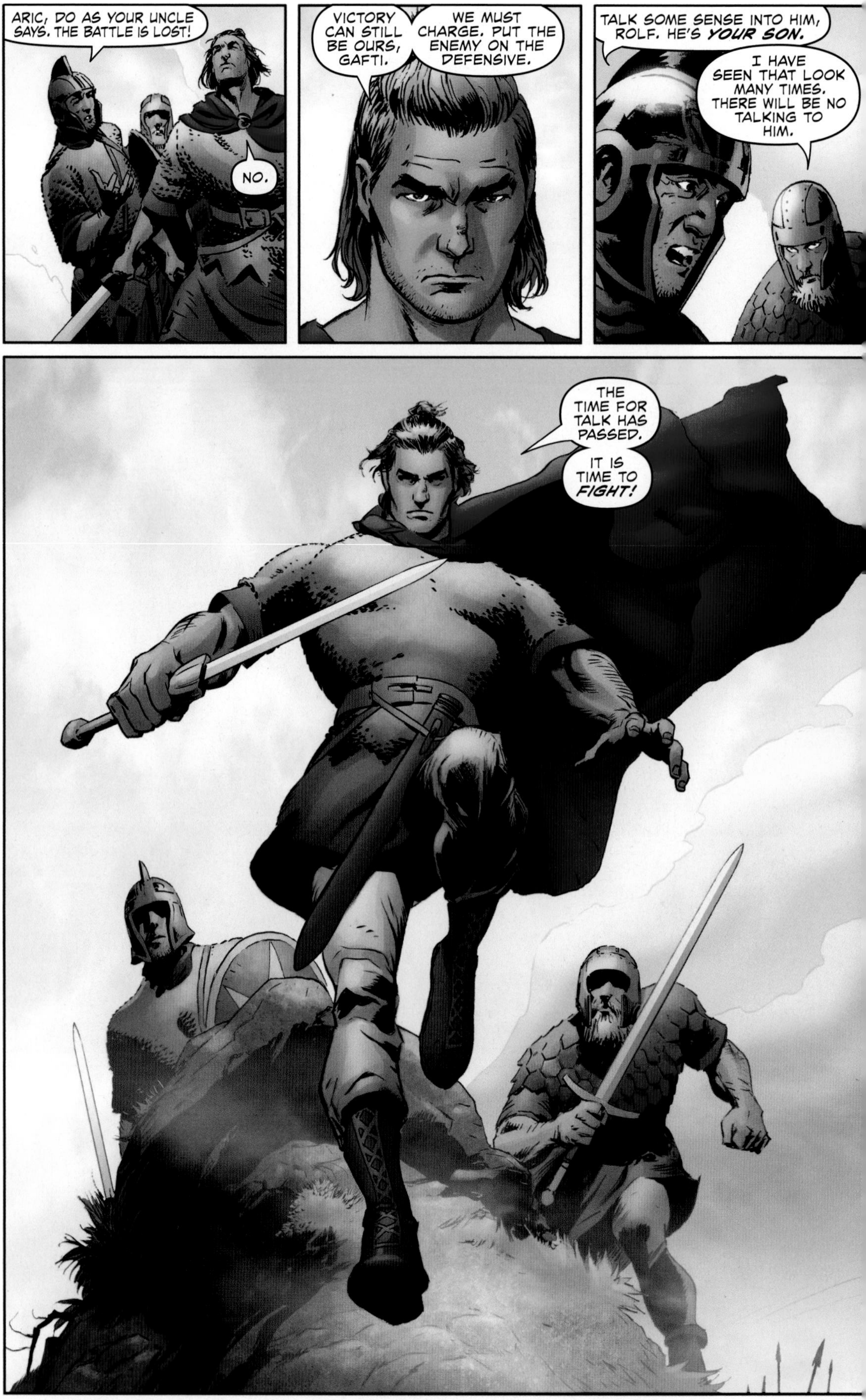

ARIC, DO AS YOUR UNCLE SAYS. THE BATTLE IS LOST!
NO.
VICTORY CAN STILL BE OURS, GAFTI.
WE MUST CHARGE. PUT THE ENEMY ON THE DEFENSIVE.
TALK SOME SENSE INTO HIM, ROLF. HE'S YOUR SON.
I HAVE SEEN THAT LOOK MANY TIMES. THERE WILL BE NO TALKING TO HIM.
THE TIME FOR TALK HAS PASSED.
IT IS TIME TO FIGHT!

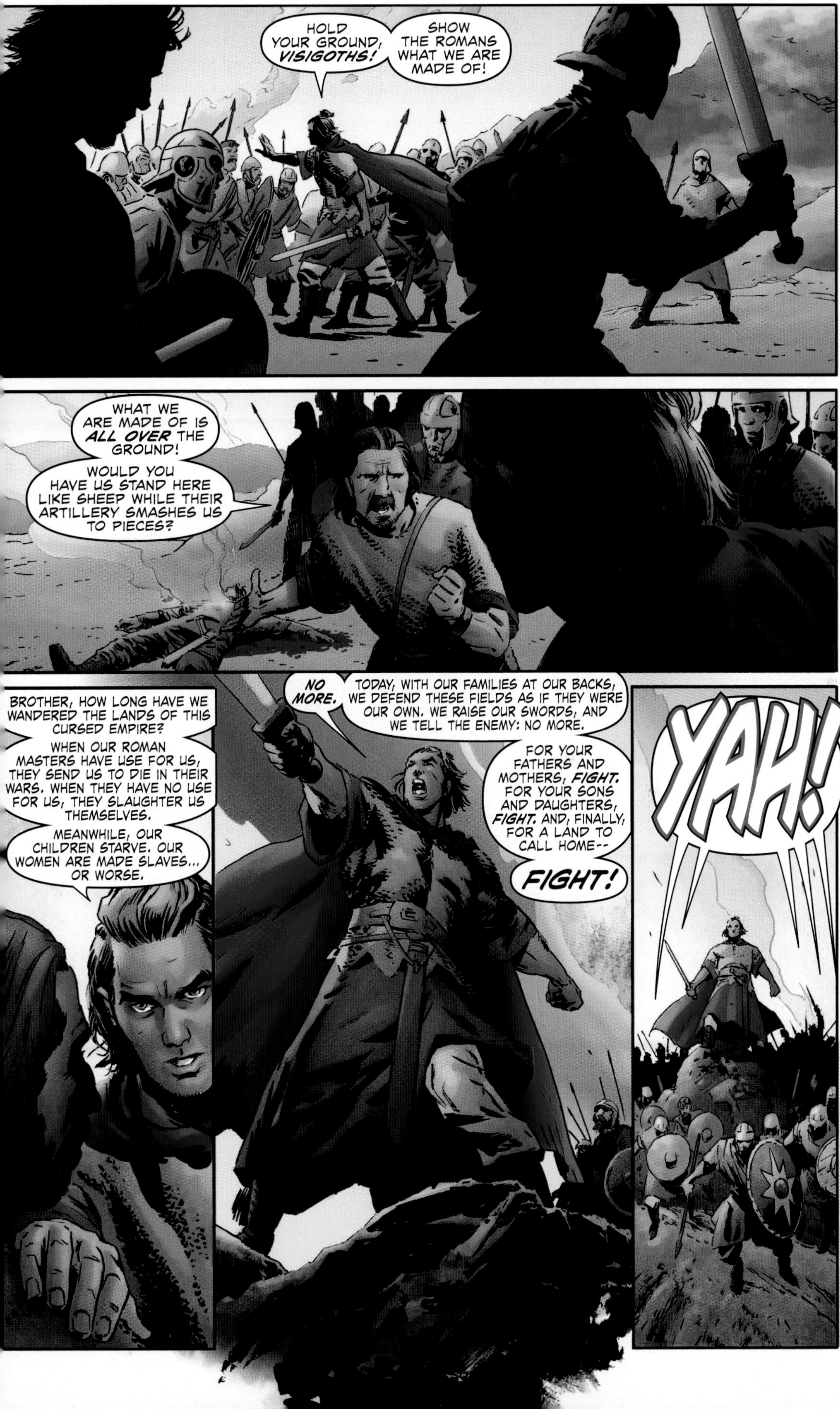

HOLD YOUR GROUND, *VISIGOTHS!*
SHOW THE ROMANS WHAT WE ARE MADE OF!
WHAT WE ARE MADE OF IS *ALL OVER* THE GROUND!
WOULD YOU HAVE US STAND HERE LIKE SHEEP WHILE THEIR ARTILLERY SMASHES US TO PIECES?
BROTHER, HOW LONG HAVE WE WANDERED THE LANDS OF THIS CURSED EMPIRE?
WHEN OUR ROMAN MASTERS HAVE USE FOR US, THEY SEND US TO DIE IN THEIR WARS. WHEN THEY HAVE NO USE FOR US, THEY SLAUGHTER US THEMSELVES.
MEANWHILE, OUR CHILDREN STARVE. OUR WOMEN ARE MADE SLAVES... OR WORSE.
NO MORE.
TODAY, WITH OUR FAMILIES AT OUR BACKS, WE DEFEND THESE FIELDS AS IF THEY WERE OUR OWN. WE RAISE OUR SWORDS, AND WE TELL THE ENEMY: NO MORE.
FOR YOUR FATHERS AND MOTHERS, *FIGHT.* FOR YOUR SONS AND DAUGHTERS, *FIGHT.* AND, FINALLY, FOR A LAND TO CALL HOME--
FIGHT!
YAH!

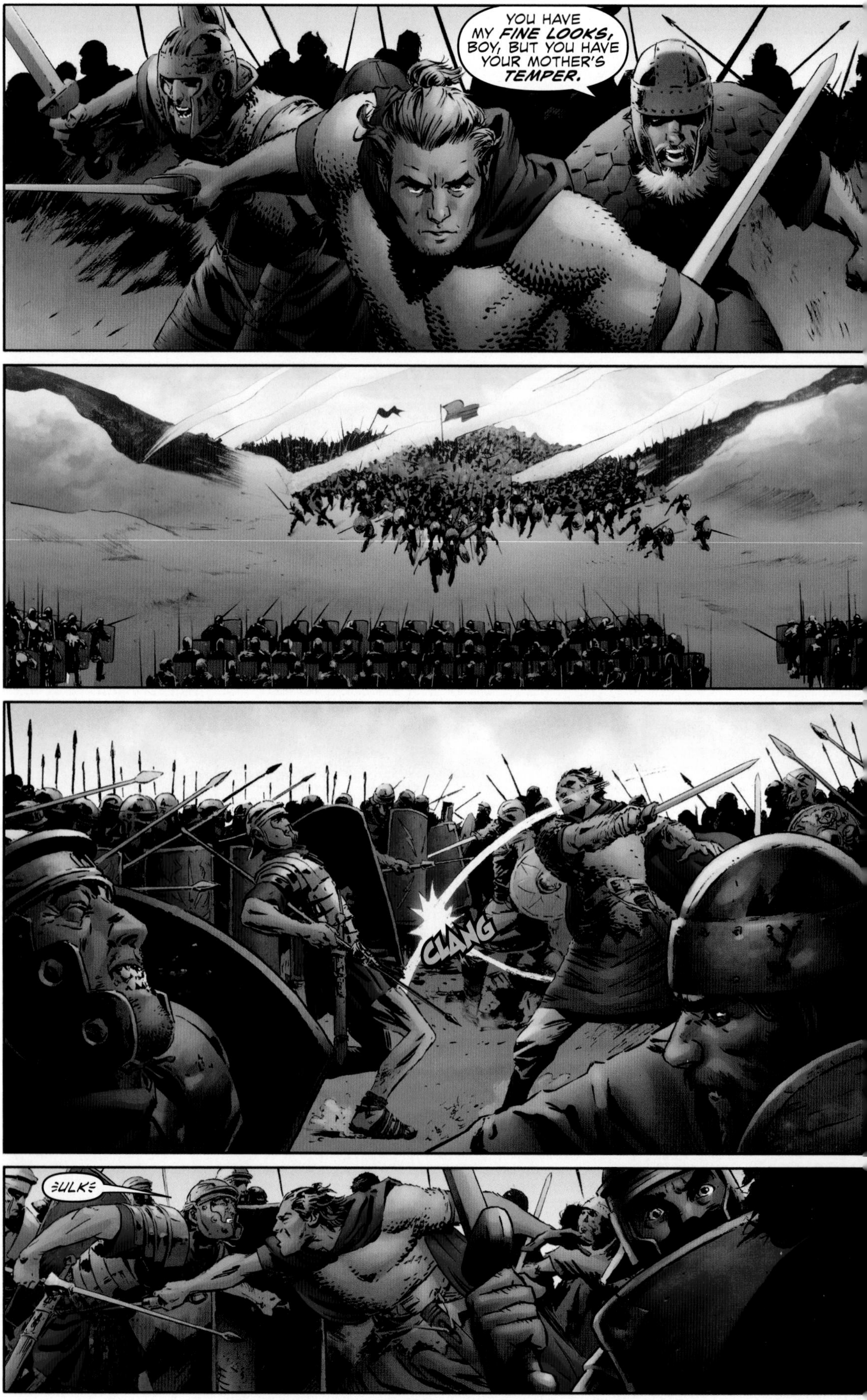
YOU HAVE MY FINE LOOKS, BOY, BUT YOU HAVE YOUR MOTHER'S TEMPER.
CLANG
ULK

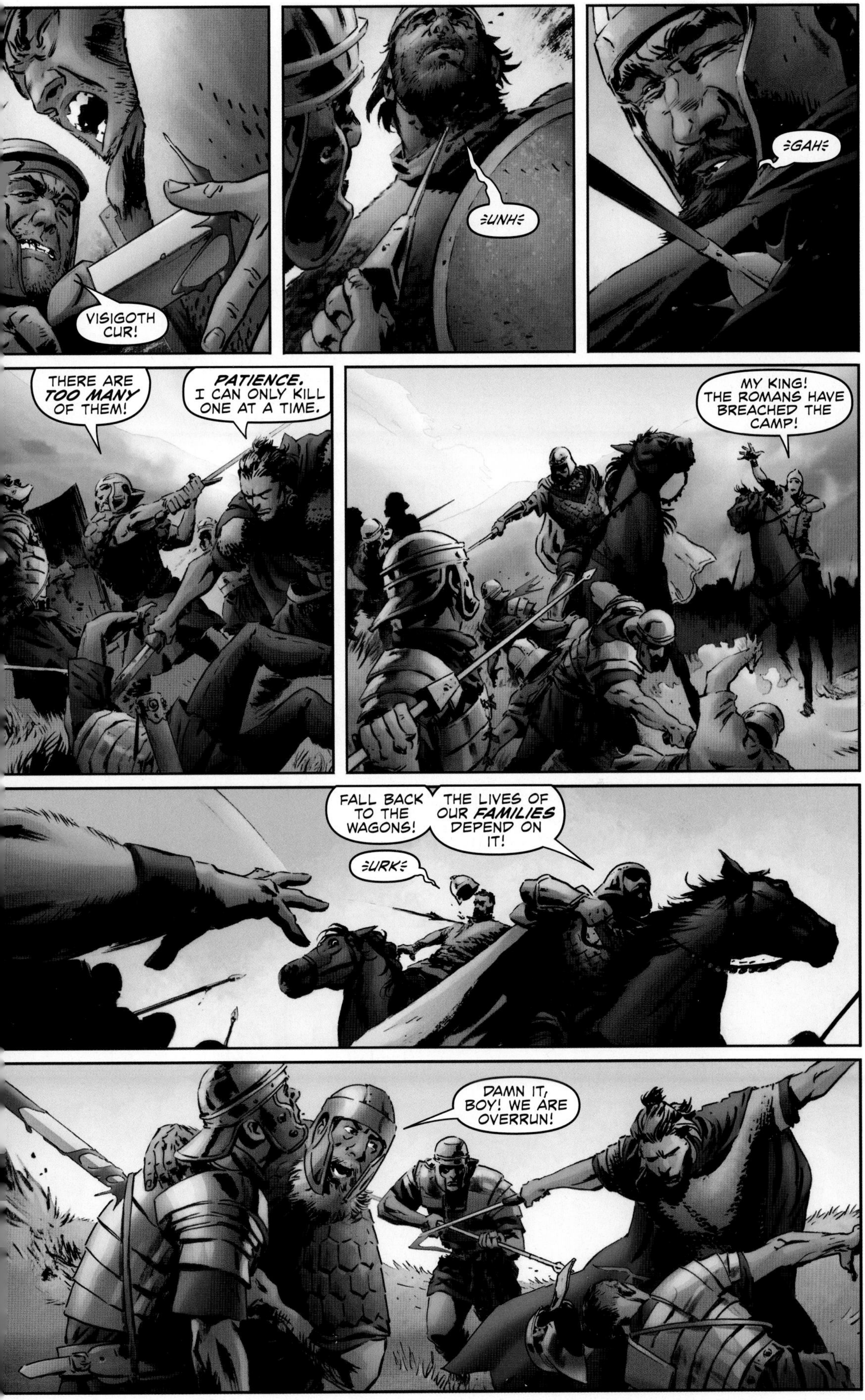

VISIGOTH CUR!
UNH
GAH
THERE ARE TOO MANY OF THEM!
PATIENCE. I CAN ONLY KILL ONE AT A TIME.
MY KING! THE ROMANS HAVE BREACHED THE CAMP!
FALL BACK TO THE WAGONS!
THE LIVES OF OUR FAMILIES DEPEND ON IT!
URK
DAMN IT, BOY! WE ARE OVERRUN!

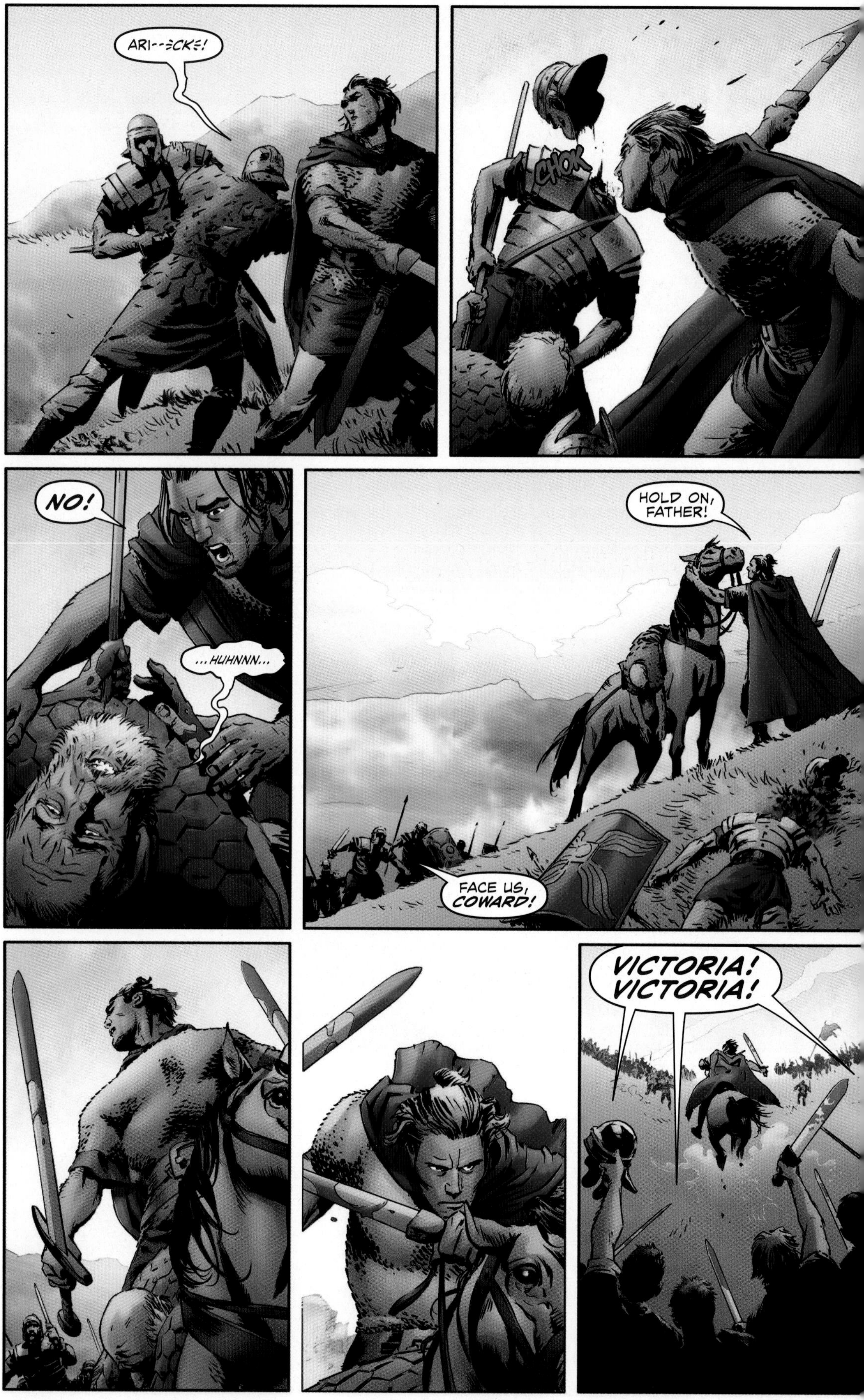
ARI--ECK!
CHOK
NO!
...HUHNNN...
HOLD ON, FATHER!
FACE US, COWARD!
VICTORIA! VICTORIA!

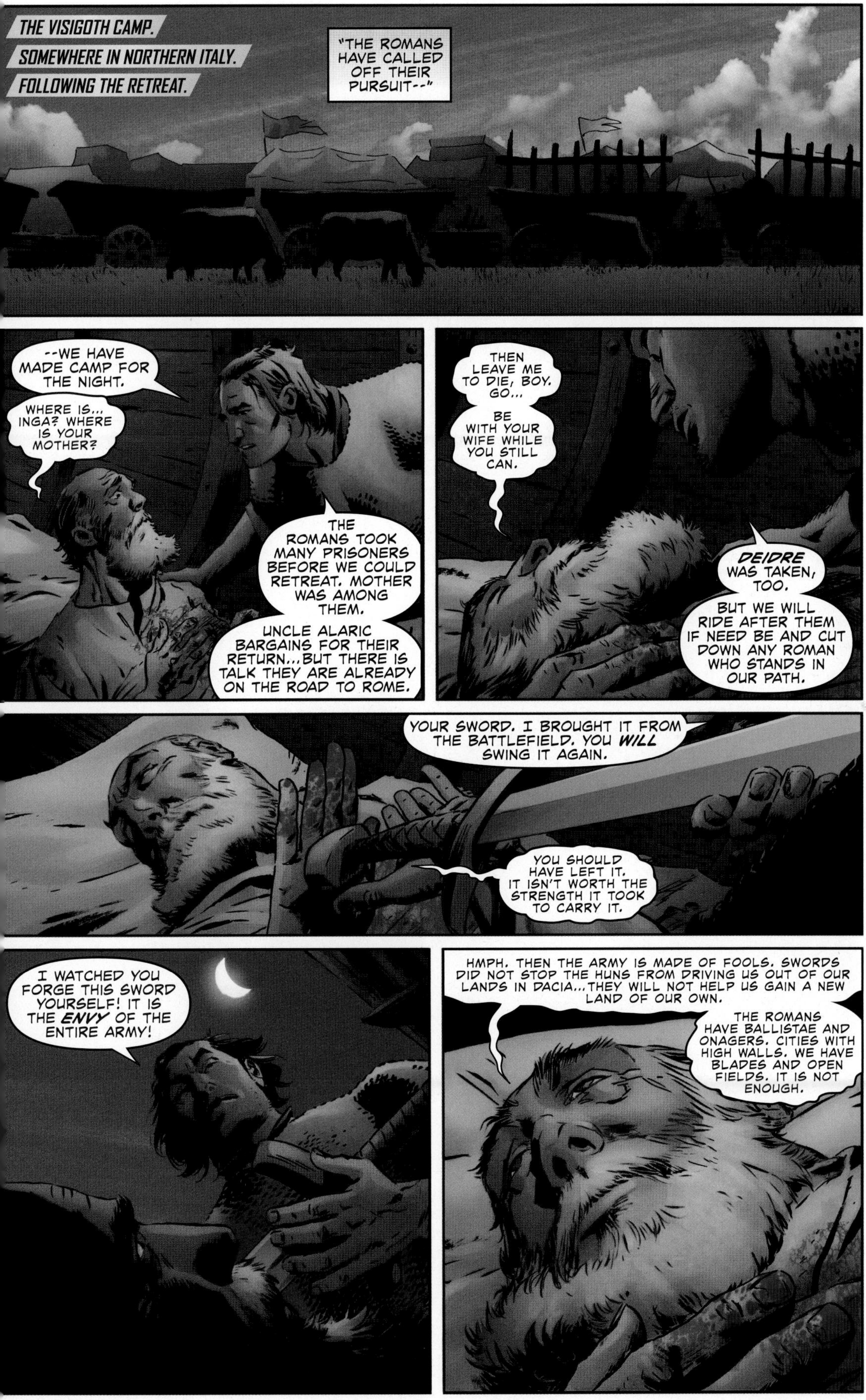
THE VISIGOTH CAMP.
SOMEWHERE IN NORTHERN ITALY.
FOLLOWING THE RETREAT.
"THE ROMANS HAVE CALLED OFF THEIR PURSUIT--"
--WE HAVE MADE CAMP FOR THE NIGHT.
WHERE IS... INGA? WHERE IS YOUR MOTHER?
THE ROMANS TOOK MANY PRISONERS BEFORE WE COULD RETREAT. MOTHER WAS AMONG THEM.
UNCLE ALARIC BARGAINS FOR THEIR RETURN...BUT THERE IS TALK THEY ARE ALREADY ON THE ROAD TO ROME.
THEN LEAVE ME TO DIE, BOY. GO...
BE WITH YOUR WIFE WHILE YOU STILL CAN.
DEIDRE WAS TAKEN, TOO.
BUT WE WILL RIDE AFTER THEM IF NEED BE AND CUT DOWN ANY ROMAN WHO STANDS IN OUR PATH.
YOUR SWORD. I BROUGHT IT FROM THE BATTLEFIELD. YOU WILL SWING IT AGAIN.
YOU SHOULD HAVE LEFT IT. IT ISN'T WORTH THE STRENGTH IT TOOK TO CARRY IT.
I WATCHED YOU FORGE THIS SWORD YOURSELF! IT IS THE ENVY OF THE ENTIRE ARMY!
HMPH. THEN THE ARMY IS MADE OF FOOLS. SWORDS DID NOT STOP THE HUNS FROM DRIVING US OUT OF OUR LANDS IN DACIA...THEY WILL NOT HELP US GAIN A NEW LAND OF OUR OWN.
THE ROMANS HAVE BALLISTAE AND ONAGERS. CITIES WITH HIGH WALLS. WE HAVE BLADES AND OPEN FIELDS. IT IS NOT ENOUGH.

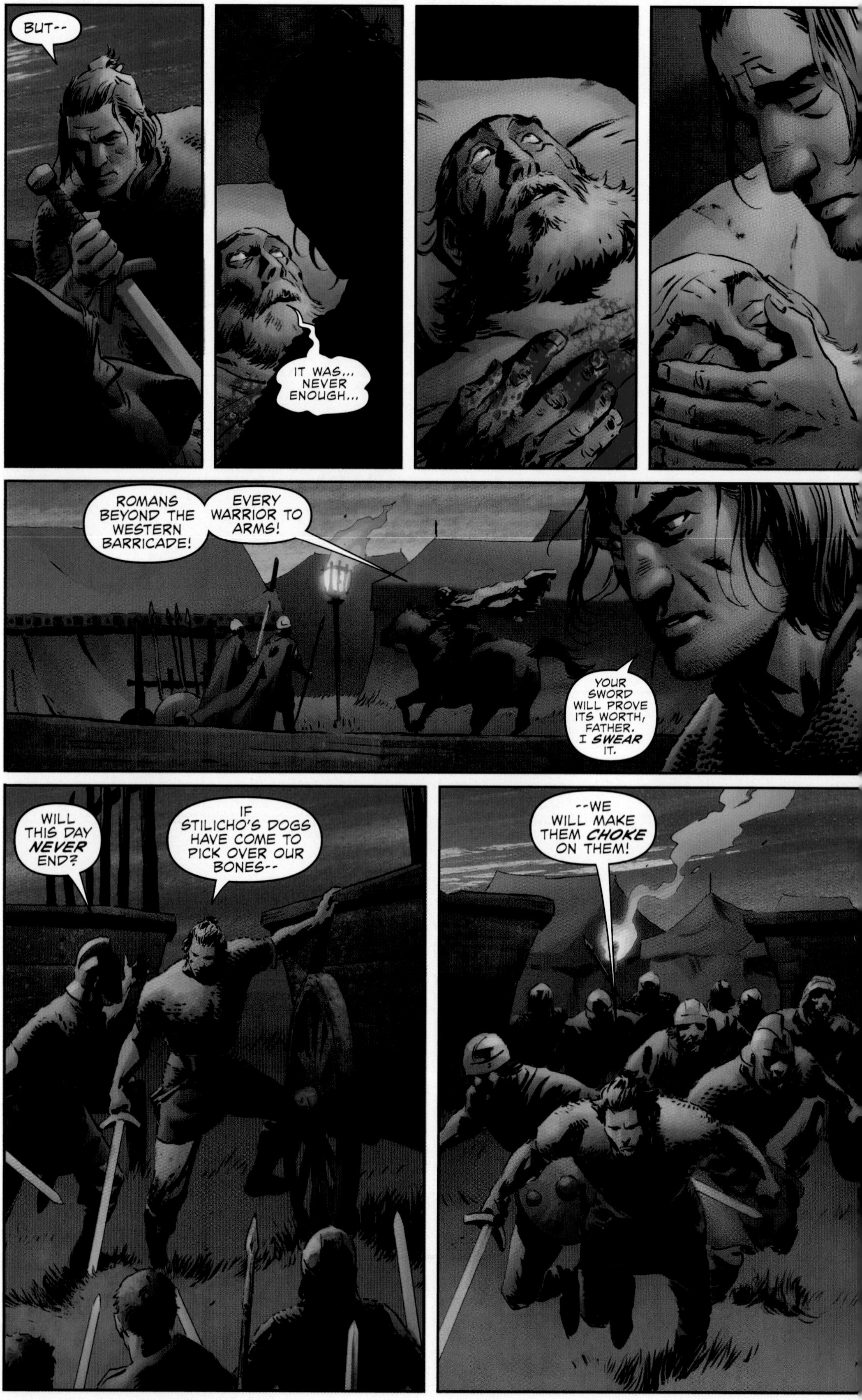
BUT--
IT WAS... NEVER ENOUGH...
ROMANS BEYOND THE WESTERN BARRICADE!
EVERY WARRIOR TO ARMS!
YOUR SWORD WILL PROVE ITS WORTH, FATHER. I *SWEAR* IT.
WILL THIS DAY *NEVER* END?
IF STILICHO'S DOGS HAVE COME TO PICK OVER OUR BONES--
--WE WILL MAKE THEM *CHOKE* ON THEM!

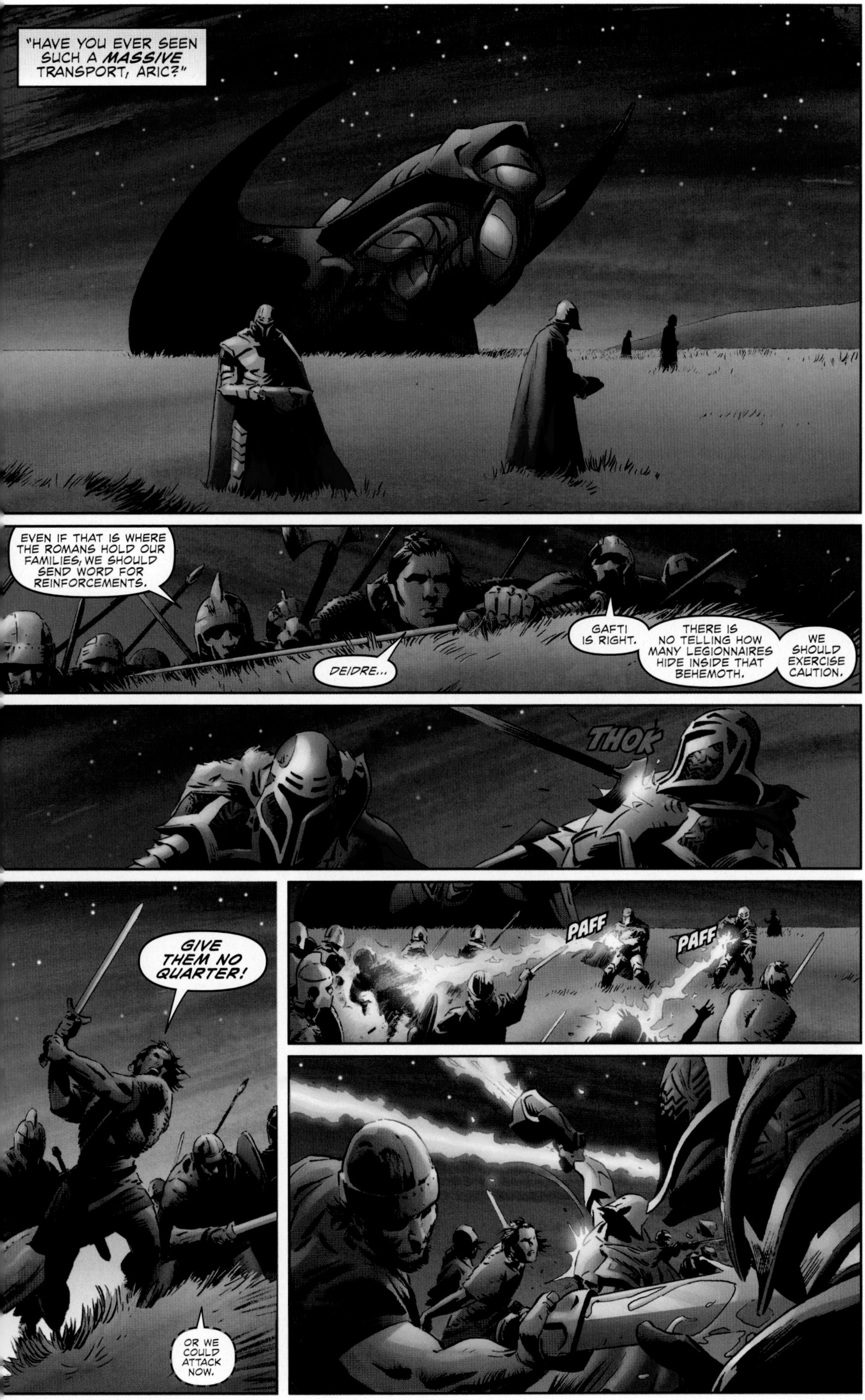
"HAVE YOU EVER SEEN SUCH A MASSIVE TRANSPORT, ARIC?"
EVEN IF THAT IS WHERE THE ROMANS HOLD OUR FAMILIES, WE SHOULD SEND WORD FOR REINFORCEMENTS.
DEIDRE...
GAFTI IS RIGHT.
THERE IS NO TELLING HOW MANY LEGIONNAIRES HIDE INSIDE THAT BEHEMOTH.
WE SHOULD EXERCISE CAUTION.
THOK
GIVE THEM NO QUARTER!
OR WE COULD ATTACK NOW.
PAFF
PAFF

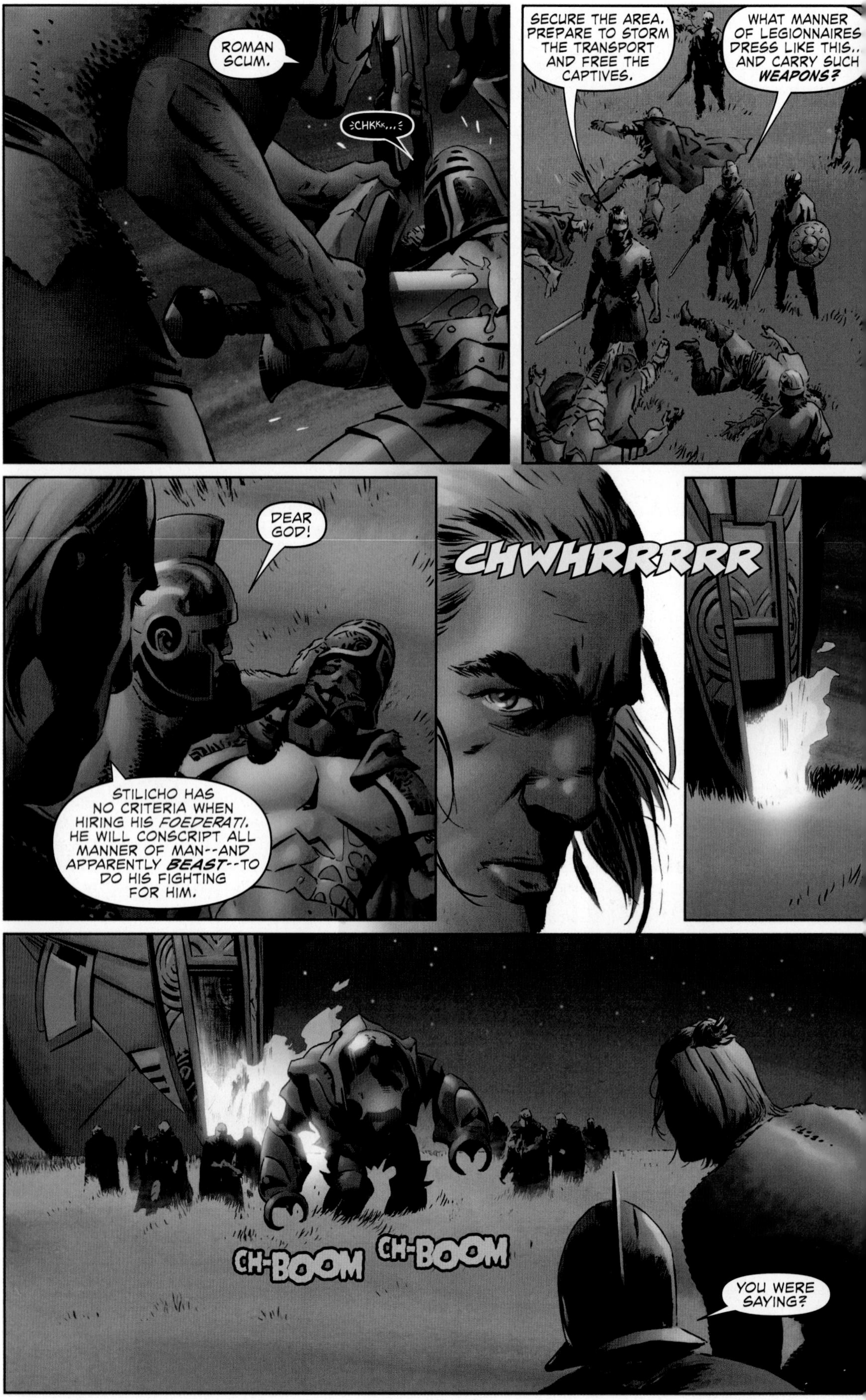
ROMAN SCUM.
CHKKK...
SECURE THE AREA. PREPARE TO STORM THE TRANSPORT AND FREE THE CAPTIVES.
WHAT MANNER OF LEGIONNAIRES DRESS LIKE THIS.. AND CARRY SUCH WEAPONS?
DEAR GOD!
CHWHRRRRRR
STILICHO HAS NO CRITERIA WHEN HIRING HIS FOEDERATI. HE WILL CONSCRIPT ALL MANNER OF MAN--AND APPARENTLY BEAST--TO DO HIS FIGHTING FOR HIM.
CH-BOOM CH-BOOM
YOU WERE SAYING?

THE VISIGOTH CAMP.

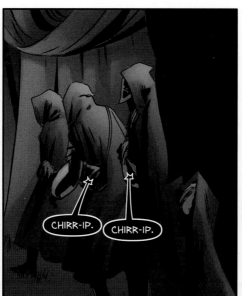

CHIRR-IP.

CHIRR-IP.

MUH MUH

CHIRR-IP.

MUH

PLUCK

WAH!

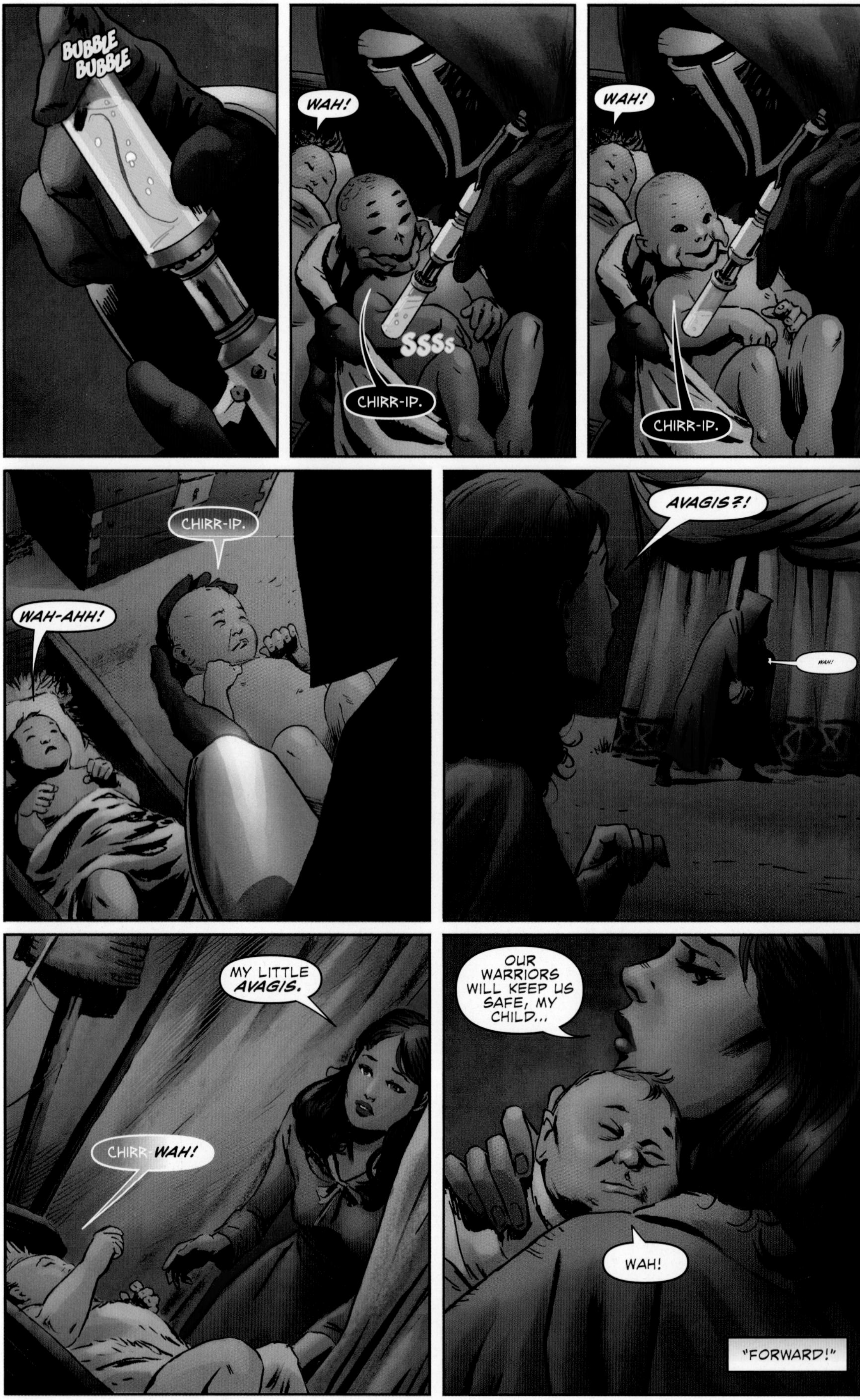

BUBBLE BUBBLE
WAH!
SSSs
CHIRR-IP.
WAH!
CHIRR-IP.
CHIRR-IP.
WAH-AHH!
AVAGIS?!
WAH!
MY LITTLE AVAGIS.
CHIRR WAH!
OUR WARRIORS WILL KEEP US SAFE, MY CHILD...
WAH!
"FORWARD!"

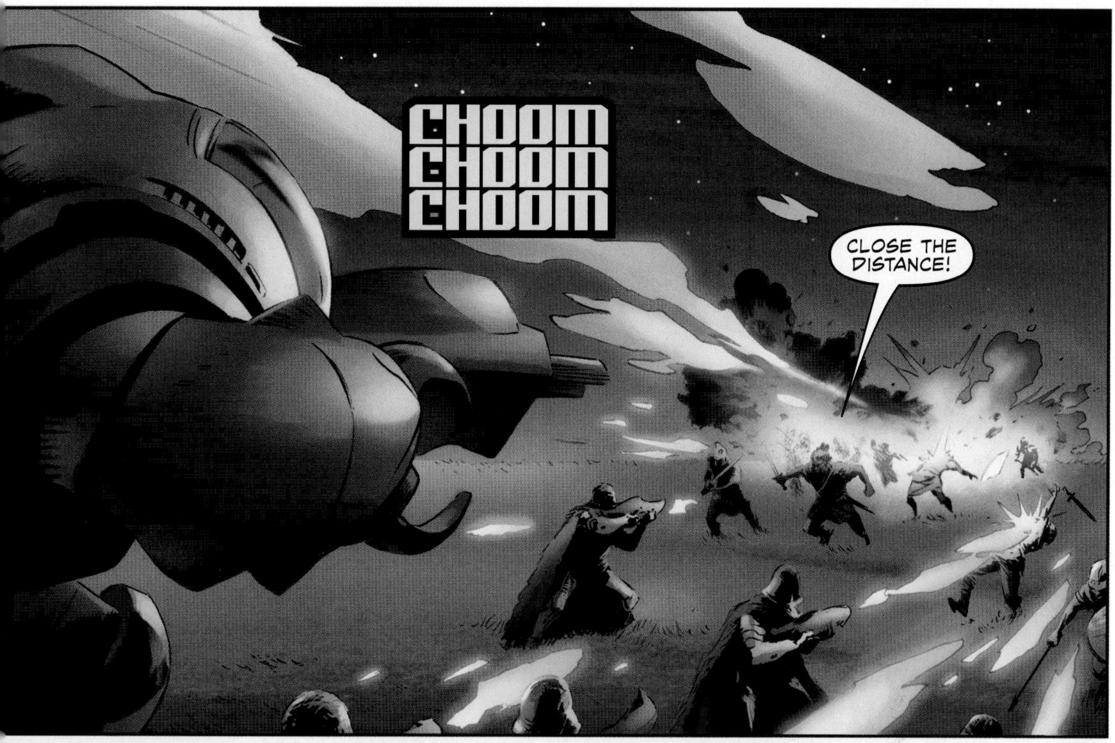
CHOOM CHOOM CHOOM
CLOSE THE DISTANCE!

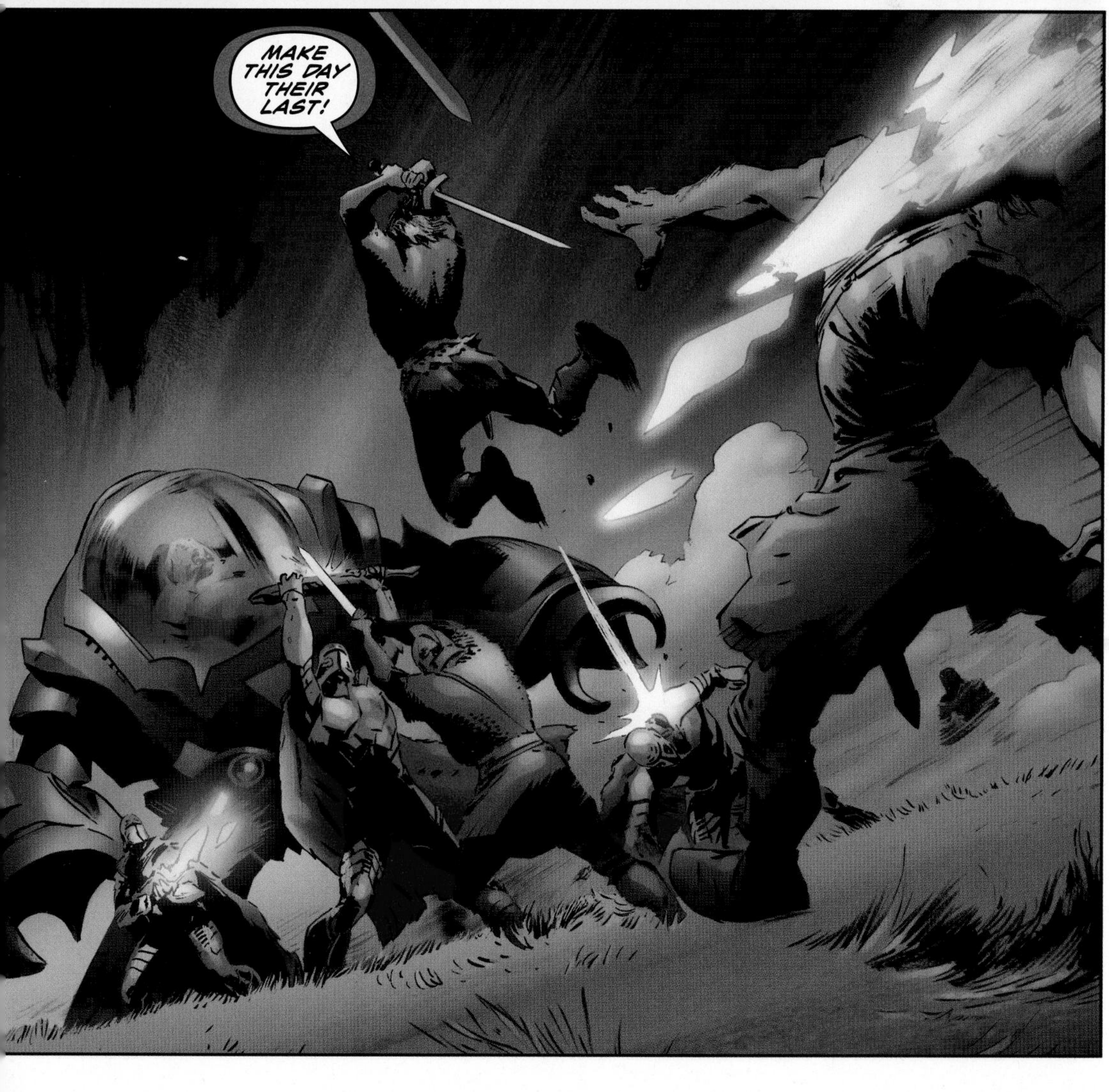
MAKE THIS DAY THEIR LAST!

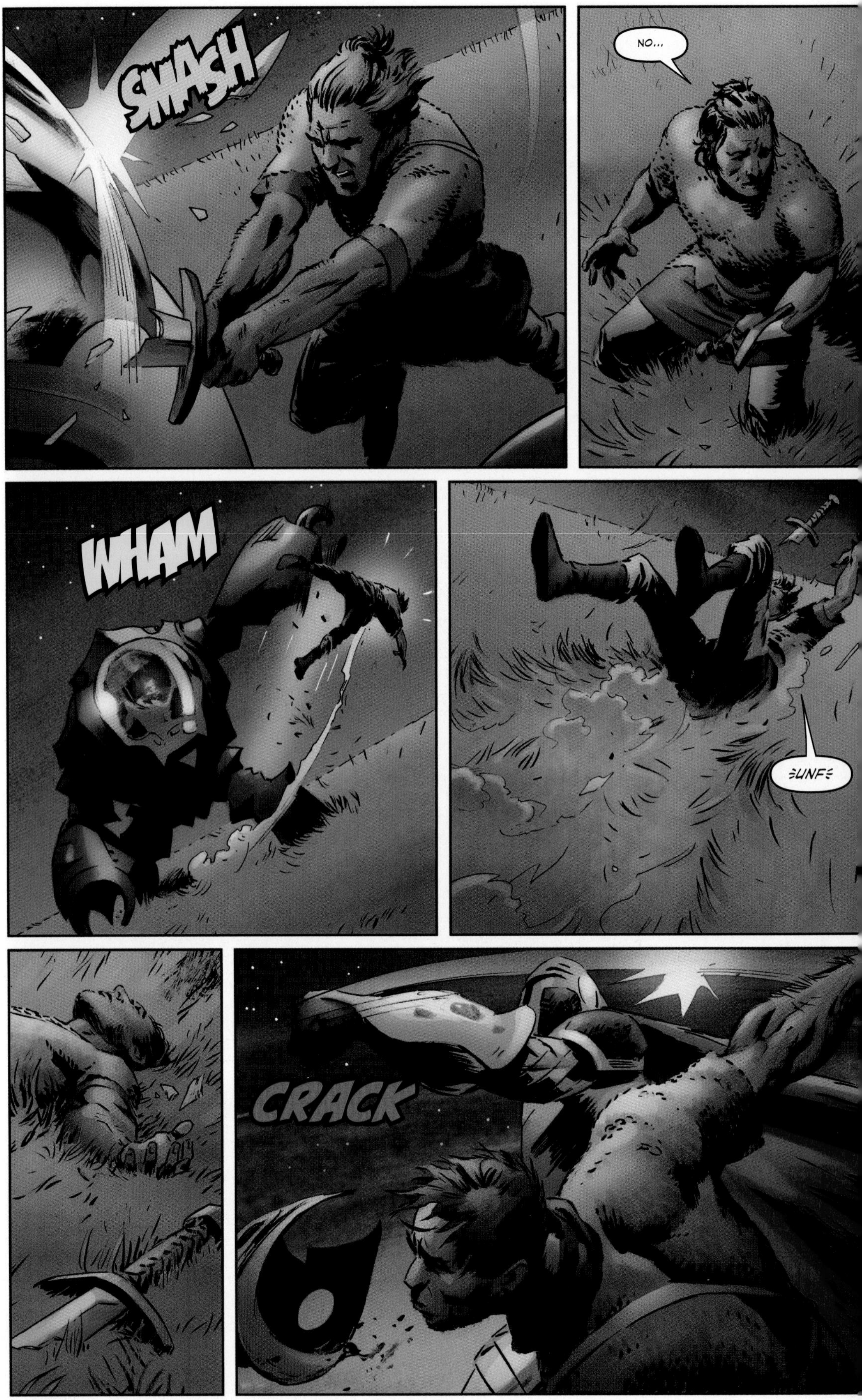
SMASH
NO...
WHAM
UNF
CRACK

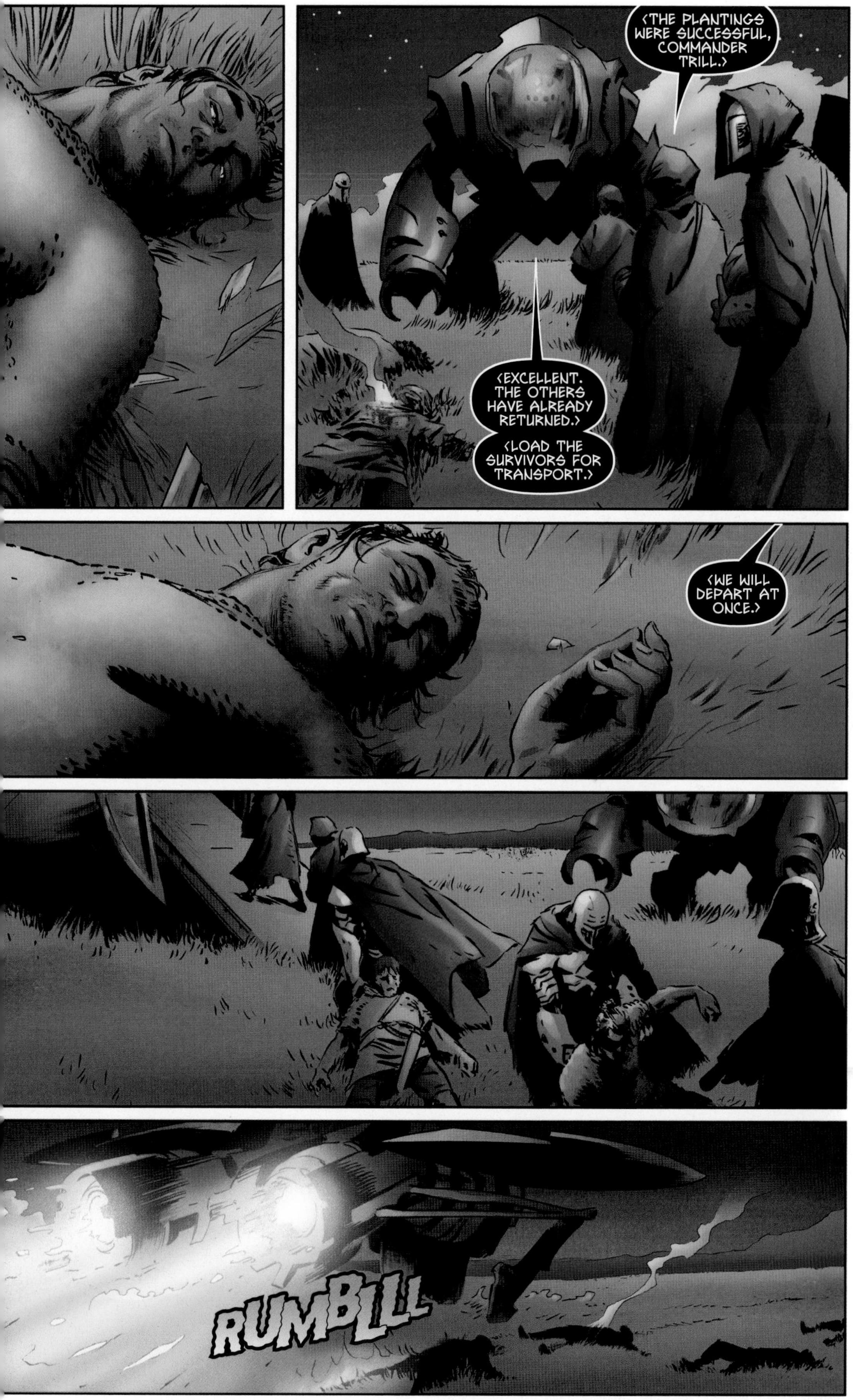

<THE PLANTINGS WERE SUCCESSFUL, COMMANDER TRILL.>
<EXCELLENT. THE OTHERS HAVE ALREADY RETURNED.>
<LOAD THE SURVIVORS FOR TRANSPORT.>
<WE WILL DEPART AT ONCE.>
RUMBLLL

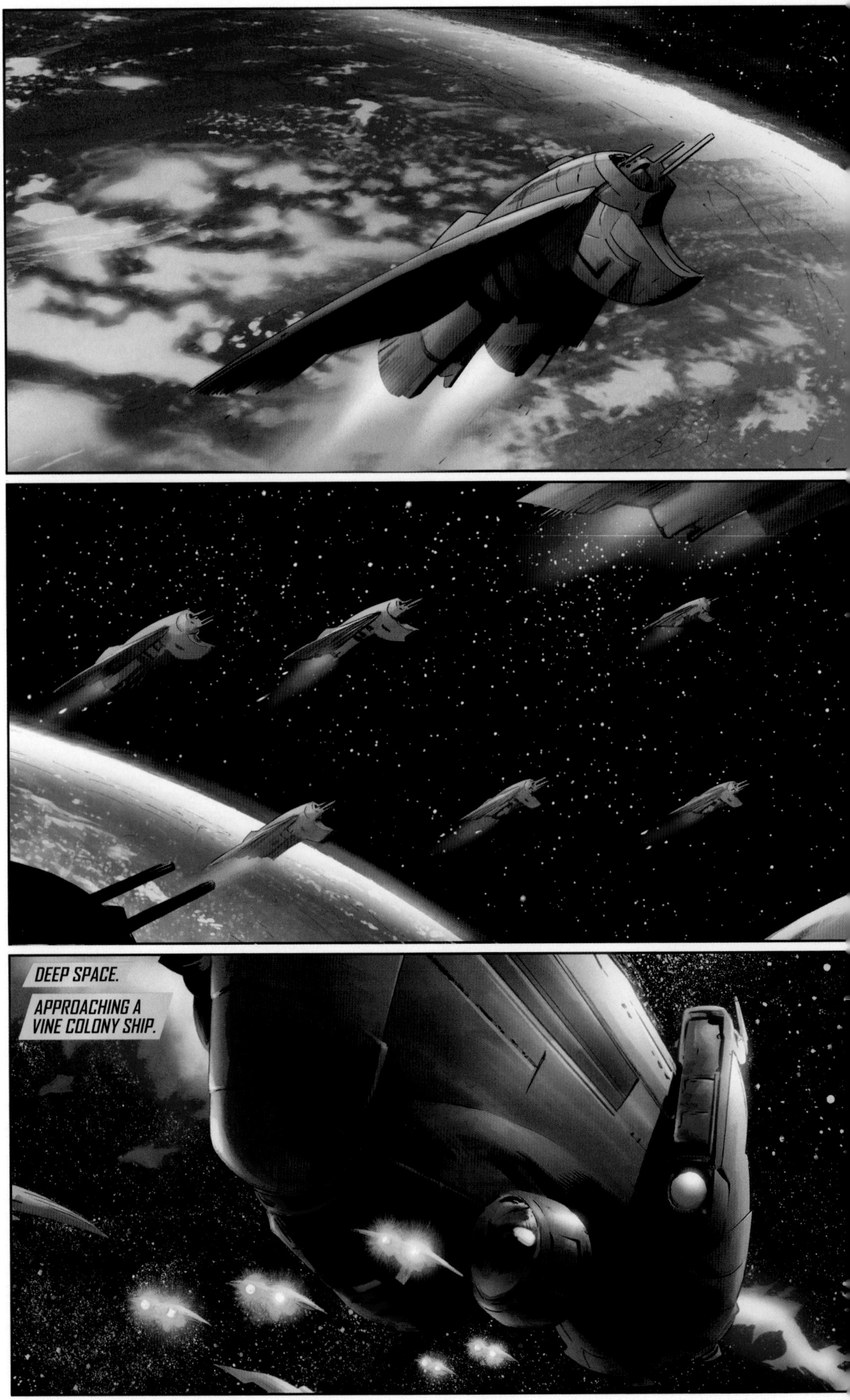
DEEP SPACE.
APPROACHING A VINE COLONY SHIP.

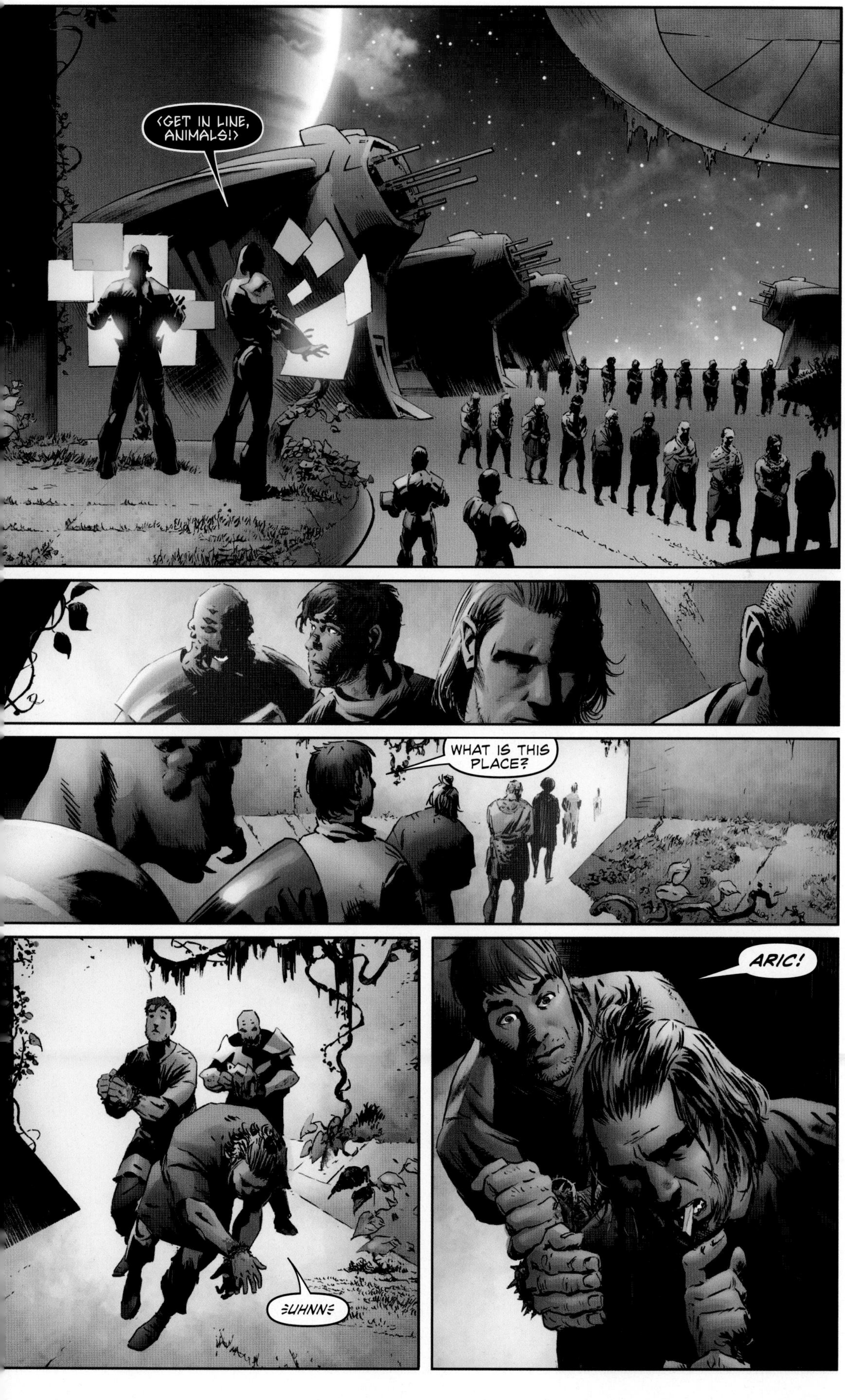

‹GET IN LINE, ANIMALS!›
WHAT IS THIS PLACE?
≡UHNN≡
ARIC!

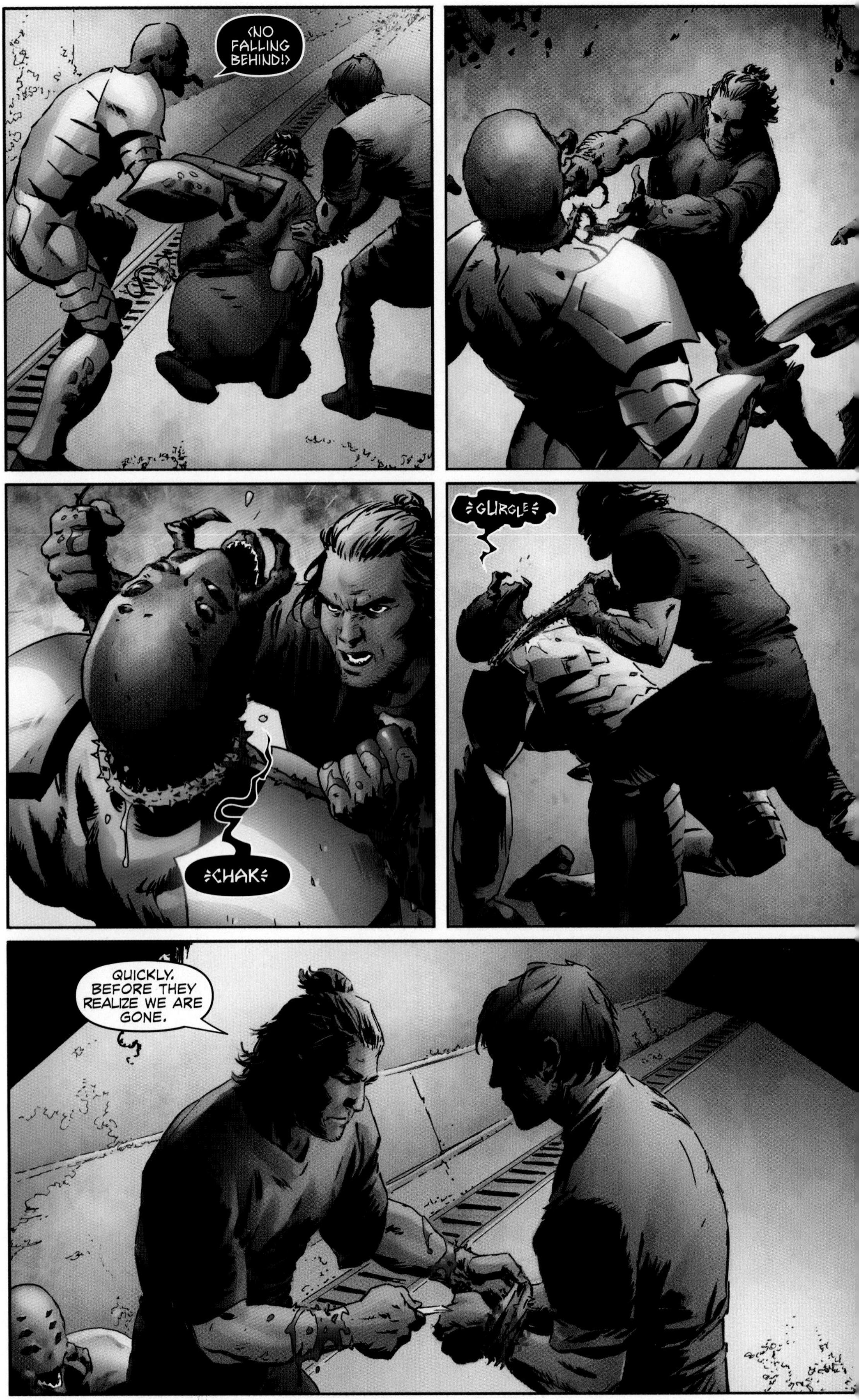

‹NO FALLING BEHIND!›
GURGLE
CHAK
QUICKLY. BEFORE THEY REALIZE WE ARE GONE.

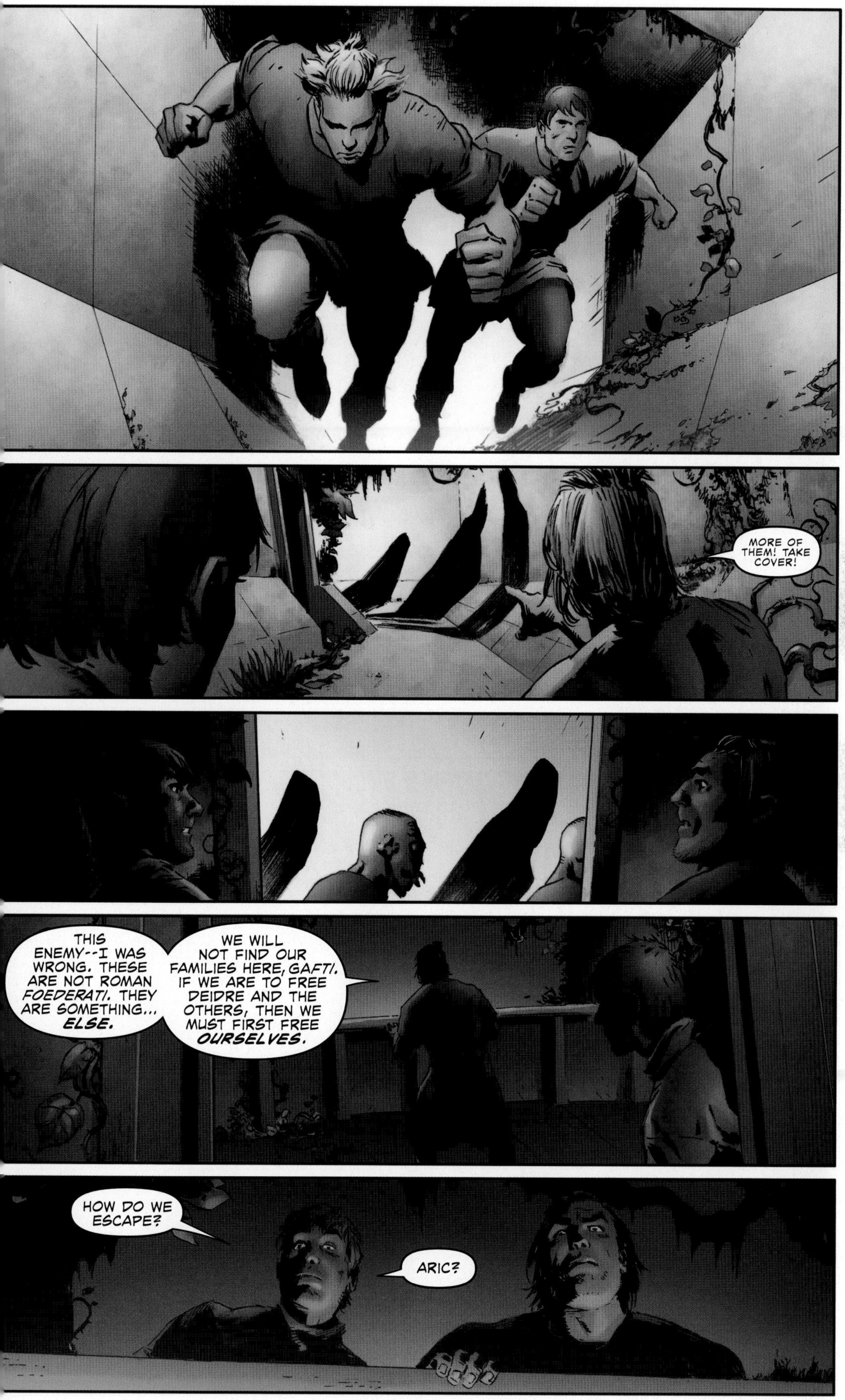
MORE OF THEM! TAKE COVER!
THIS ENEMY--I WAS WRONG. THESE ARE NOT ROMAN *FOEDERATI*. THEY ARE SOMETHING... ***ELSE.***
WE WILL NOT FIND OUR FAMILIES HERE, GAFTI. IF WE ARE TO FREE DEIDRE AND THE OTHERS, THEN WE MUST FIRST FREE ***OURSELVES.***
HOW DO WE ESCAPE?
ARIC?

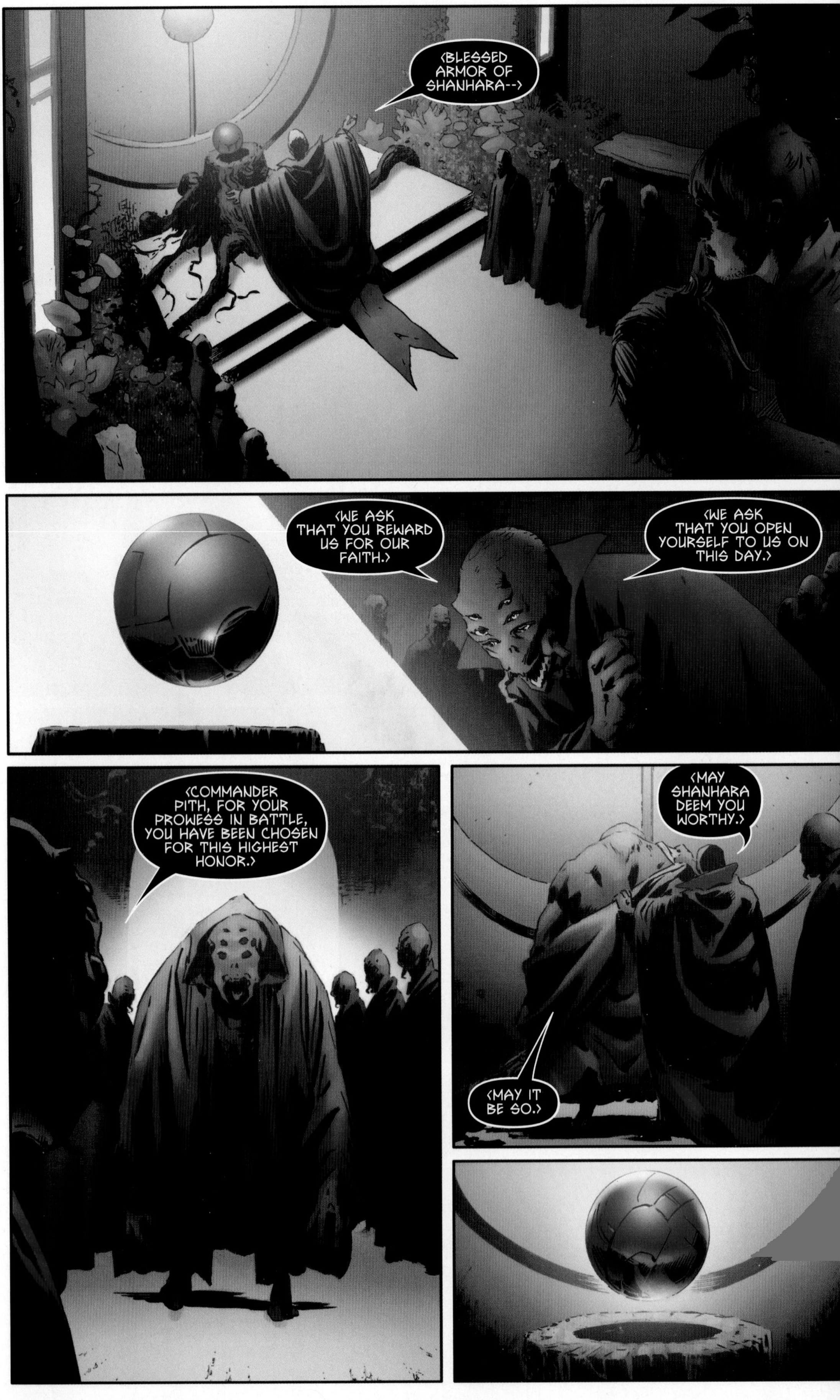

<BLESSED ARMOR OF SHANHARA-->
<WE ASK THAT YOU REWARD US FOR OUR FAITH.>
<WE ASK THAT YOU OPEN YOURSELF TO US ON THIS DAY.>
<COMMANDER PITH, FOR YOUR PROWESS IN BATTLE, YOU HAVE BEEN CHOSEN FOR THIS HIGHEST HONOR.>
<MAY SHANHARA DEEM YOU WORTHY.>
<MAY IT BE SO.>

THE METAL... IT MOVES ON ITS OWN. HAVE YOU EVER HEARD OF SUCH A THING?

NOT EVEN IN THE *MYTHS*.

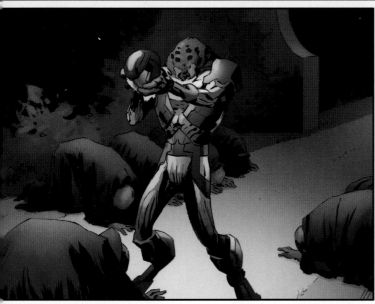

IS THAT THEIR KING?

IS IT THE CREATURE THEY BOW TO... OR THE ARMOR?

‹SHALL WE EXECUTE THE SLAVES, COMMANDER TRILL?›

KRAK

YOU BEASTS WILL FIND ME MUCH HARDER TO DEFEAT WITHOUT YOUR MACHINES.

‹YOU ARE AN OBSTINATE ONE.›

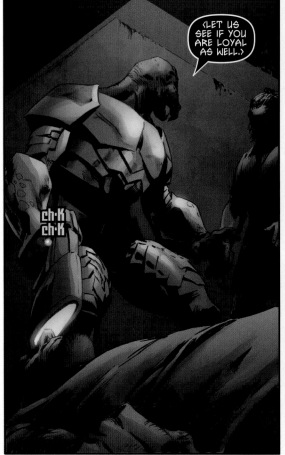

‹LET US SEE IF YOU ARE LOYAL AS WELL.›

ch·K
ch·K

THE DAY WILL COME.

‹PUT THEM IN THE PENS WITH THE OTHERS.›

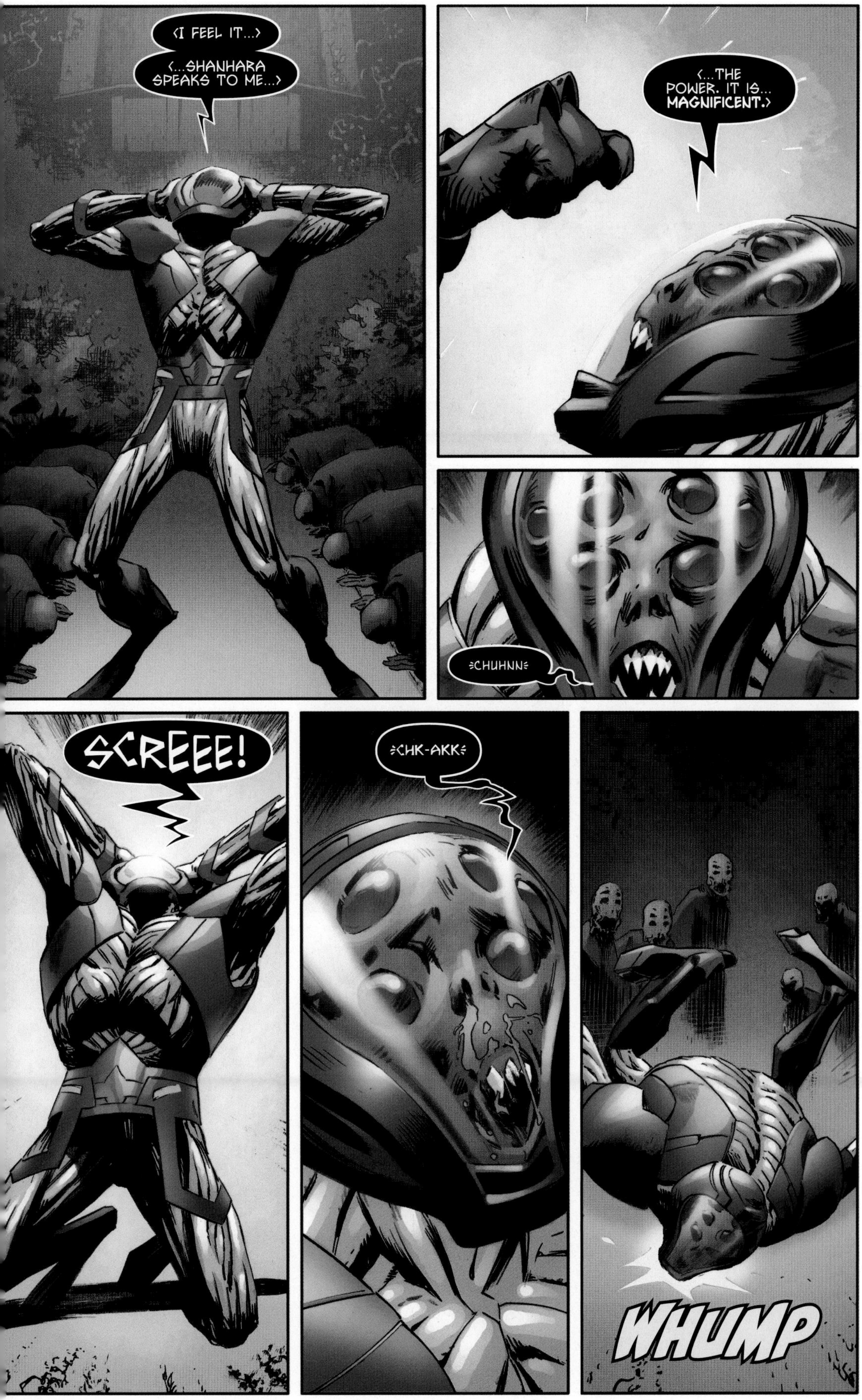

‹I FEEL IT...›
‹...SHANHARA SPEAKS TO ME...›
‹...THE POWER. IT IS... MAGNIFICENT.›
≈CHUHNN≈
SCREEE!
≈CHK-AKK≈
WHUMP

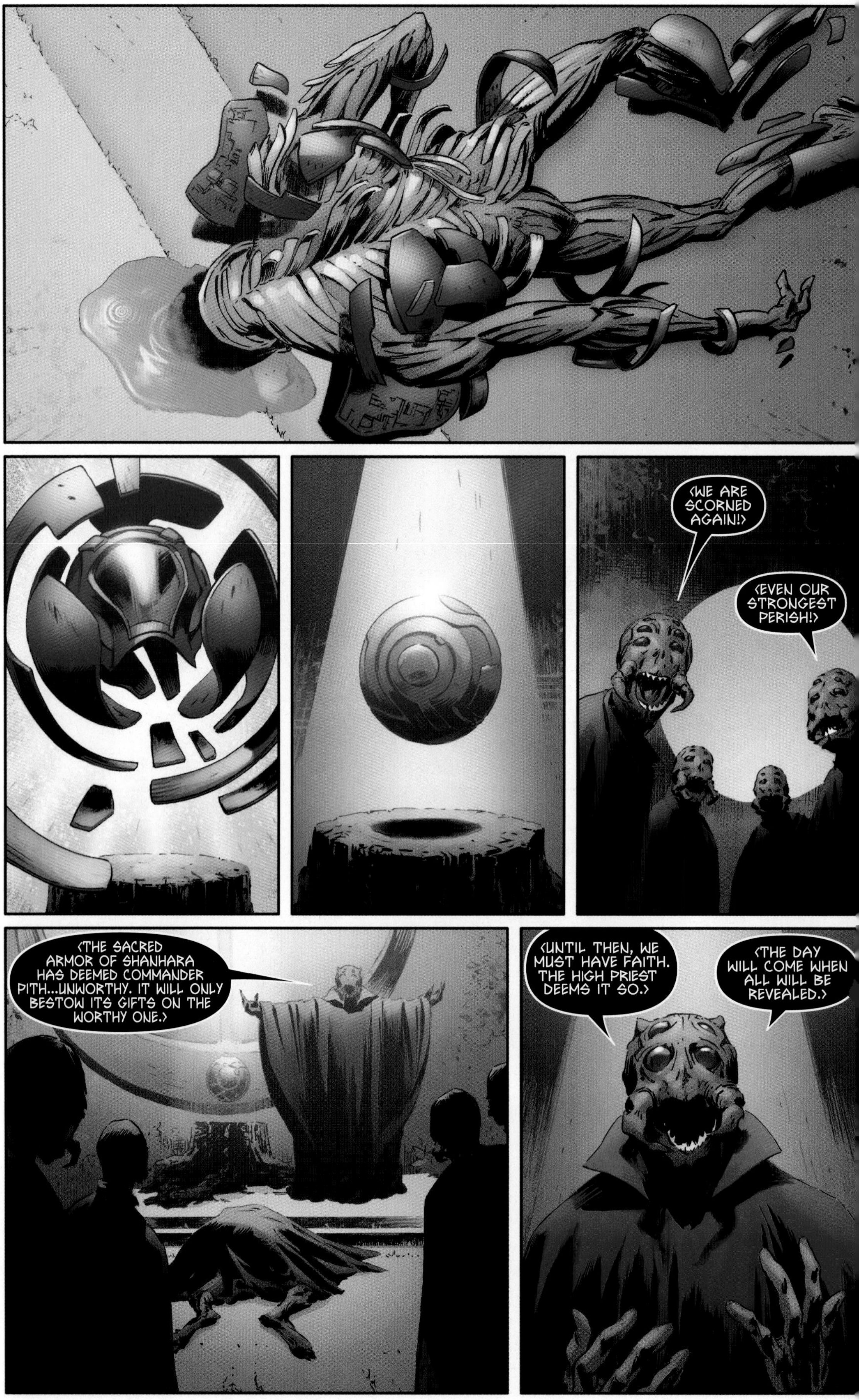
‹WE ARE SCORNED AGAIN!›
‹EVEN OUR STRONGEST PERISH!›
‹THE SACRED ARMOR OF SHANHARA HAS DEEMED COMMANDER PITH...UNWORTHY. IT WILL ONLY BESTOW ITS GIFTS ON THE WORTHY ONE.›
‹UNTIL THEN, WE MUST HAVE FAITH. THE HIGH PRIEST DEEMS IT SO.›
‹THE DAY WILL COME WHEN ALL WILL BE REVEALED.›

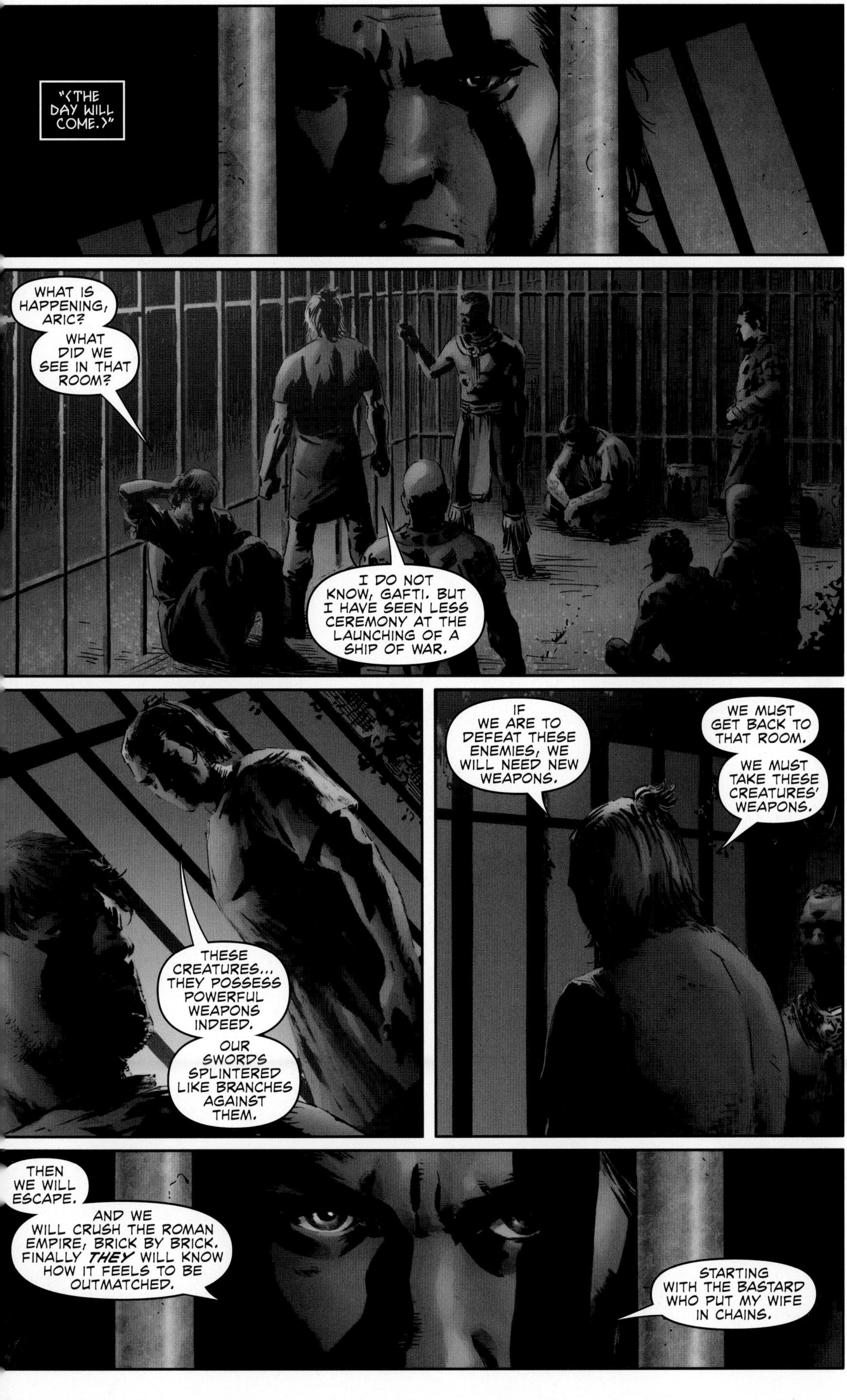
"<THE DAY WILL COME.>"
WHAT IS HAPPENING, ARIC?
WHAT DID WE SEE IN THAT ROOM?
I DO NOT KNOW, GAFTI. BUT I HAVE SEEN LESS CEREMONY AT THE LAUNCHING OF A SHIP OF WAR.
THESE CREATURES... THEY POSSESS POWERFUL WEAPONS INDEED.
OUR SWORDS SPLINTERED LIKE BRANCHES AGAINST THEM.
IF WE ARE TO DEFEAT THESE ENEMIES, WE WILL NEED NEW WEAPONS.
WE MUST GET BACK TO THAT ROOM.
WE MUST TAKE THESE CREATURES' WEAPONS.
THEN WE WILL ESCAPE.
AND WE WILL CRUSH THE ROMAN EMPIRE, BRICK BY BRICK. FINALLY *THEY* WILL KNOW HOW IT FEELS TO BE OUTMATCHED.
STARTING WITH THE BASTARD WHO PUT MY WIFE IN CHAINS.

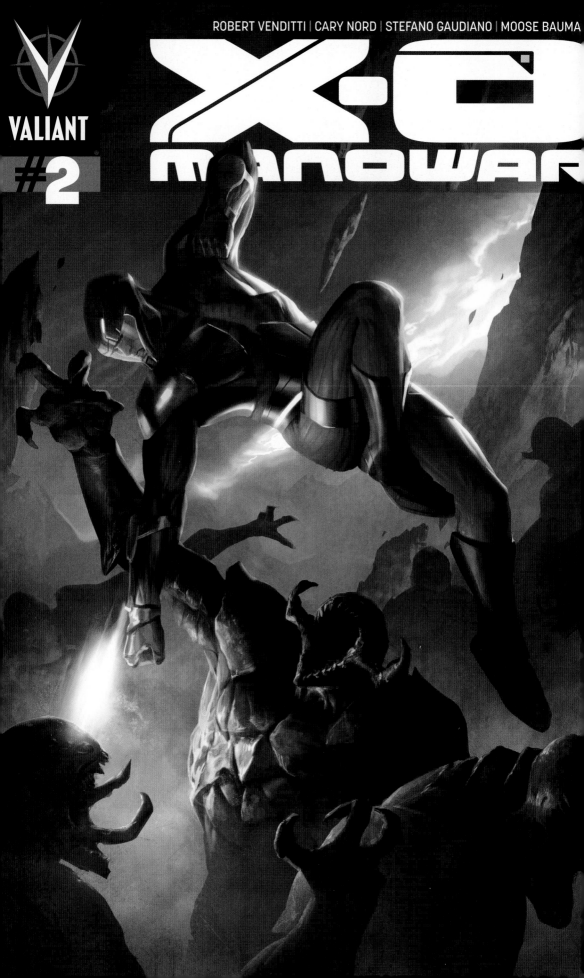

ROBERT VENDITTI | CARY NORD | STEFANO GAUDIANO | MOOSE BAUMA

X·O MANOWAR

VALIANT

#2

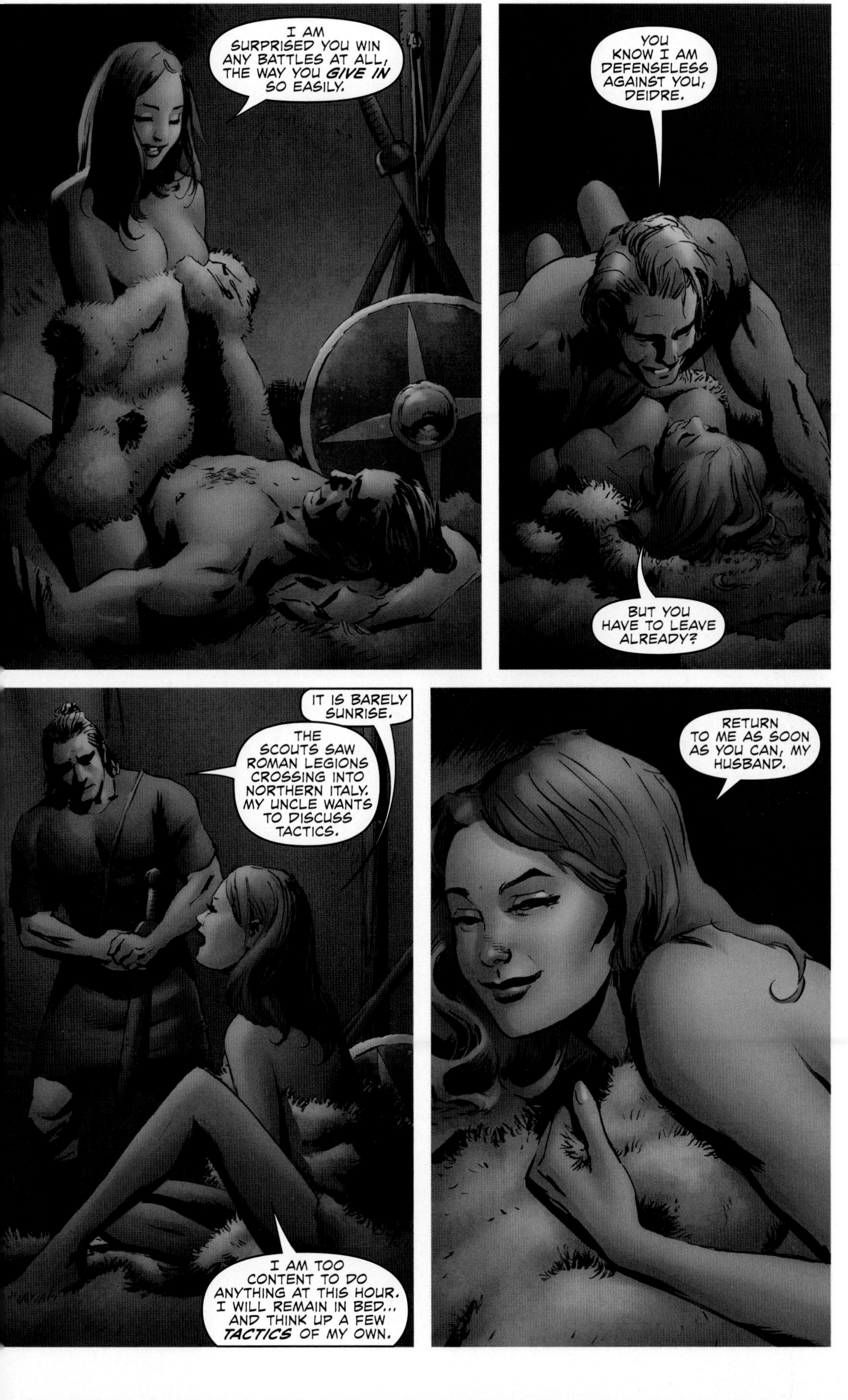
I AM SURPRISED YOU WIN ANY BATTLES AT ALL, THE WAY YOU *GIVE IN* SO EASILY.
YOU KNOW I AM DEFENSELESS AGAINST YOU, DEIDRE.
BUT YOU HAVE TO LEAVE ALREADY?
IT IS BARELY SUNRISE.
THE SCOUTS SAW ROMAN LEGIONS CROSSING INTO NORTHERN ITALY. MY UNCLE WANTS TO DISCUSS TACTICS.
I AM TOO CONTENT TO DO ANYTHING AT THIS HOUR. I WILL REMAIN IN BED... AND THINK UP A FEW *TACTICS* OF MY OWN.
RETURN TO ME AS SOON AS YOU CAN, MY HUSBAND.

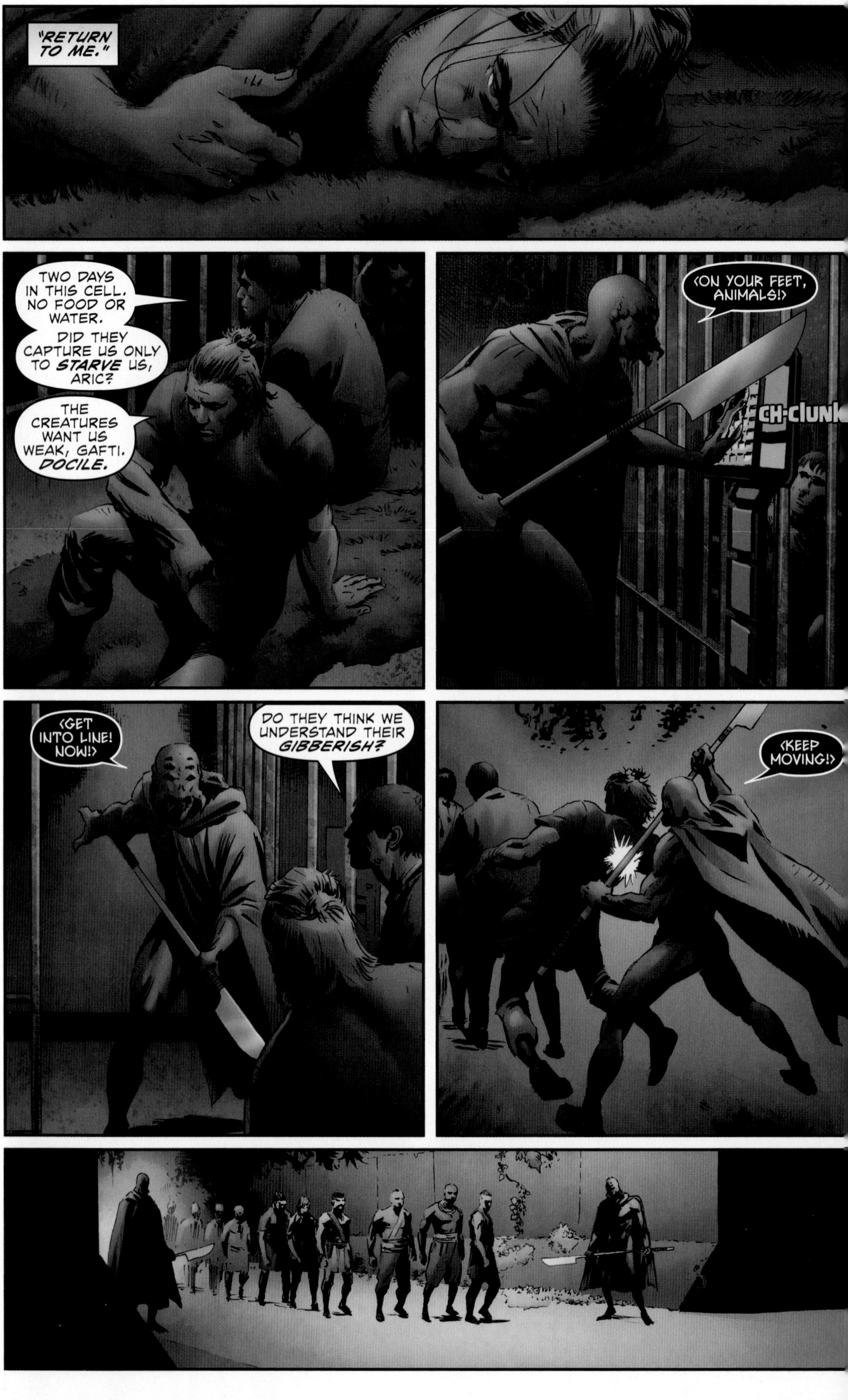
"RETURN TO ME."
TWO DAYS IN THIS CELL. NO FOOD OR WATER.
DID THEY CAPTURE US ONLY TO STARVE US, ARIC?
THE CREATURES WANT US WEAK, GAFTI. DOCILE.
‹ON YOUR FEET, ANIMALS!›
CH-CLUNK
‹GET INTO LINE! NOW!›
DO THEY THINK WE UNDERSTAND THEIR GIBBERISH?
‹KEEP MOVING!›

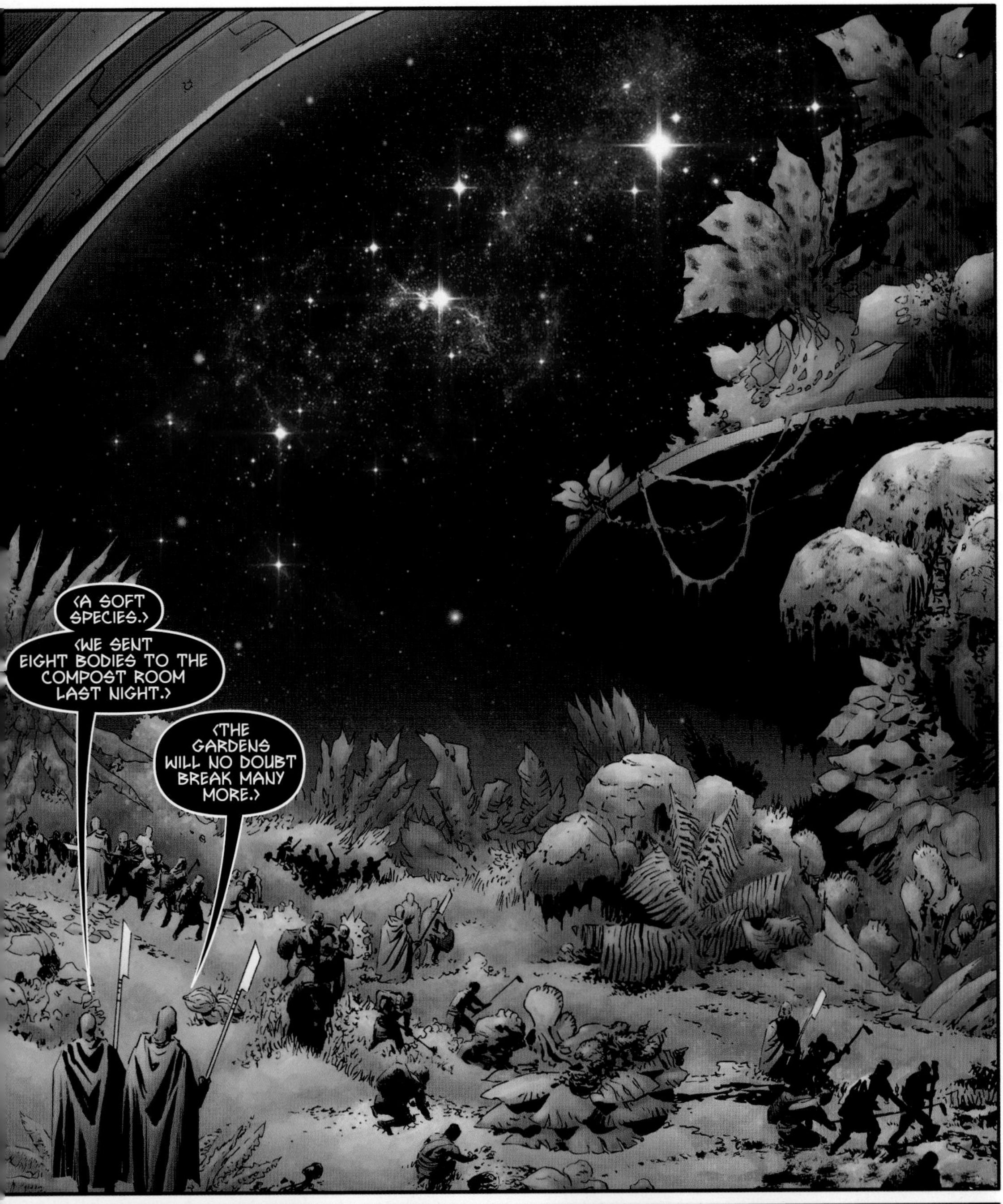

‹A SOFT SPECIES.›
‹WE SENT EIGHT BODIES TO THE COMPOST ROOM LAST NIGHT.›
‹THE GARDENS WILL NO DOUBT BREAK MANY MORE.›

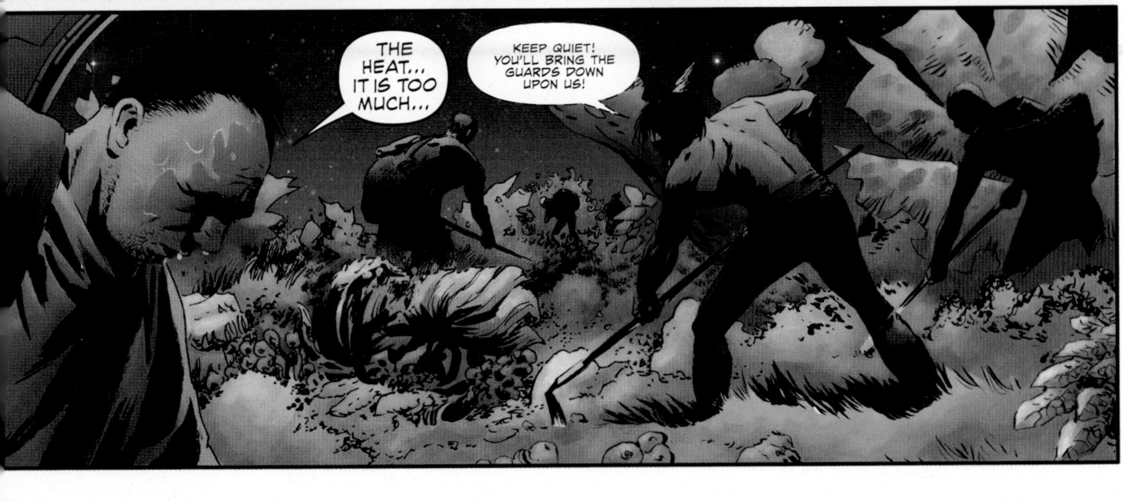

THE HEAT... IT IS TOO MUCH...
KEEP QUIET! YOU'LL BRING THE GUARDS DOWN UPON US!

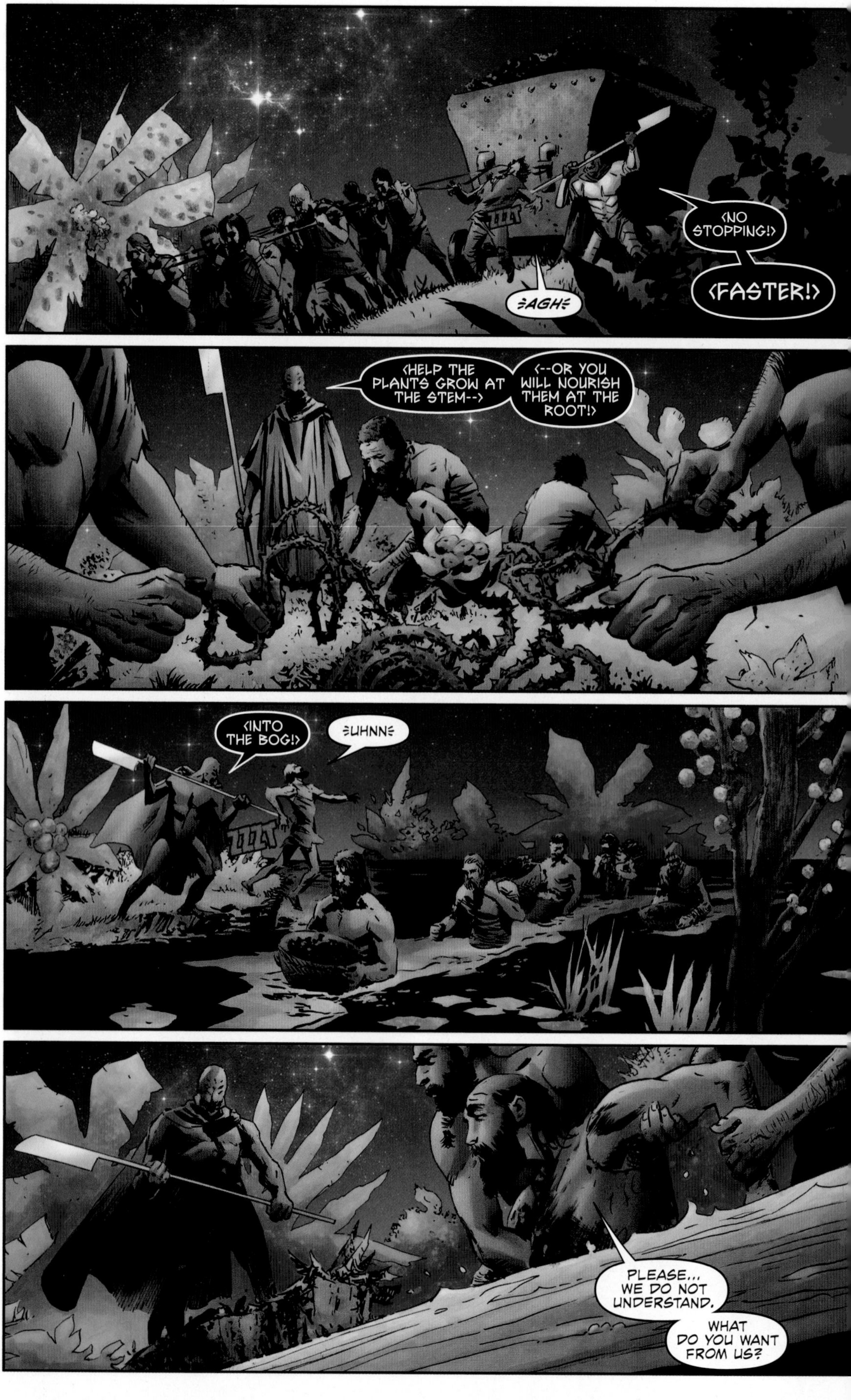
‹NO STOPPING!›
‹FASTER!›
AGH
‹HELP THE PLANTS GROW AT THE STEM--›
‹--OR YOU WILL NOURISH THEM AT THE ROOT!›
‹INTO THE BOG!›
UHNN
PLEASE... WE DO NOT UNDERSTAND.
WHAT DO YOU WANT FROM US?

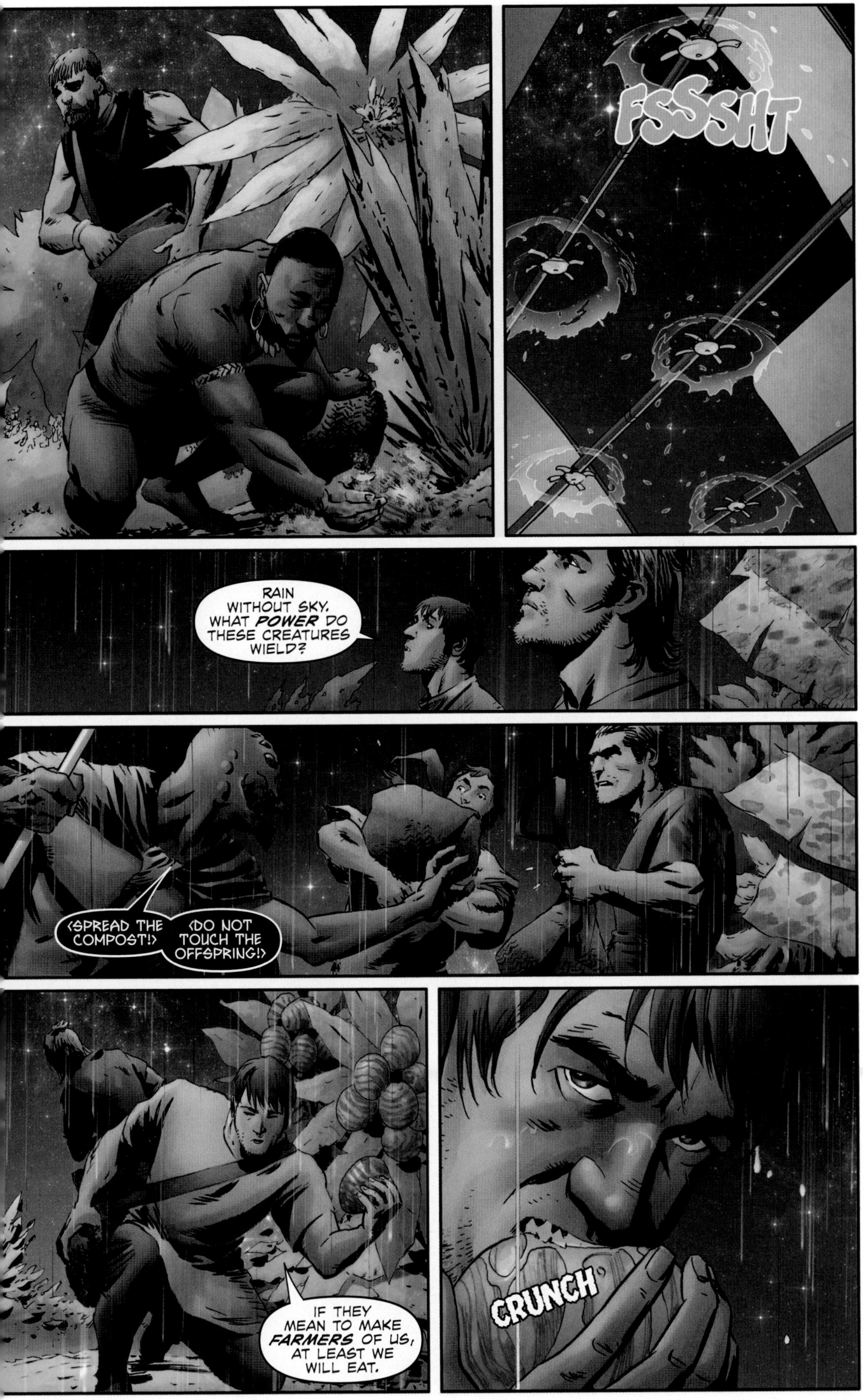
FSSSHT
RAIN WITHOUT SKY. WHAT POWER DO THESE CREATURES WIELD?
‹SPREAD THE COMPOST!›
‹DO NOT TOUCH THE OFFSPRING!›
IF THEY MEAN TO MAKE FARMERS OF US, AT LEAST WE WILL EAT.
CRUNCH

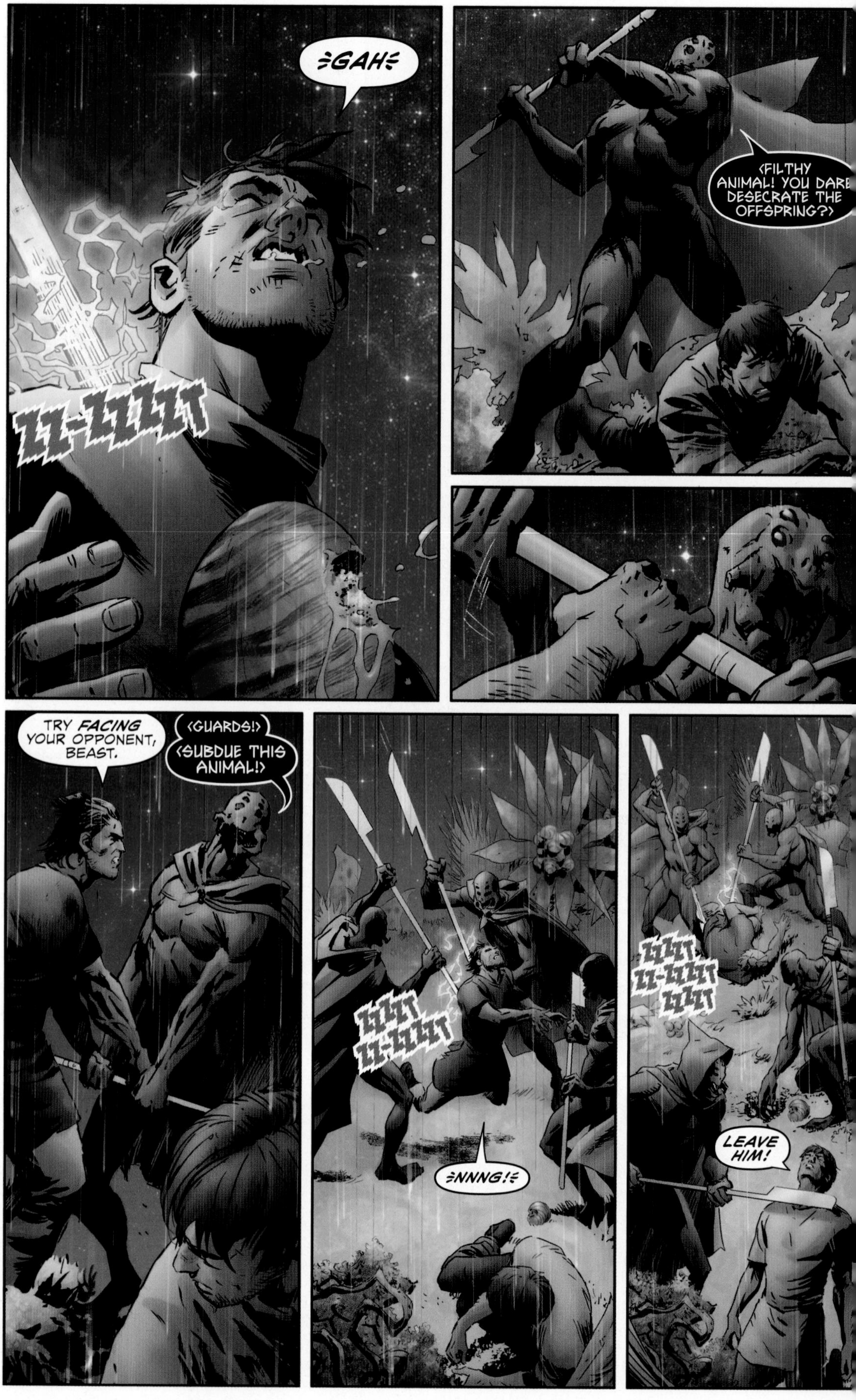
GAH
ZZ-ZZZZT
‹FILTHY ANIMAL! YOU DARE DESECRATE THE OFFSPRING?›
TRY *FACING* YOUR OPPONENT, BEAST.
‹GUARDS!›
‹SUBDUE THIS ANIMAL!›
NNNG!
LEAVE HIM!

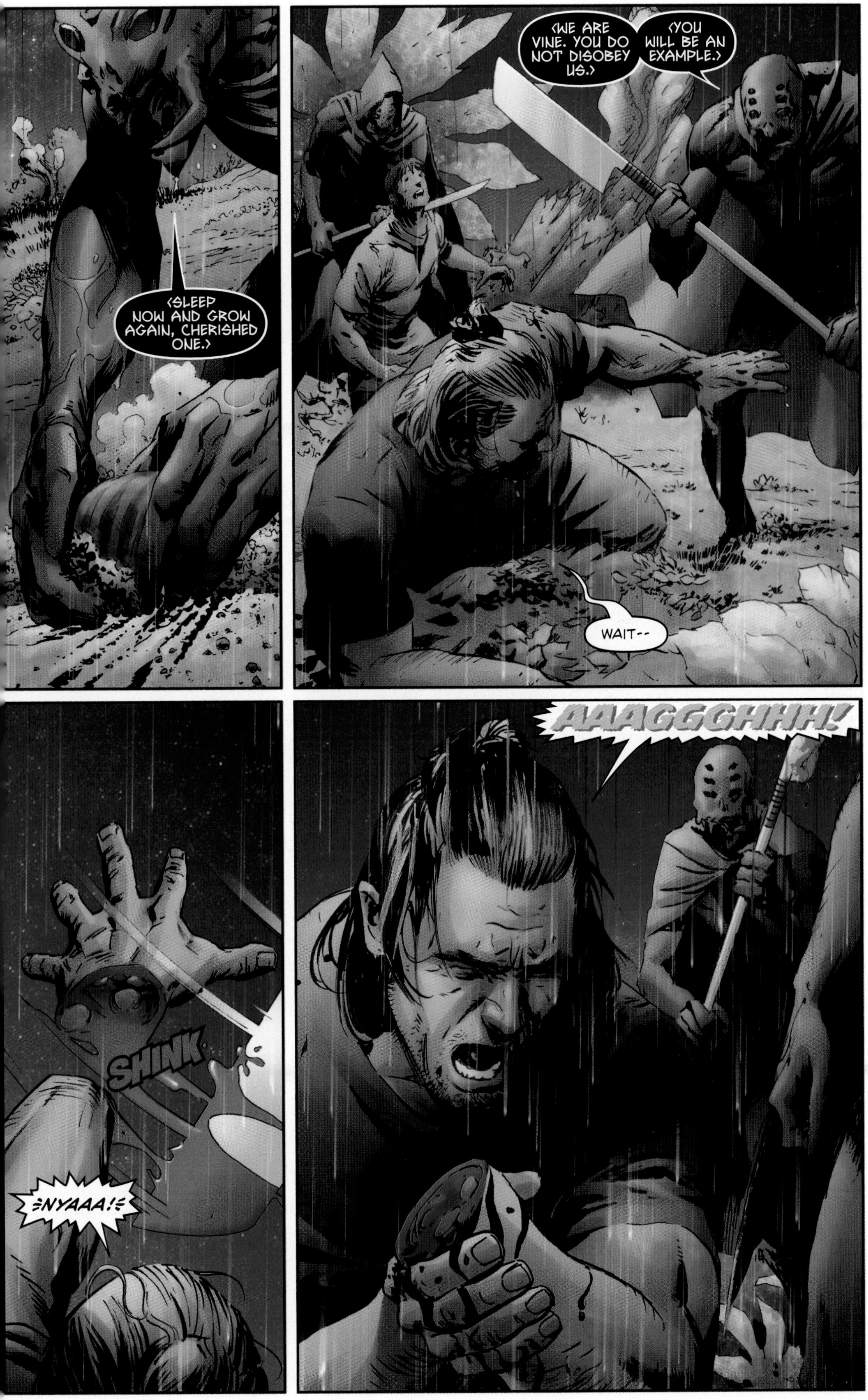

<SLEEP NOW AND GROW AGAIN, CHERISHED ONE.>
<WE ARE VINE. YOU DO NOT DISOBEY US.>
<YOU WILL BE AN EXAMPLE.>
WAIT--
SHINK
NYAAA!
AAAGGGHHH!

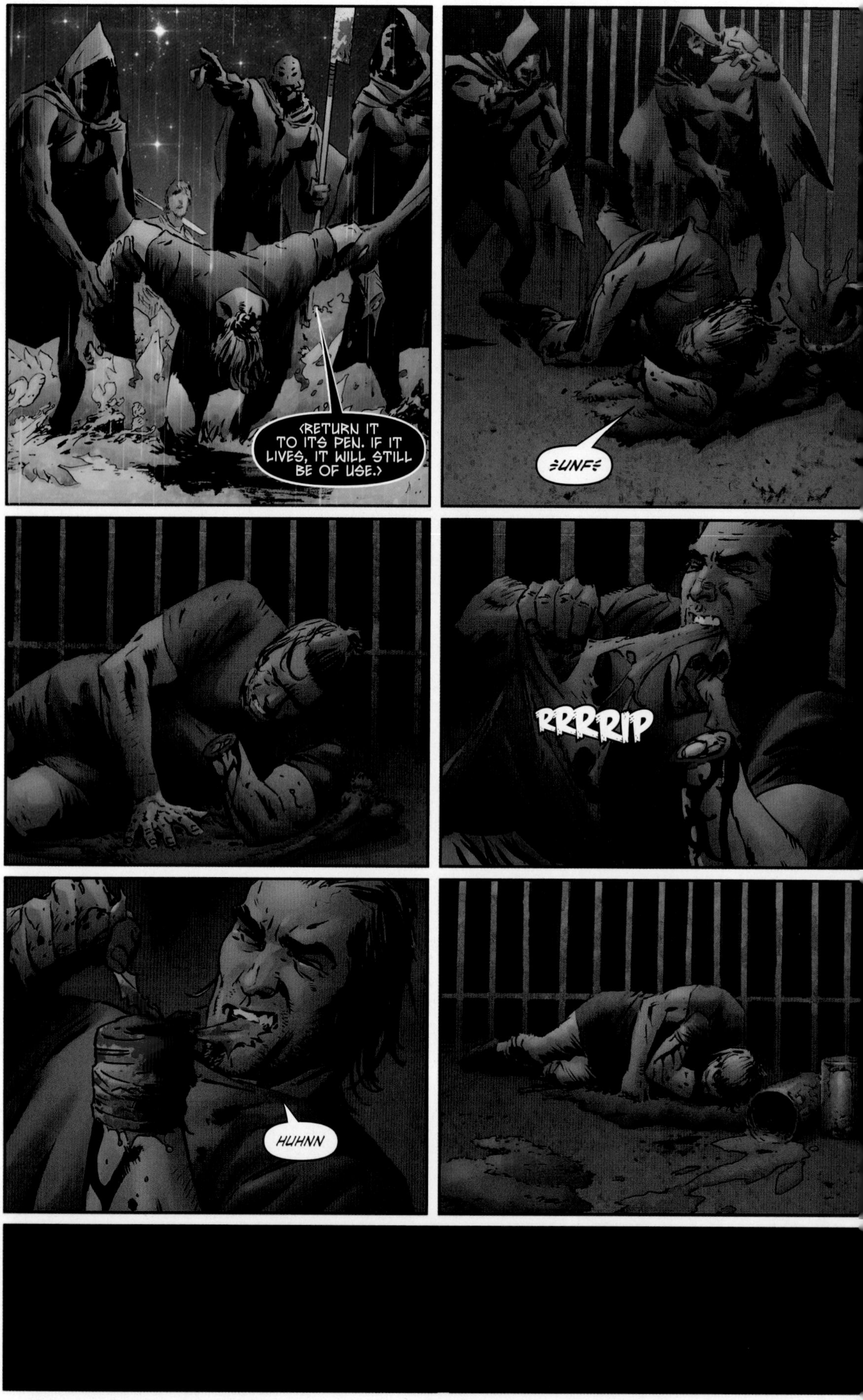
‹RETURN IT TO ITS PEN. IF IT LIVES, IT WILL STILL BE OF USE.›
UNF
RRRRIP
HUHNN

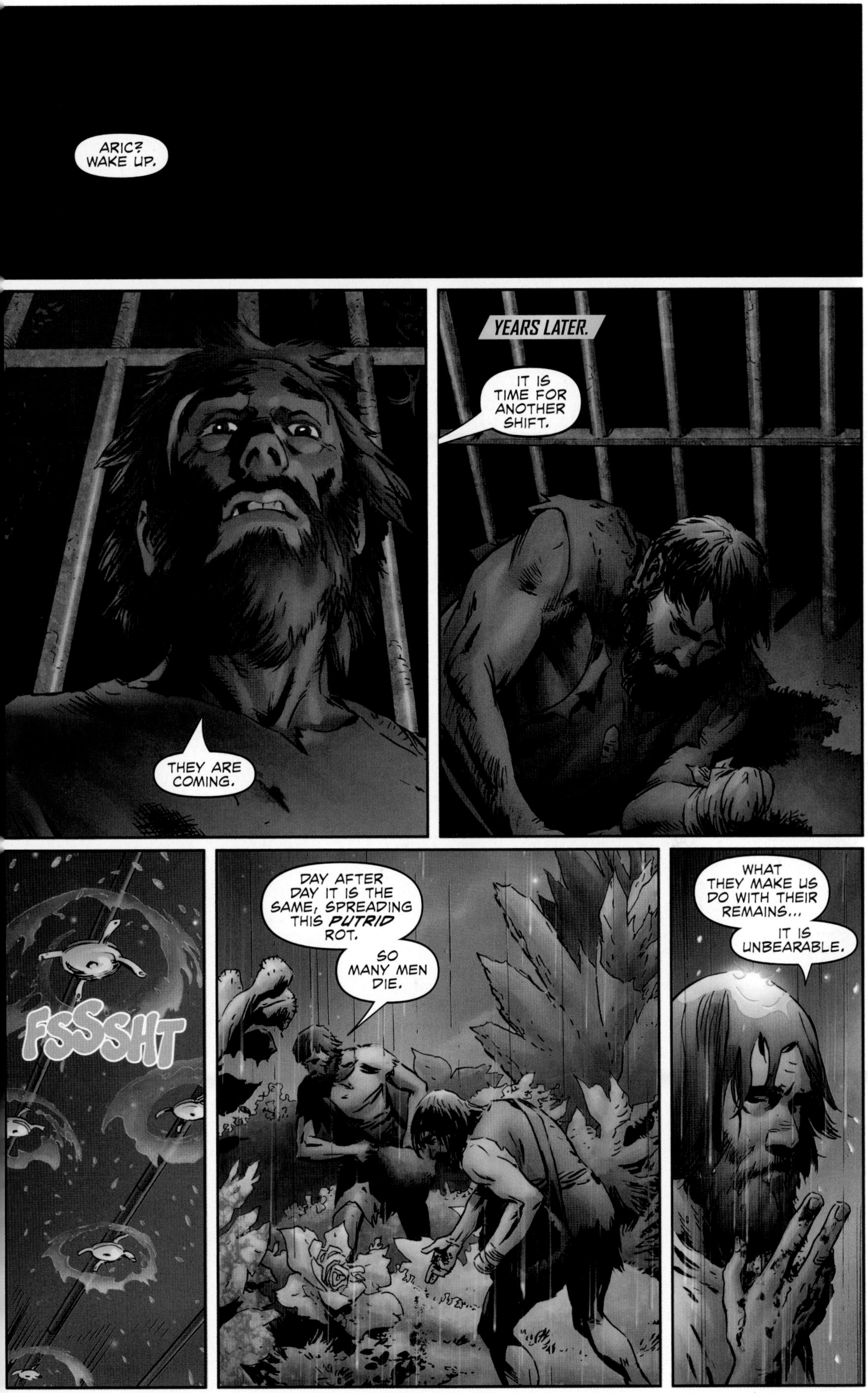
ARIC? WAKE UP.
THEY ARE COMING.
YEARS LATER.
IT IS TIME FOR ANOTHER SHIFT.
FSSSHT
DAY AFTER DAY IT IS THE SAME, SPREADING THIS PUTRID ROT.
SO MANY MEN DIE.
WHAT THEY MAKE US DO WITH THEIR REMAINS...
IT IS UNBEARABLE.

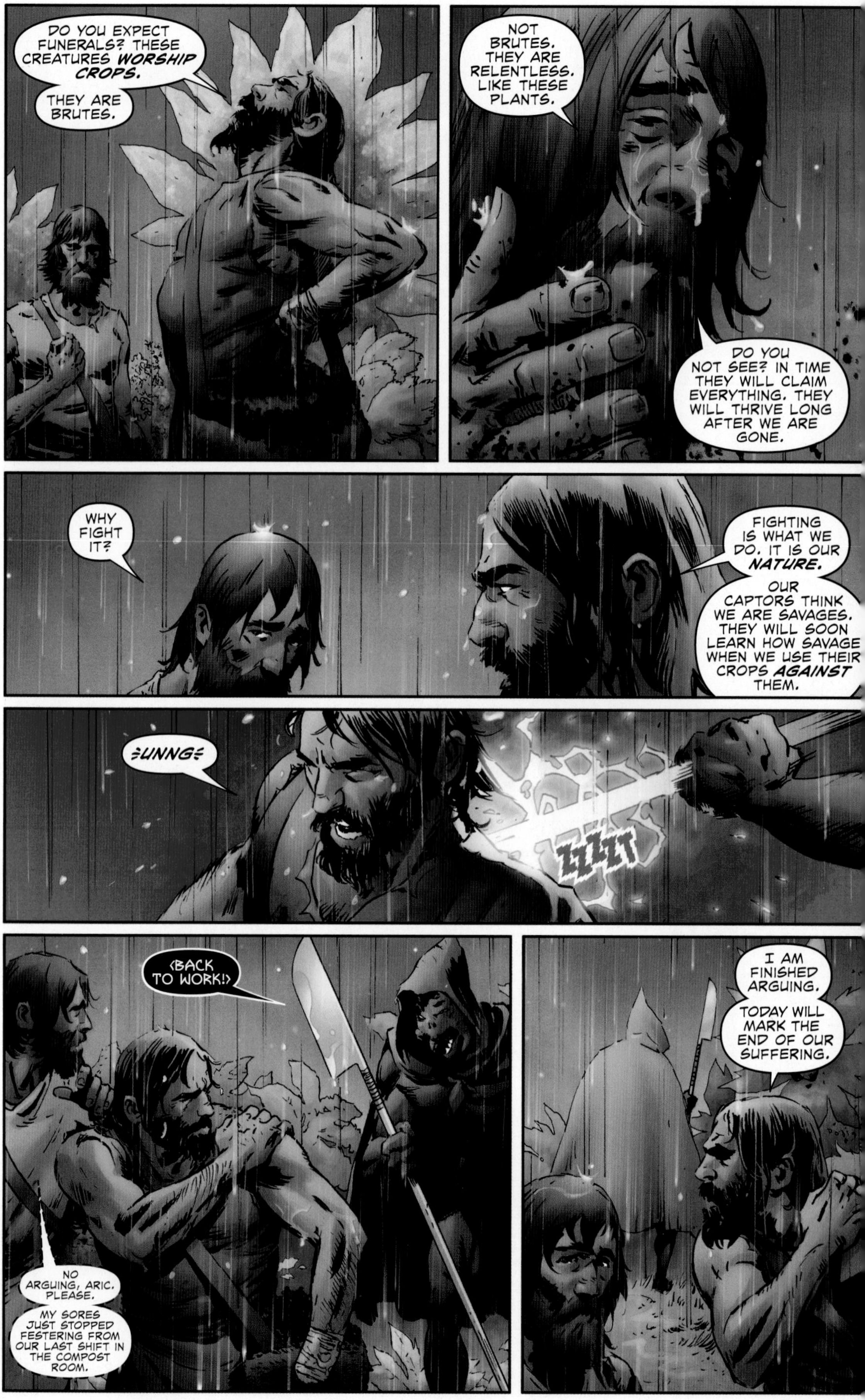

DO YOU EXPECT FUNERALS? THESE CREATURES ***WORSHIP CROPS.***
THEY ARE BRUTES.
NOT BRUTES. THEY ARE RELENTLESS. LIKE THESE PLANTS.
DO YOU NOT SEE? IN TIME THEY WILL CLAIM EVERYTHING. THEY WILL THRIVE LONG AFTER WE ARE GONE.
WHY FIGHT IT?
FIGHTING IS WHAT WE DO. IT IS OUR ***NATURE.***
OUR CAPTORS THINK WE ARE SAVAGES. THEY WILL SOON LEARN HOW SAVAGE WHEN WE USE THEIR CROPS ***AGAINST*** THEM.
UNNG
ZZZZT
<BACK TO WORK!>
NO ARGUING, ARIC. PLEASE.
MY SORES JUST STOPPED FESTERING FROM OUR LAST SHIFT IN THE COMPOST ROOM.
I AM FINISHED ARGUING.
TODAY WILL MARK THE END OF OUR SUFFERING.

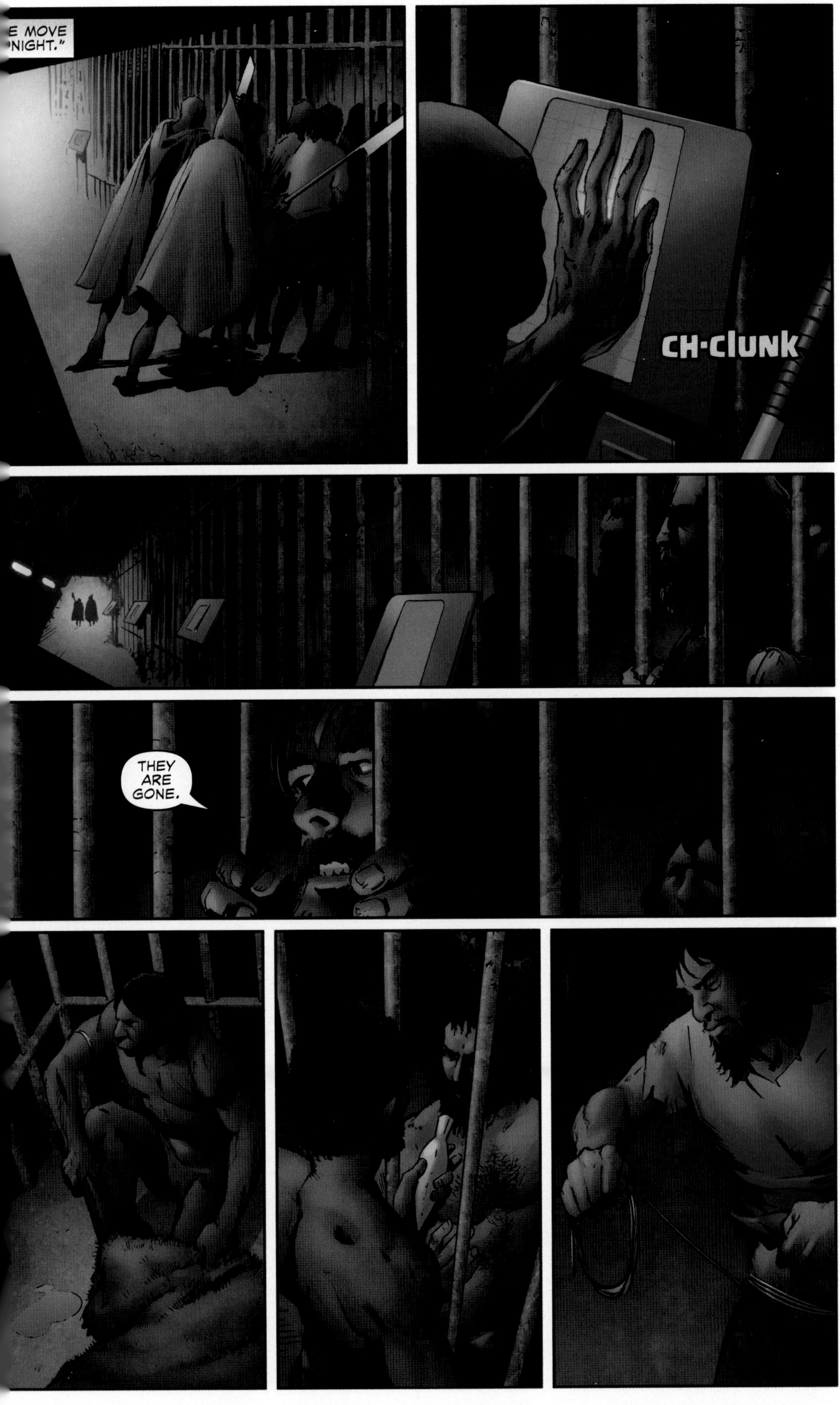
E MOVE
NIGHT."
CH-CLUNK
THEY ARE GONE.

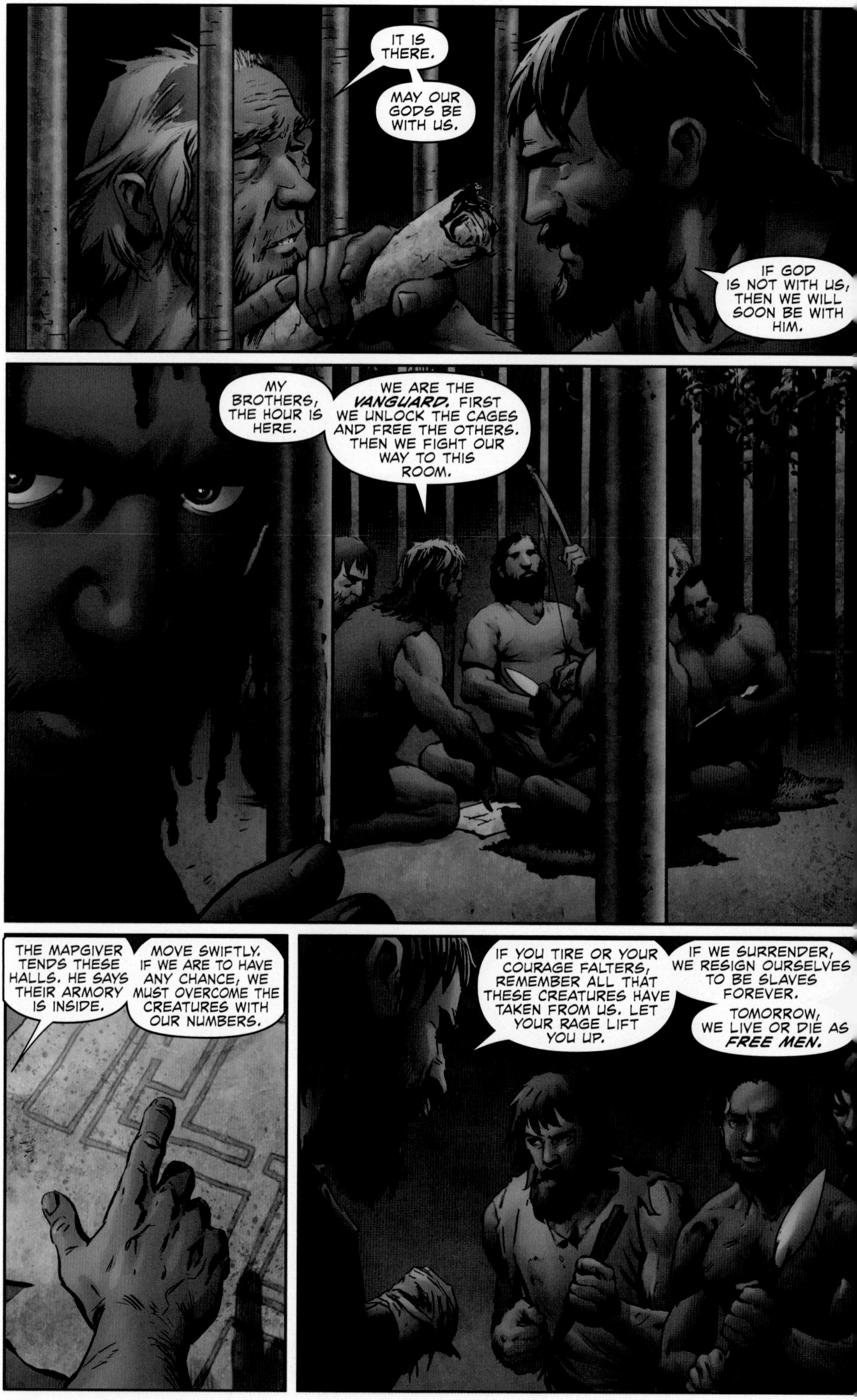
IT IS THERE.
MAY OUR GODS BE WITH US.
IF GOD IS NOT WITH US, THEN WE WILL SOON BE WITH HIM.
MY BROTHERS, THE HOUR IS HERE.
WE ARE THE ***VANGUARD.*** FIRST WE UNLOCK THE CAGES AND FREE THE OTHERS. THEN WE FIGHT OUR WAY TO THIS ROOM.
THE MAPGIVER TENDS THESE HALLS. HE SAYS THEIR ARMORY IS INSIDE.
MOVE SWIFTLY. IF WE ARE TO HAVE ANY CHANCE, WE MUST OVERCOME THE CREATURES WITH OUR NUMBERS.
IF YOU TIRE OR YOUR COURAGE FALTERS, REMEMBER ALL THAT THESE CREATURES HAVE TAKEN FROM US. LET YOUR RAGE LIFT YOU UP.
IF WE SURRENDER, WE RESIGN OURSELVES TO BE SLAVES FOREVER.
TOMORROW, WE LIVE OR DIE AS ***FREE MEN.***

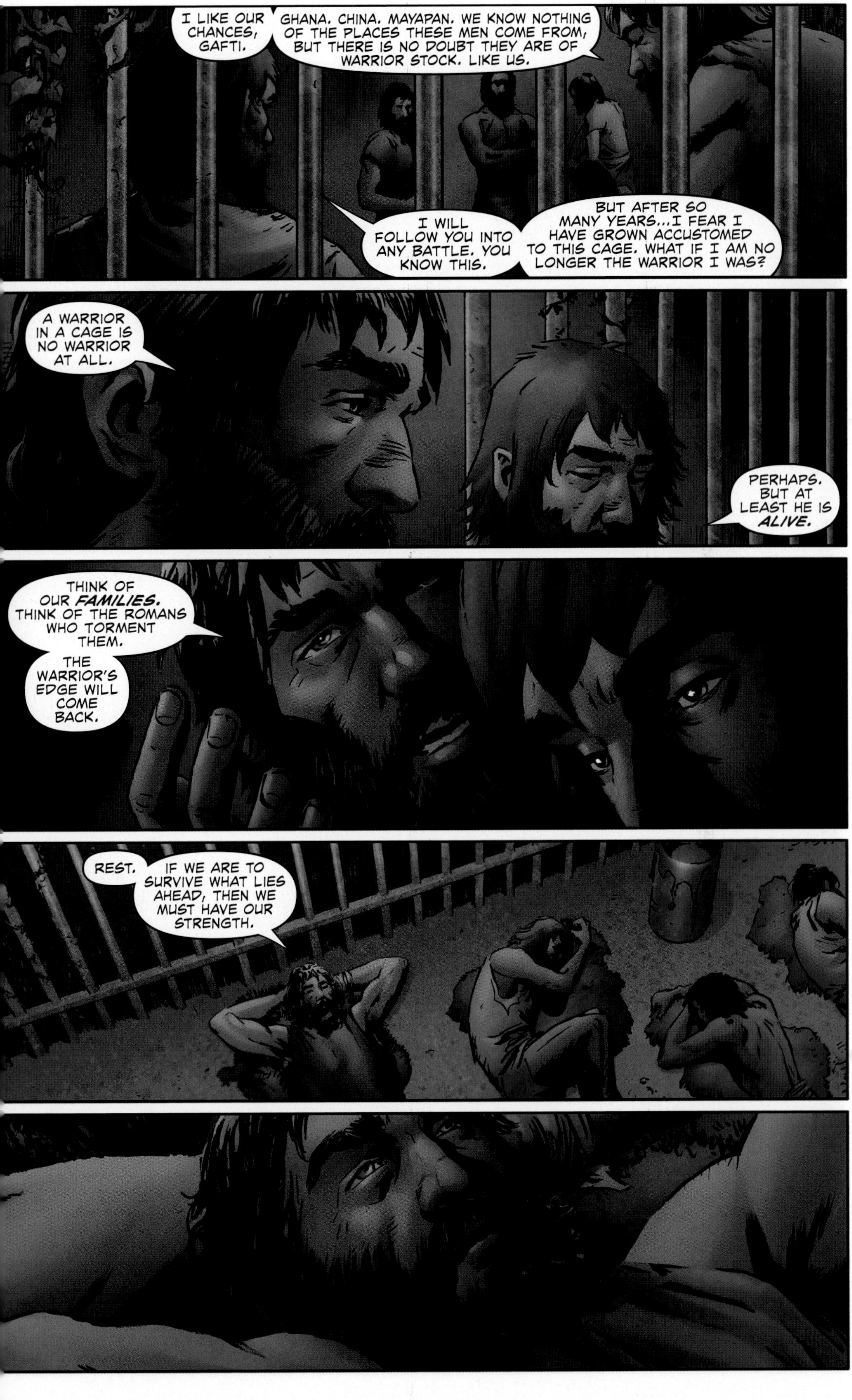

I LIKE OUR CHANCES, GAFTI.
GHANA. CHINA. MAYAPAN. WE KNOW NOTHING OF THE PLACES THESE MEN COME FROM, BUT THERE IS NO DOUBT THEY ARE OF WARRIOR STOCK. LIKE US.
I WILL FOLLOW YOU INTO ANY BATTLE. YOU KNOW THIS.
BUT AFTER SO MANY YEARS...I FEAR I HAVE GROWN ACCUSTOMED TO THIS CAGE. WHAT IF I AM NO LONGER THE WARRIOR I WAS?
A WARRIOR IN A CAGE IS NO WARRIOR AT ALL.
PERHAPS. BUT AT LEAST HE IS *ALIVE.*
THINK OF OUR ***FAMILIES.*** THINK OF THE ROMANS WHO TORMENT THEM.
THE WARRIOR'S EDGE WILL COME BACK.
REST.
IF WE ARE TO SURVIVE WHAT LIES AHEAD, THEN WE MUST HAVE OUR STRENGTH.

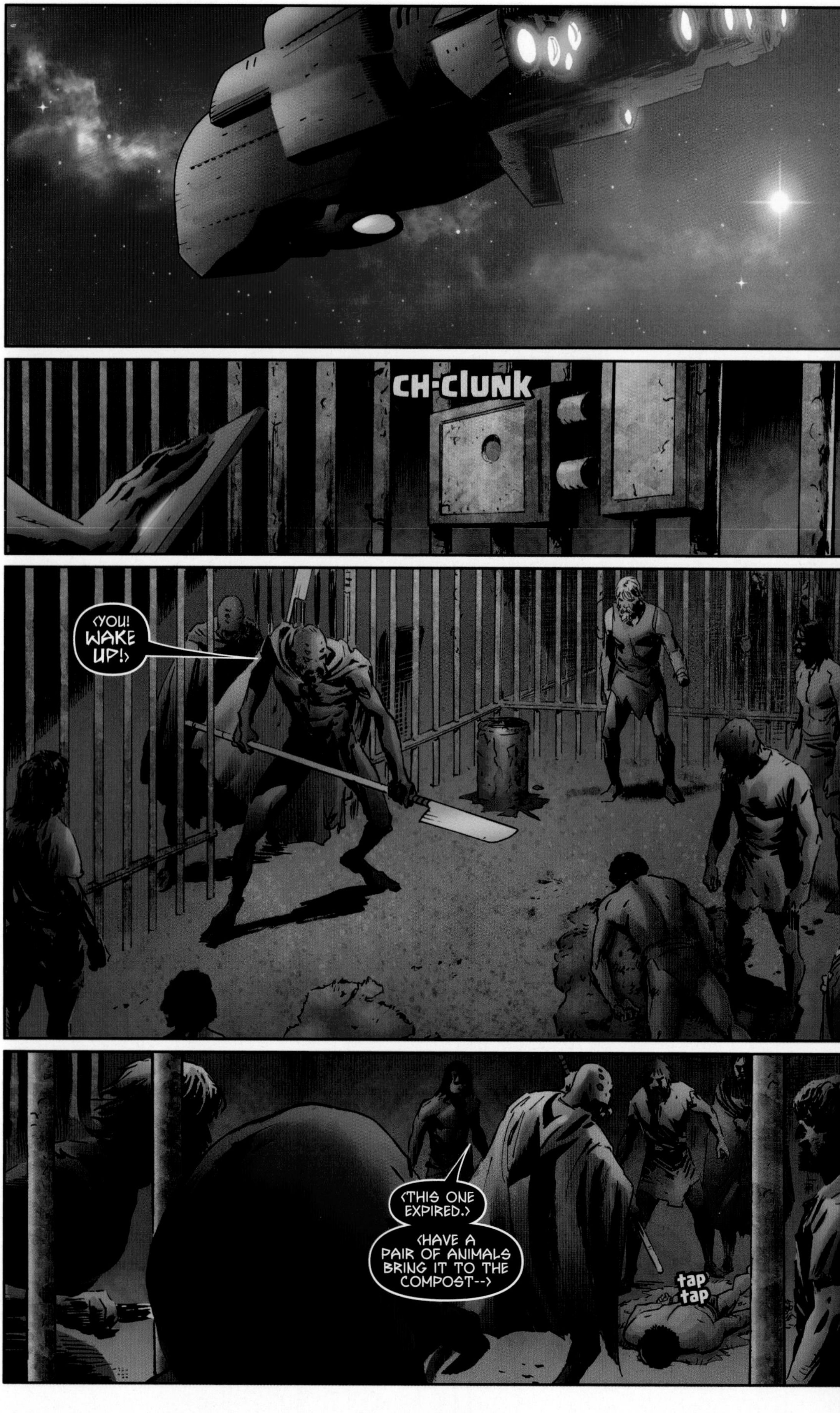
CH-CLUNK
‹YOU! WAKE UP!›
‹THIS ONE EXPIRED.›
‹HAVE A PAIR OF ANIMALS BRING IT TO THE COMPOST--›
tap tap

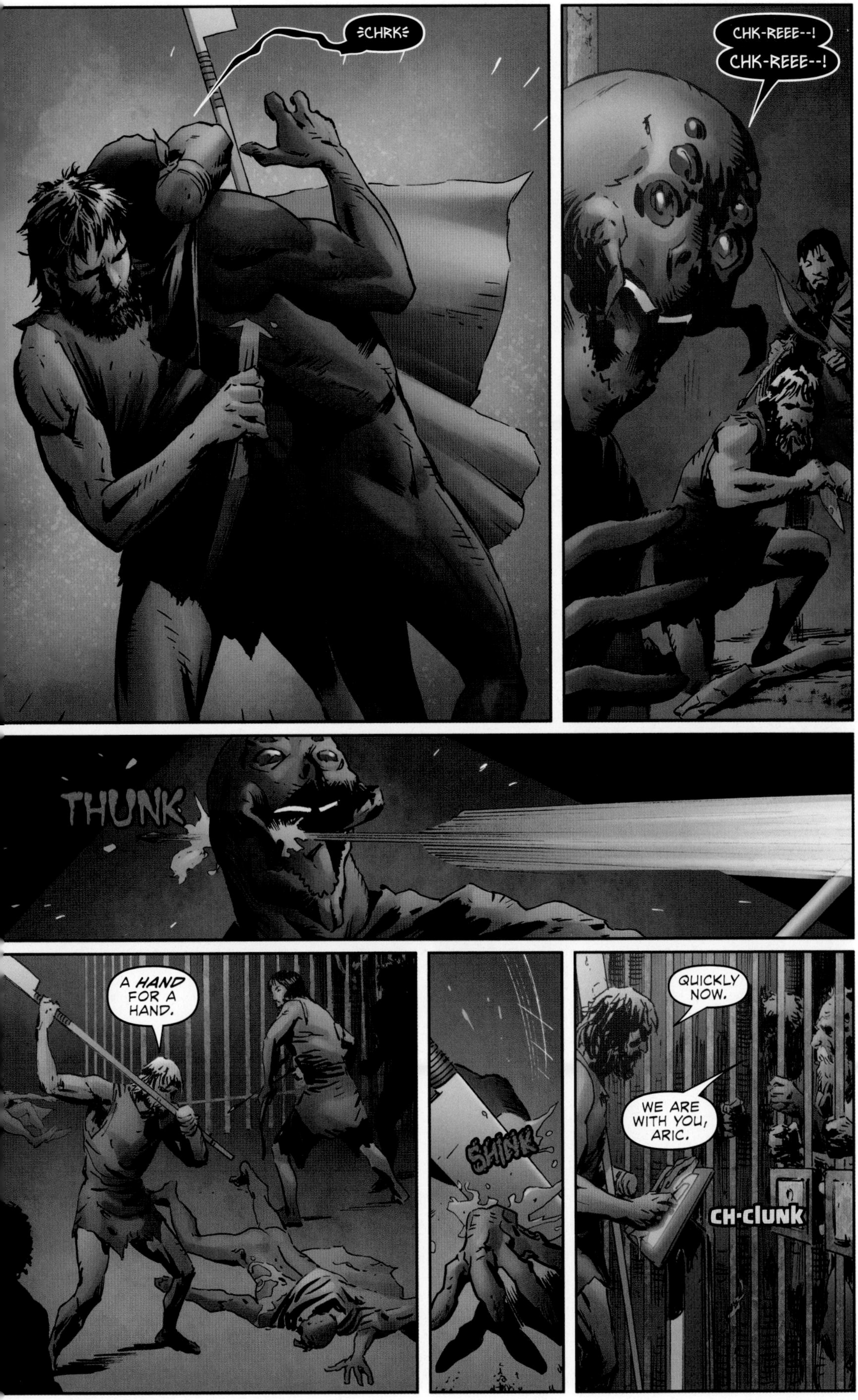
CHRK
CHK-REEE--!
CHK-REEE--!
THUNK
A HAND FOR A HAND.
SHINK
QUICKLY NOW.
WE ARE WITH YOU, ARIC.
CH-CLUNK

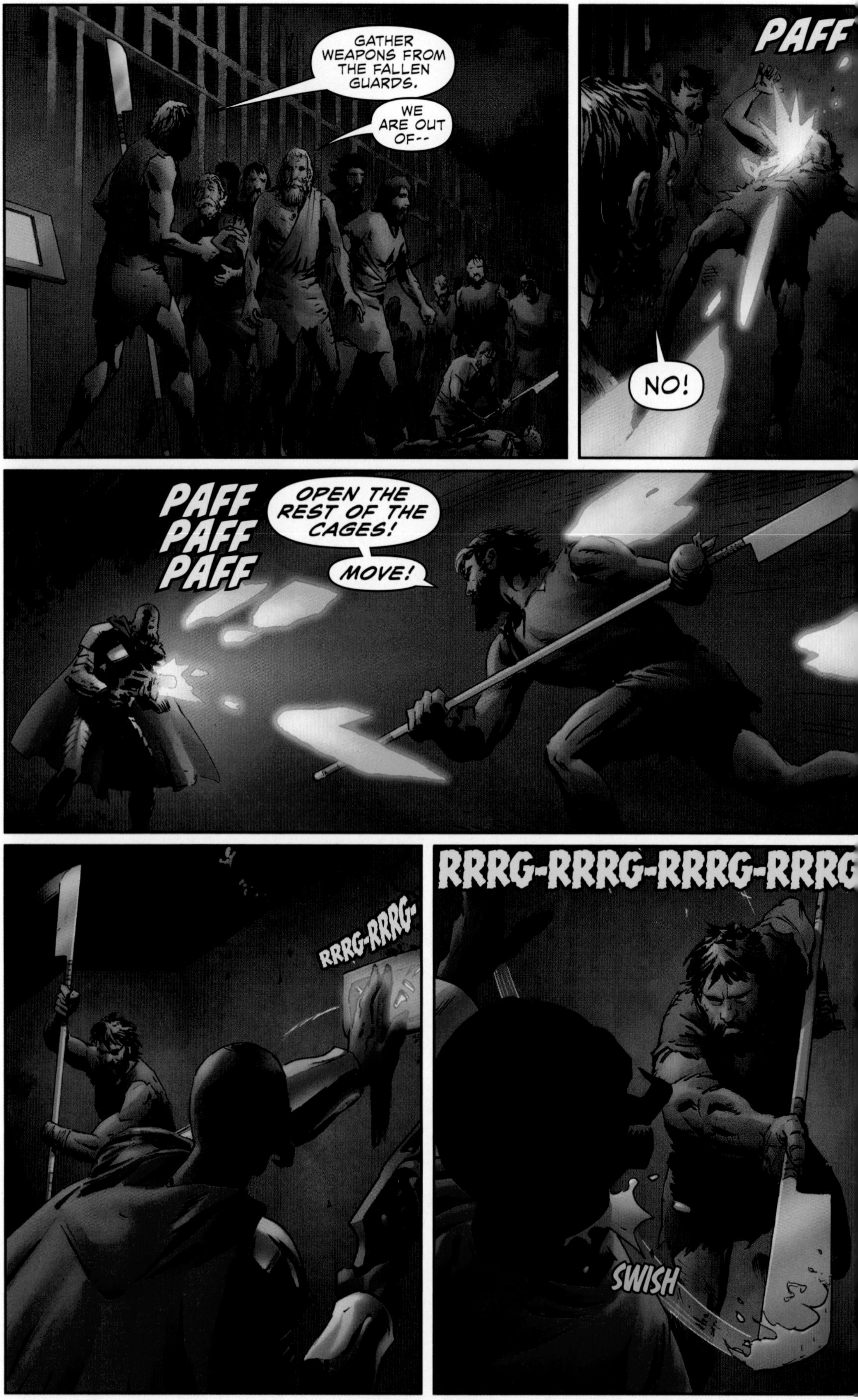
GATHER WEAPONS FROM THE FALLEN GUARDS.
WE ARE OUT OF--
PAFF
NO!
PAFF PAFF PAFF
OPEN THE REST OF THE CAGES!
MOVE!
RRRG-RRRG-
RRRG-RRRG-RRRG-RRRG
SWISH

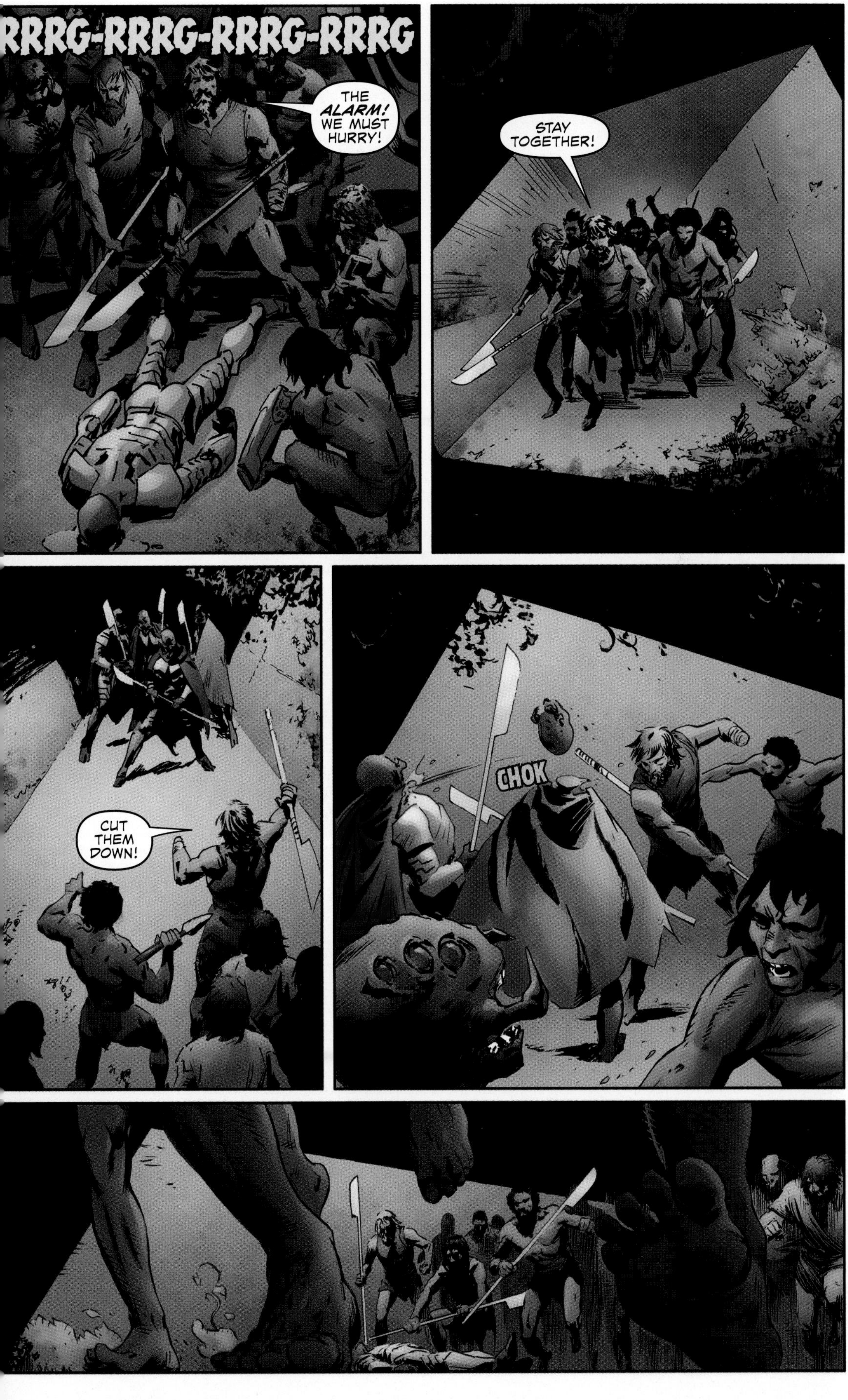
RRRG-RRRG-RRRG-RRRG
THE ALARM! WE MUST HURRY!
STAY TOGETHER!
CUT THEM DOWN!
CHOK

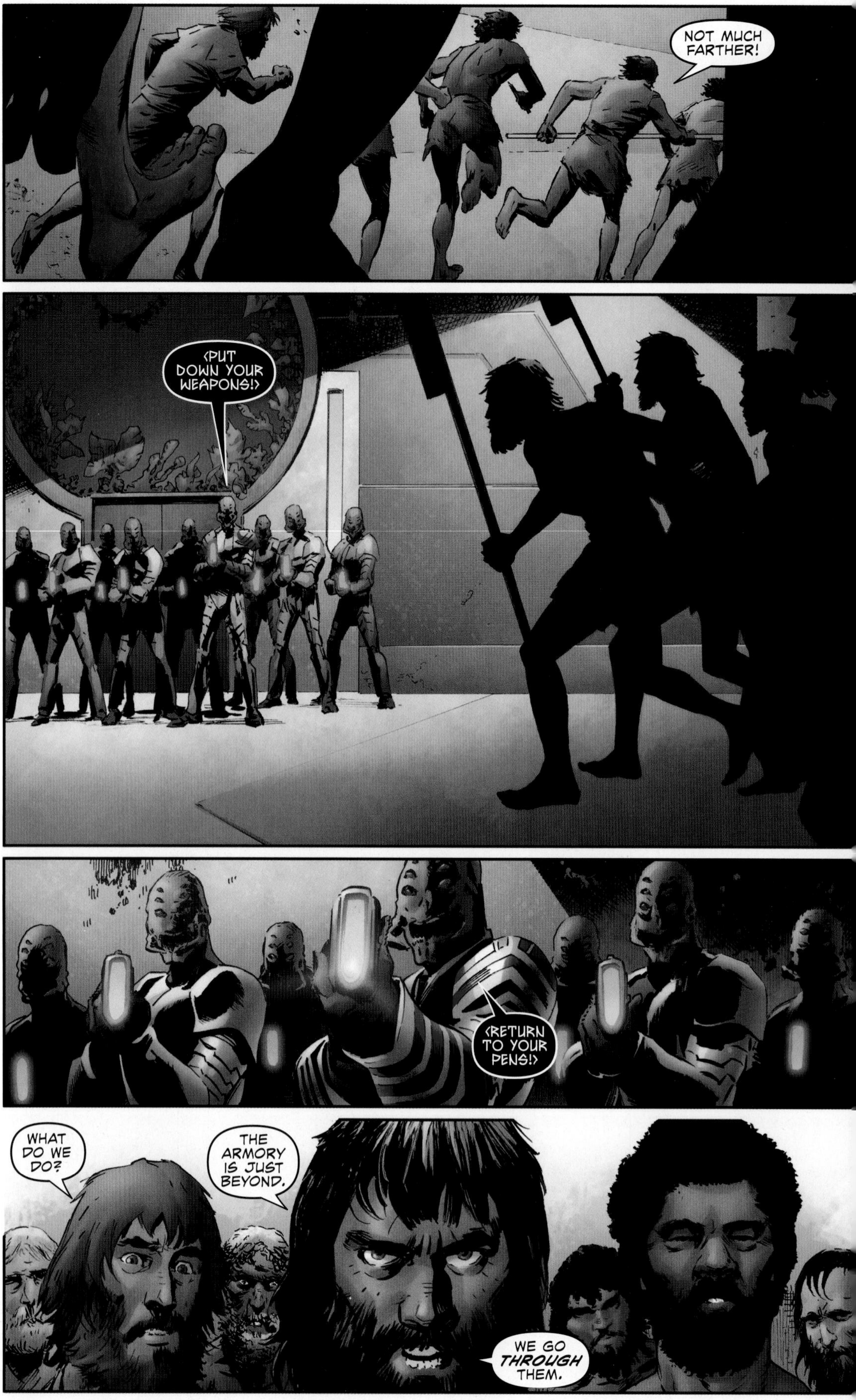
NOT MUCH FARTHER!
‹PUT DOWN YOUR WEAPONS!›
‹RETURN TO YOUR PENS!›
WHAT DO WE DO?
THE ARMORY IS JUST BEYOND.
WE GO *THROUGH* THEM.

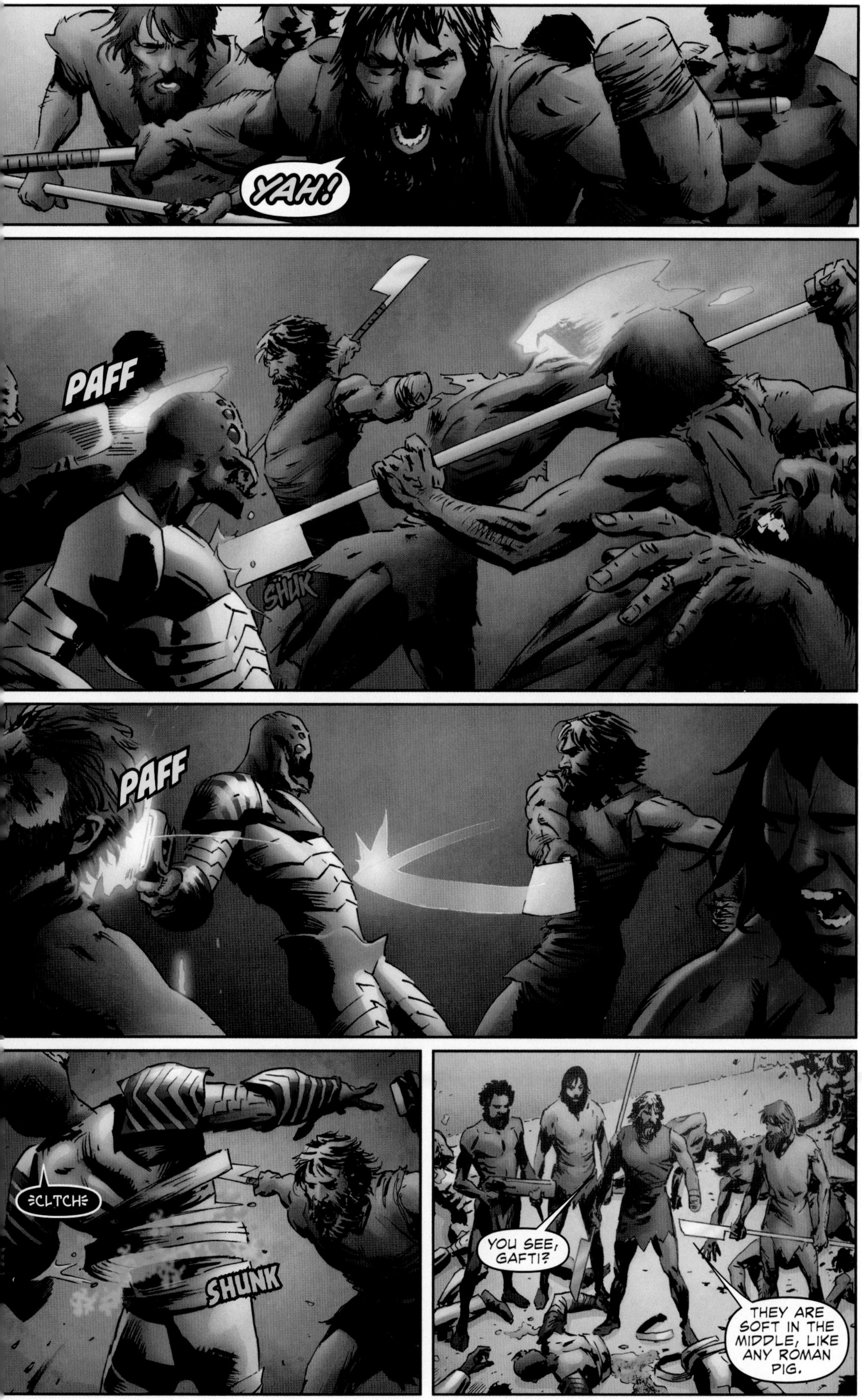
YAH!
PAFF
SHUK
PAFF
CLTCH
SHUNK
YOU SEE, GAFTI?
THEY ARE SOFT IN THE MIDDLE, LIKE ANY ROMAN PIG.

BACK AWAY.

IF THIS IS AN *ARMORY*, IT IS DECIDELY *LACKING* IN ARMOR. IS THERE JUST THE ONE?

ONE WILL HAVE TO BE ENOUGH.

MY GOD...

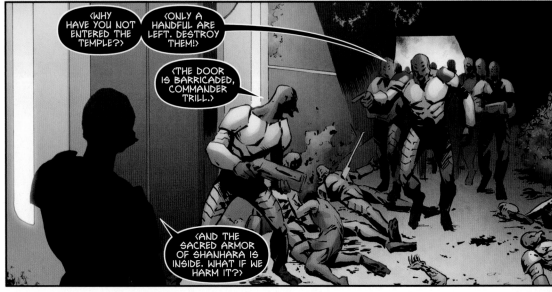

‹WHY HAVE YOU NOT ENTERED THE TEMPLE?›

‹ONLY A HANDFUL ARE LEFT. DESTROY THEM!›

‹THE DOOR IS BARRICADED, COMMANDER TRILL.›

‹AND THE SACRED ARMOR OF SHANHARA IS INSIDE. WHAT IF WE HARM IT?›

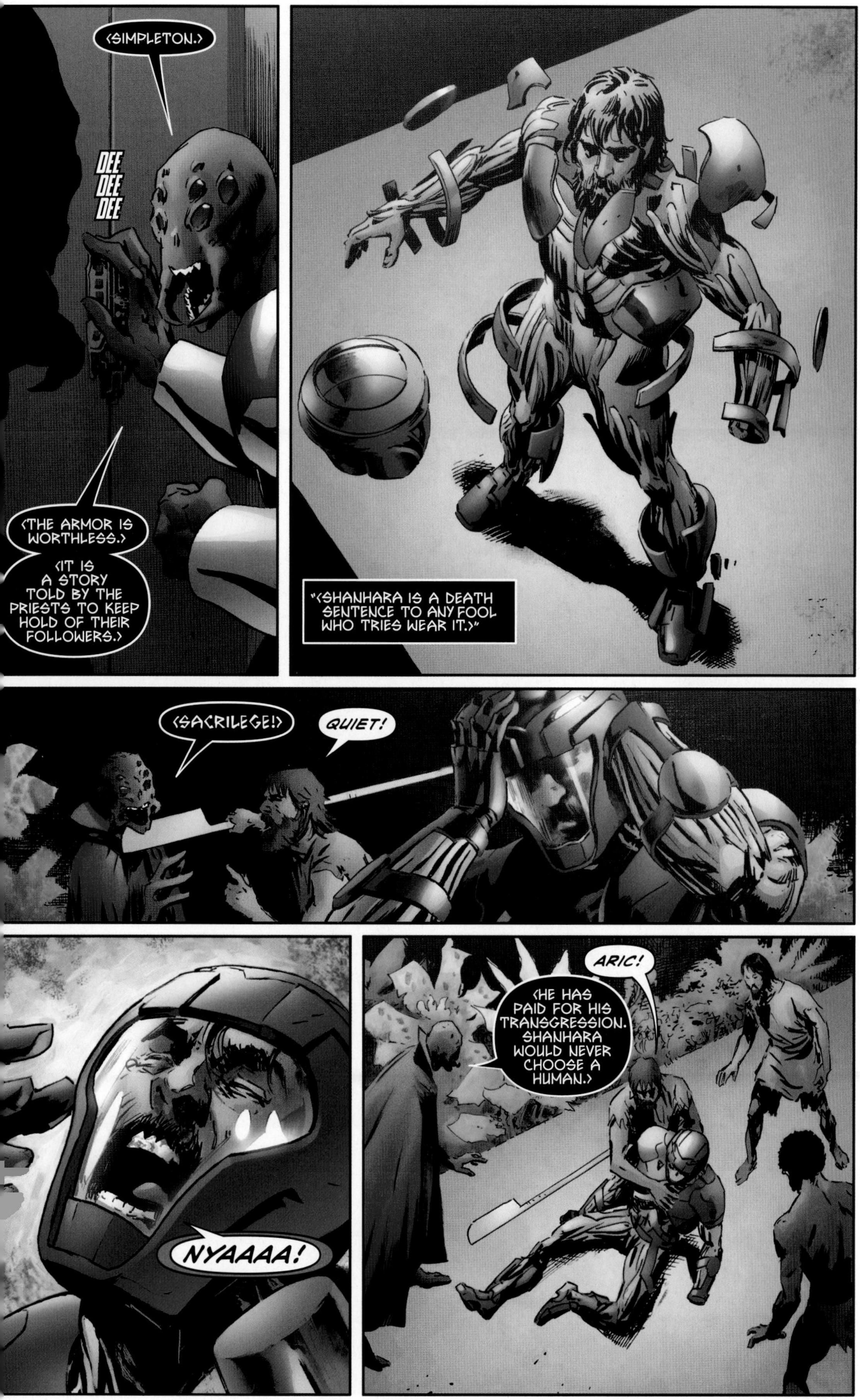

<SIMPLETON.>
DEE DEE DEE
<THE ARMOR IS WORTHLESS.>
<IT IS A STORY TOLD BY THE PRIESTS TO KEEP HOLD OF THEIR FOLLOWERS.>
"<SHANHARA IS A DEATH SENTENCE TO ANY FOOL WHO TRIES WEAR IT.>"
<SACRILEGE!>
QUIET!
NYAAAA!
ARIC!
<HE HAS PAID FOR HIS TRANSGRESSION. SHANHARA WOULD NEVER CHOOSE A HUMAN.>

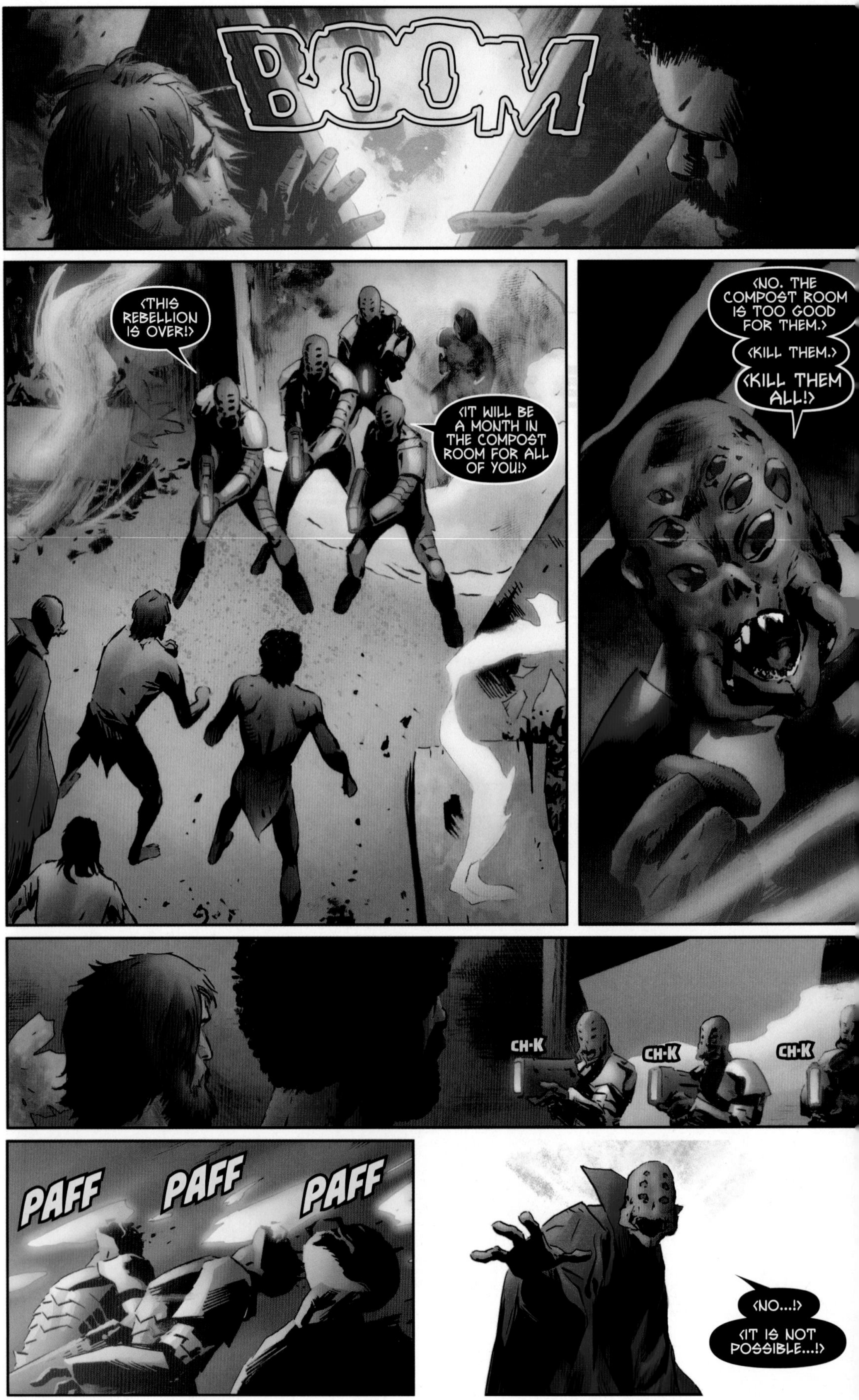
BOOM
‹THIS REBELLION IS OVER!›
‹IT WILL BE A MONTH IN THE COMPOST ROOM FOR ALL OF YOU!›
‹NO. THE COMPOST ROOM IS TOO GOOD FOR THEM.›
‹KILL THEM.›
‹KILL THEM ALL!›
CH-K
CH-K
CH-K
PAFF
PAFF
PAFF
‹NO...!›
‹IT IS NOT POSSIBLE...!›

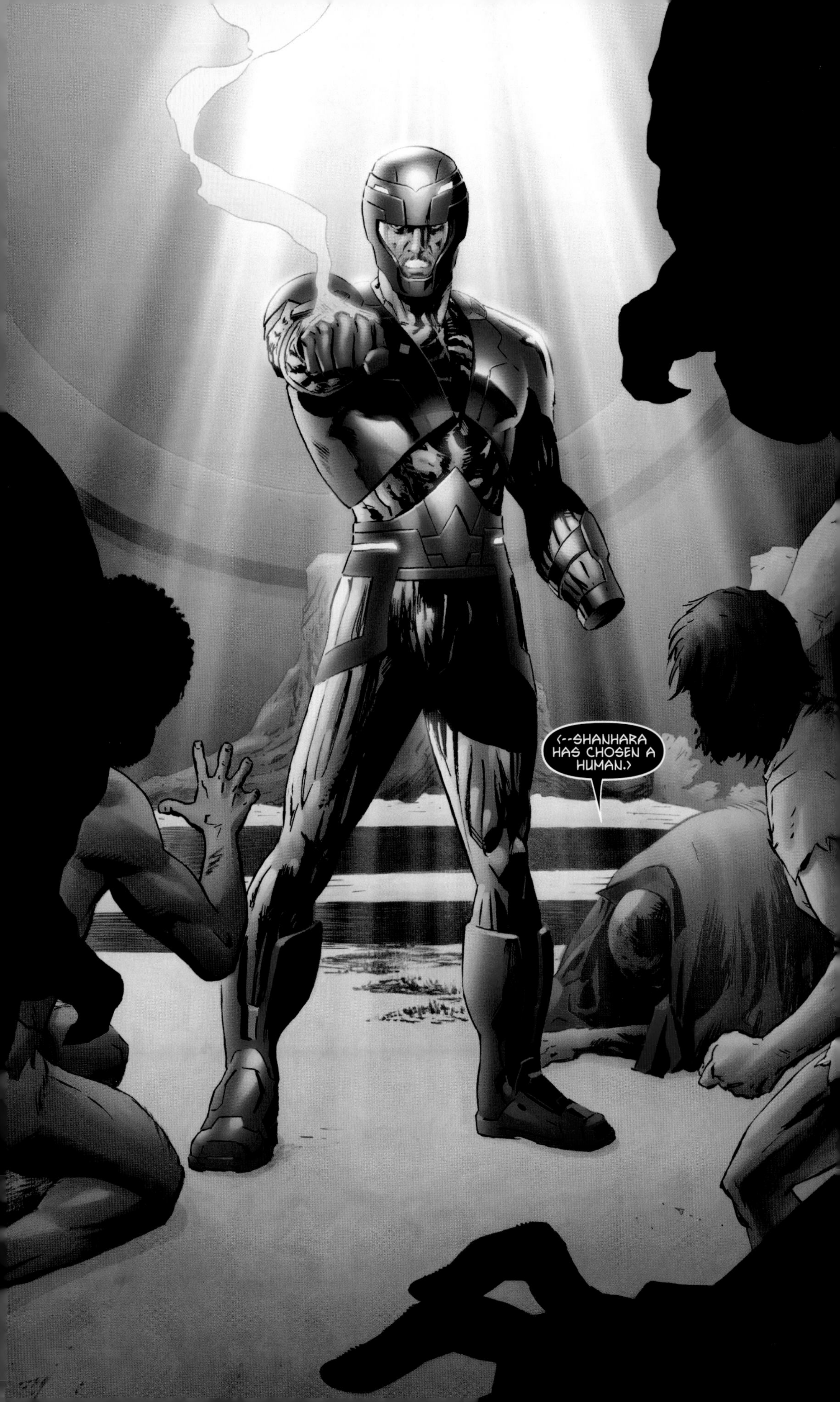
‹--SHANHARA HAS CHOSEN A HUMAN.›

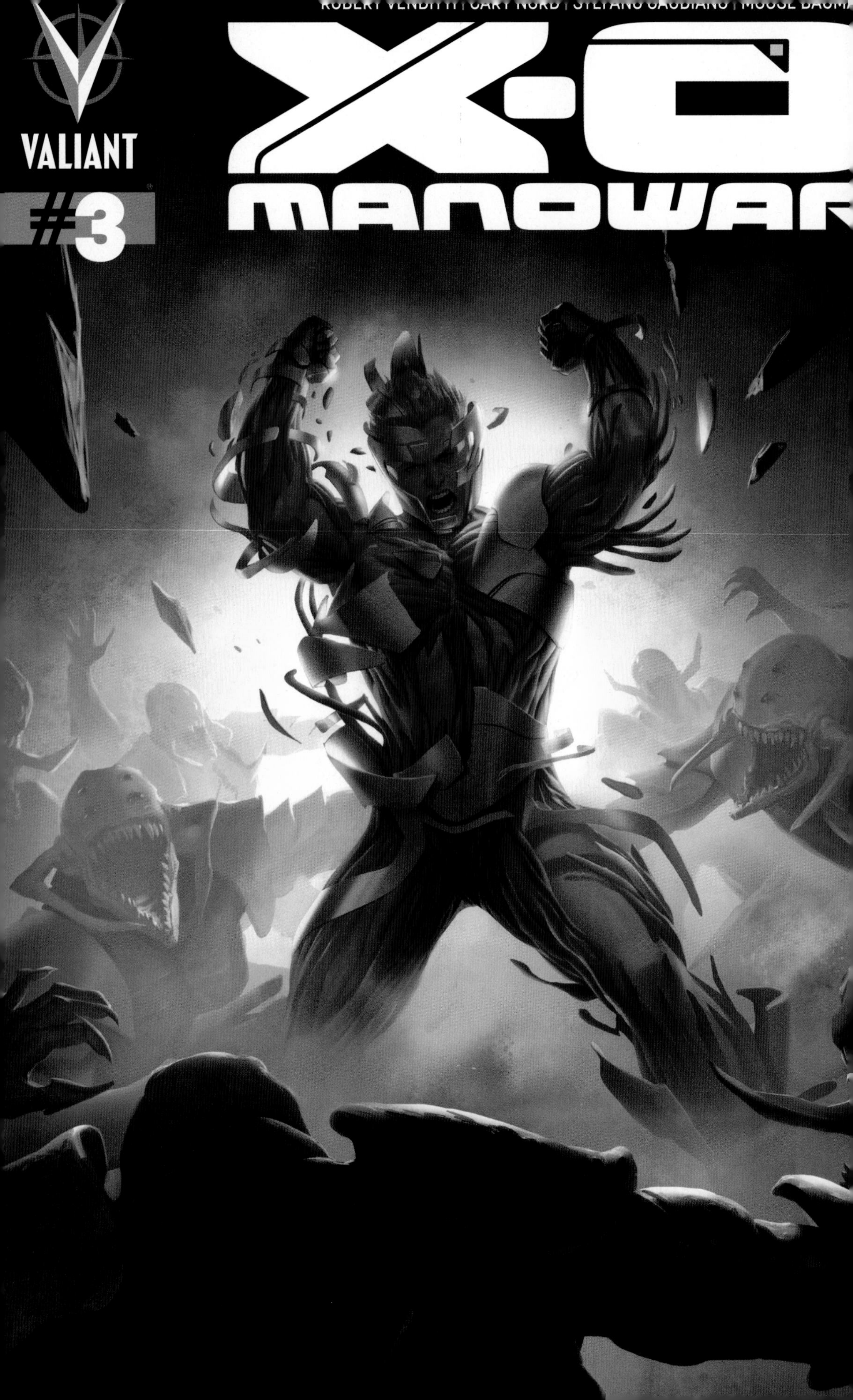
VALIANT
X-O
MANOWAR
#3

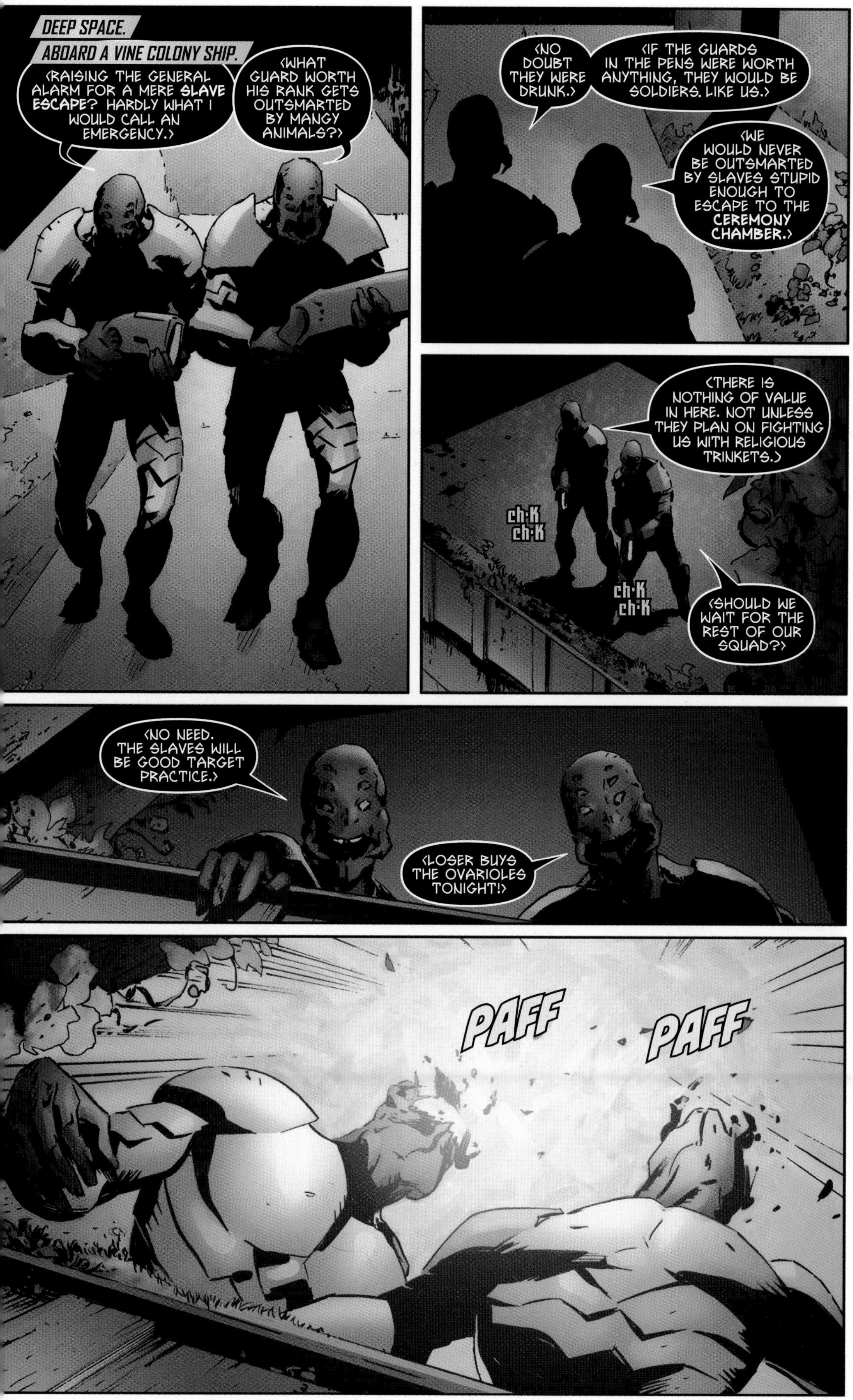
DEEP SPACE.
ABOARD A VINE COLONY SHIP.
<RAISING THE GENERAL ALARM FOR A MERE **SLAVE ESCAPE**? HARDLY WHAT I WOULD CALL AN EMERGENCY.>
<WHAT GUARD WORTH HIS RANK GETS OUTSMARTED BY MANGY ANIMALS?>
<NO DOUBT THEY WERE DRUNK.>
<IF THE GUARDS IN THE PENS WERE WORTH ANYTHING, THEY WOULD BE SOLDIERS. LIKE US.>
<WE WOULD NEVER BE OUTSMARTED BY SLAVES STUPID ENOUGH TO ESCAPE TO THE **CEREMONY CHAMBER.**>
<THERE IS NOTHING OF VALUE IN HERE. NOT UNLESS THEY PLAN ON FIGHTING US WITH RELIGIOUS TRINKETS.>
ch·K ch·K
ch·K ch·K
<SHOULD WE WAIT FOR THE REST OF OUR SQUAD?>
<NO NEED. THE SLAVES WILL BE GOOD TARGET PRACTICE.>
<LOSER BUYS THE OVARIOLES TONIGHT!>
PAFF
PAFF

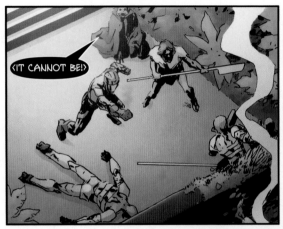

〈IT CANNOT BE!〉

〈THE SACRED ARMOR OF SHANHARA HAS KILLED ALL WHO HAVE WORN IT.〉

〈YET A SLAVE FROM THE PENS SURVIVES.〉

〈HOW?〉

KSSH

THUD

SPLLTCH

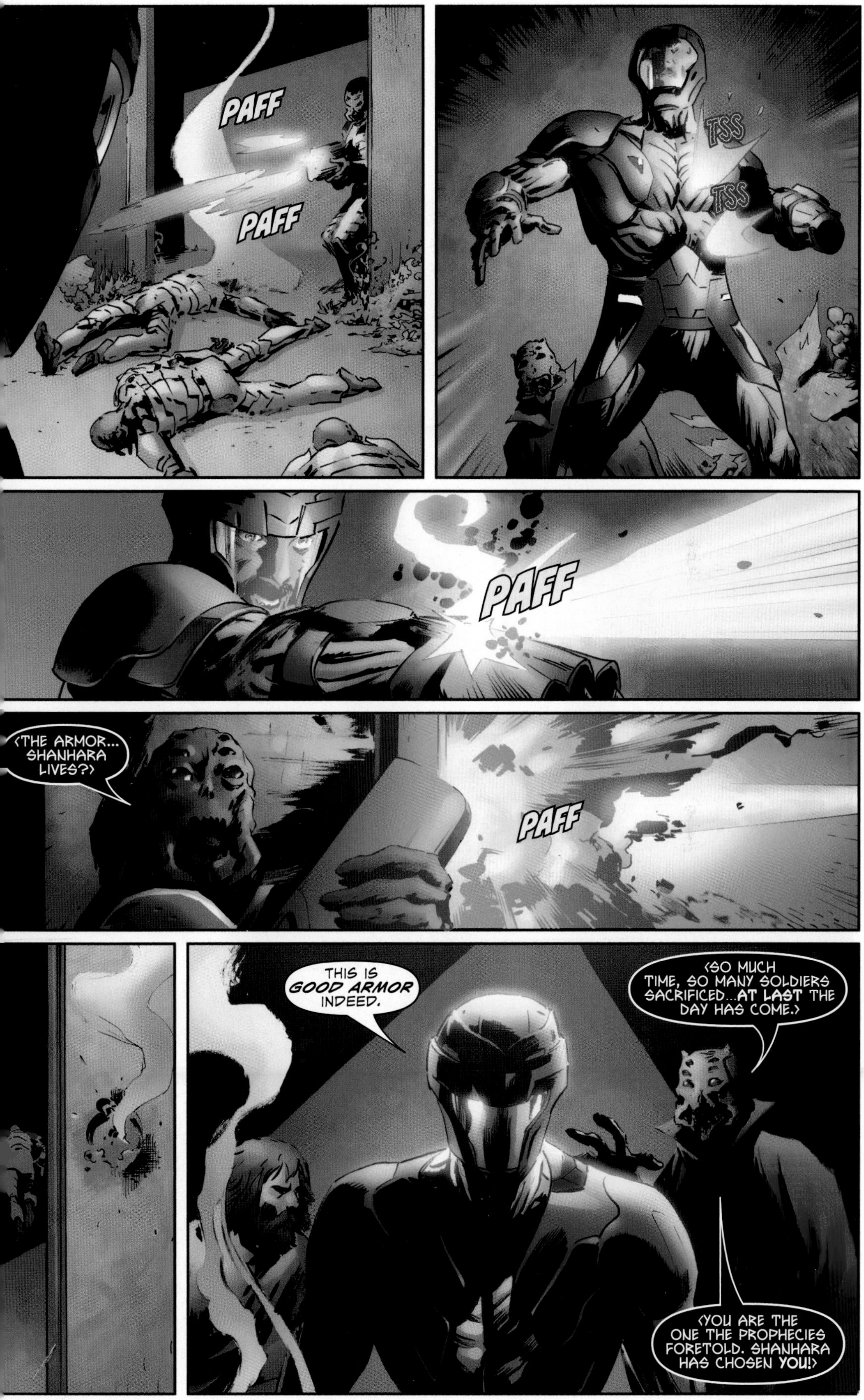
PAFF
PAFF
TSS
TSS
PAFF
‹THE ARMOR... SHANHARA LIVES?›
PAFF
THIS IS GOOD ARMOR INDEED.
‹SO MUCH TIME, SO MANY SOLDIERS SACRIFICED...AT LAST THE DAY HAS COME.›
‹YOU ARE THE ONE THE PROPHECIES FORETOLD. SHANHARA HAS CHOSEN YOU!›

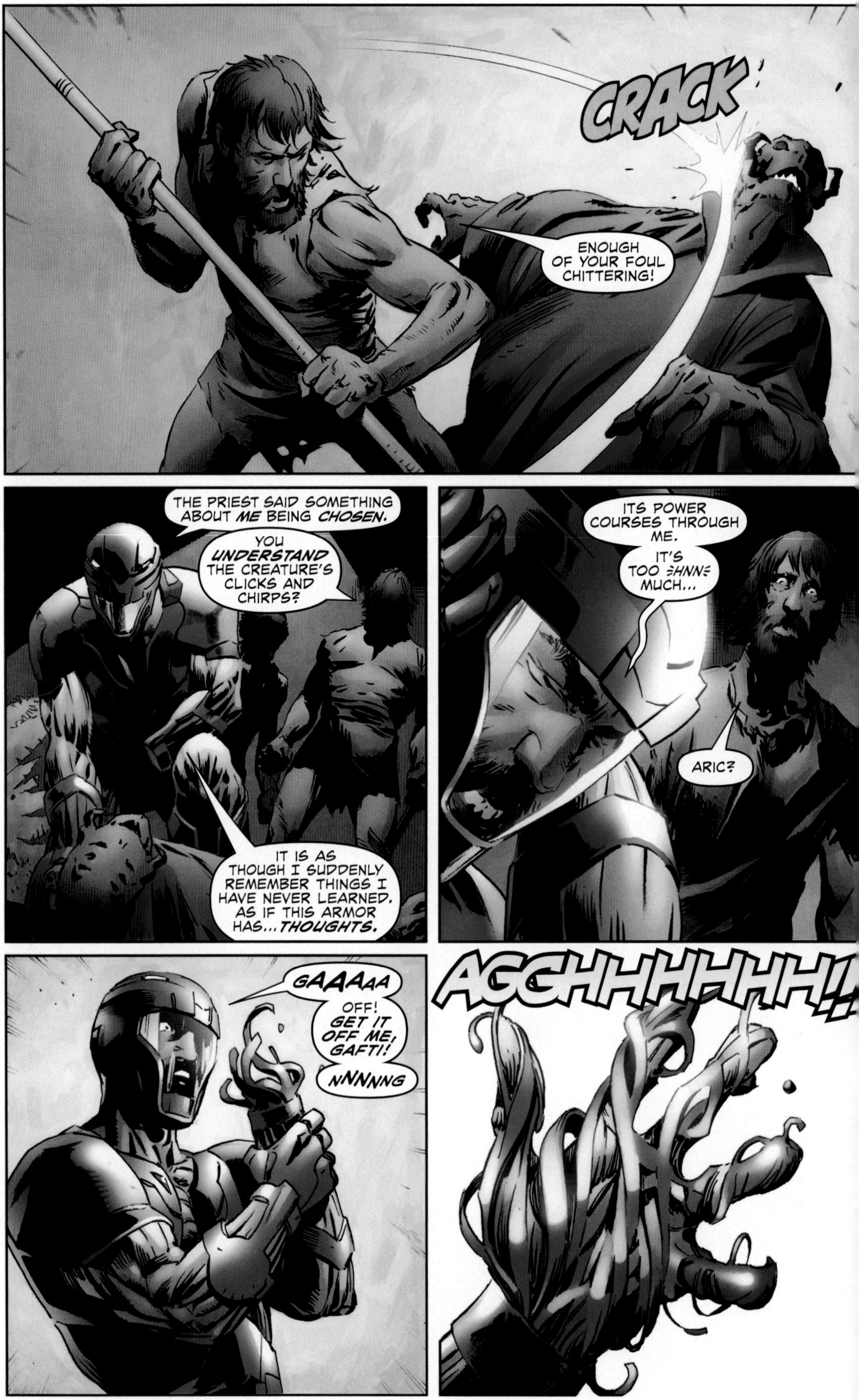
CRACK
ENOUGH OF YOUR FOUL CHITTERING!
THE PRIEST SAID SOMETHING ABOUT ME BEING CHOSEN.
YOU UNDERSTAND THE CREATURE'S CLICKS AND CHIRPS?
IT IS AS THOUGH I SUDDENLY REMEMBER THINGS I HAVE NEVER LEARNED. AS IF THIS ARMOR HAS...THOUGHTS.
ITS POWER COURSES THROUGH ME.
IT'S TOO =HNN= MUCH...
ARIC?
GAAAAA
OFF! GET IT OFF ME, GAFTI!
NNNNNG
AGGHHHHHH!!

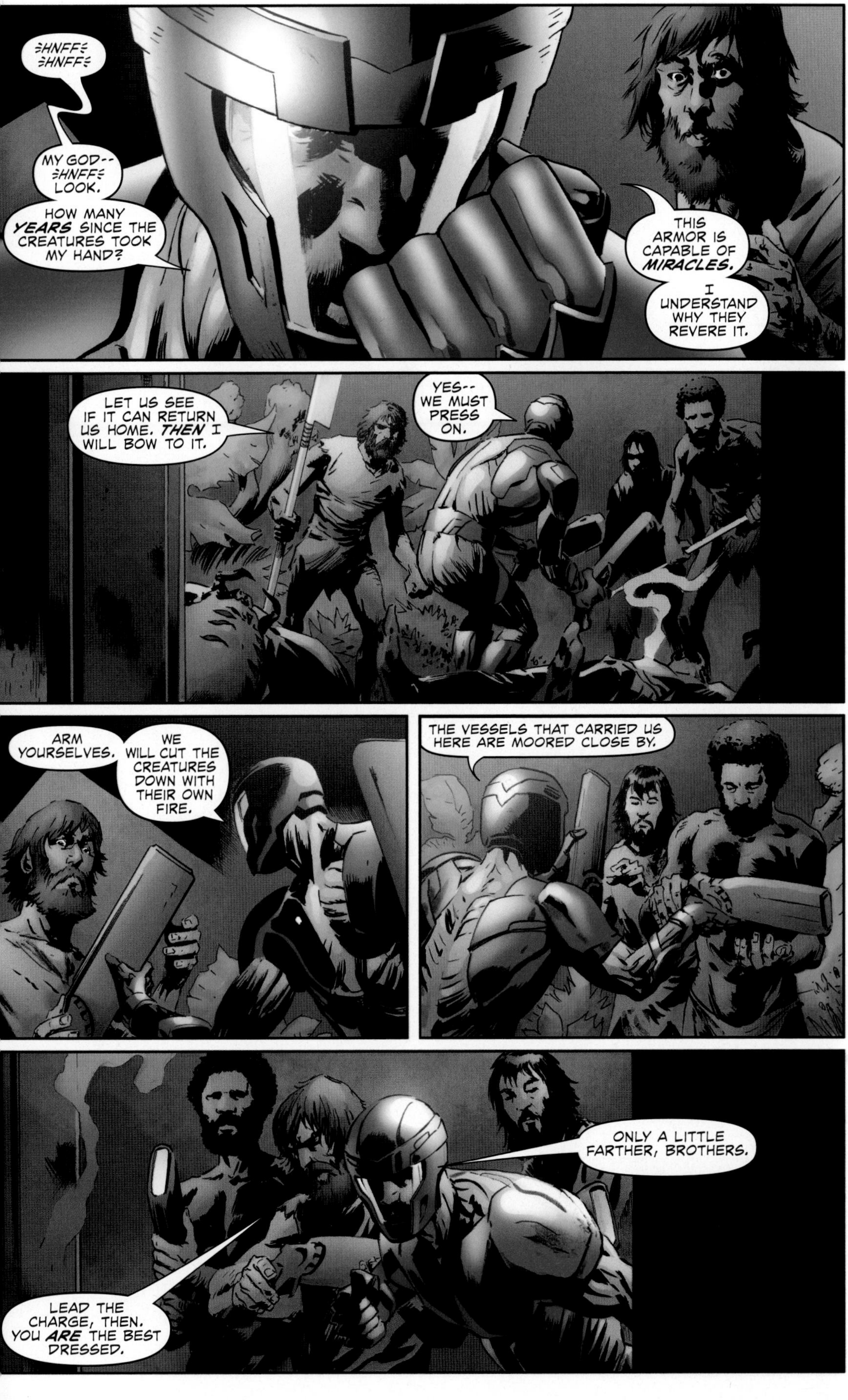

≈HNFF≈ ≈HNFF≈
MY GOD-- ≈HNFF≈ LOOK.
HOW MANY YEARS SINCE THE CREATURES TOOK MY HAND?
THIS ARMOR IS CAPABLE OF MIRACLES.
I UNDERSTAND WHY THEY REVERE IT.
LET US SEE IF IT CAN RETURN US HOME. THEN I WILL BOW TO IT.
YES-- WE MUST PRESS ON.
ARM YOURSELVES.
WE WILL CUT THE CREATURES DOWN WITH THEIR OWN FIRE.
THE VESSELS THAT CARRIED US HERE ARE MOORED CLOSE BY.
ONLY A LITTLE FARTHER, BROTHERS.
LEAD THE CHARGE, THEN. YOU ARE THE BEST DRESSED.

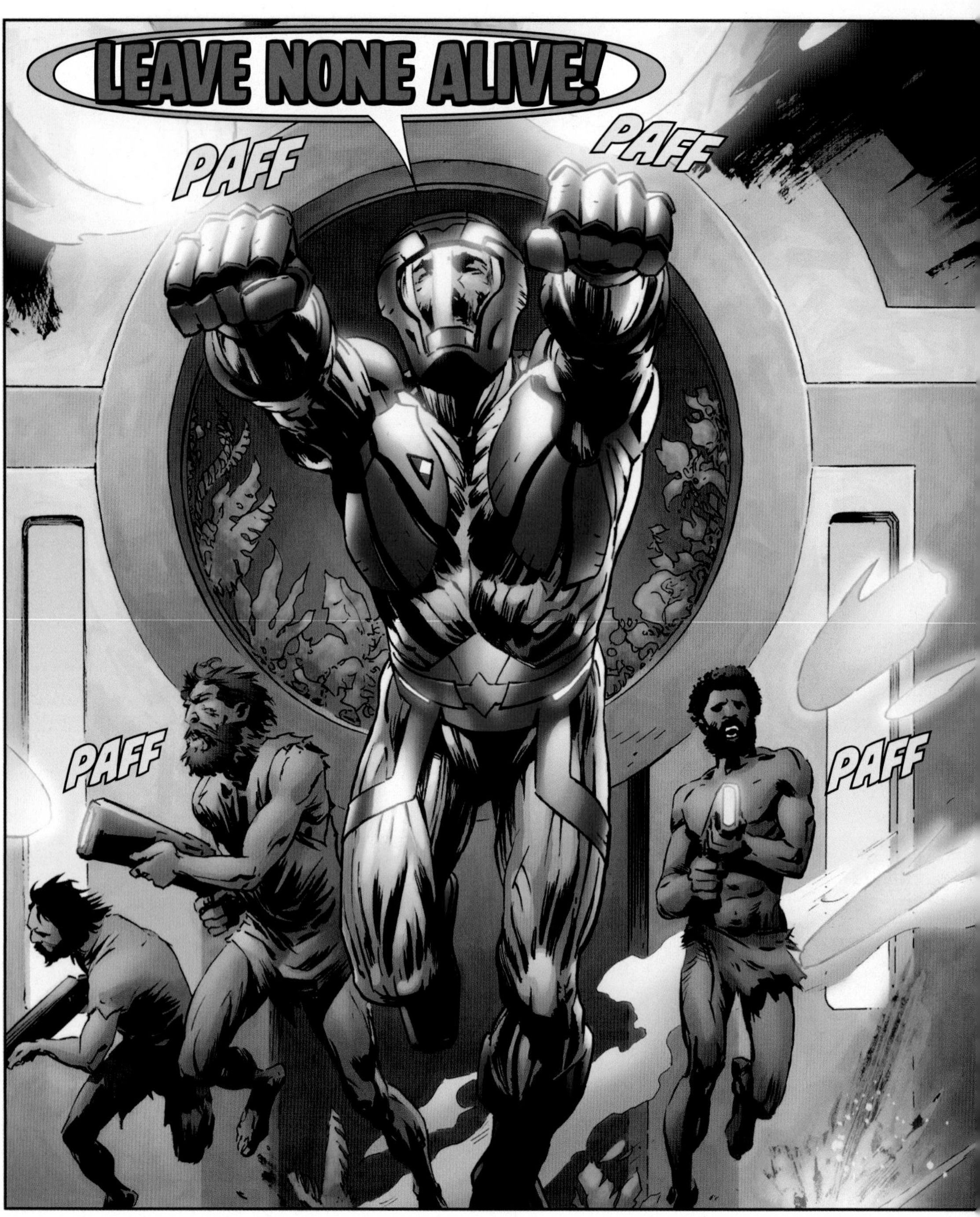
LEAVE NONE ALIVE!
PAFF
PAFF
PAFF
PAFF

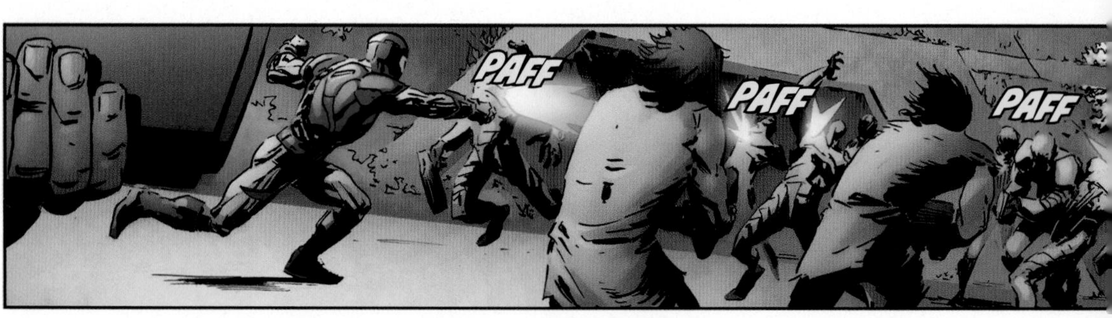
PAFF
PAFF
PAFF

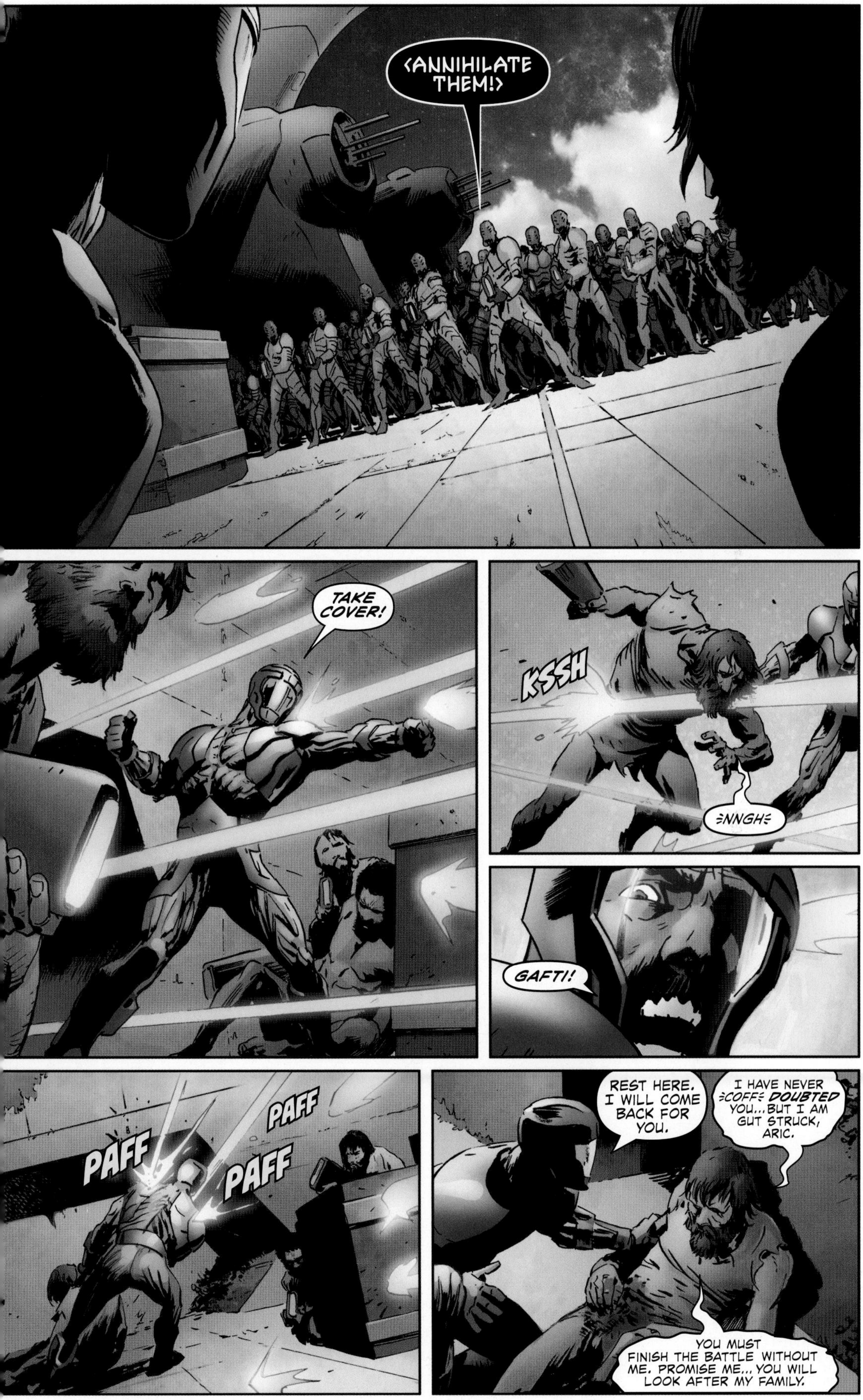
‹ANNIHILATE THEM!›
TAKE COVER!
KSSH
=NNGH=
GAFTI!
PAFF
PAFF
PAFF
REST HERE. I WILL COME BACK FOR YOU.
I HAVE NEVER =COFF= DOUBTED YOU... BUT I AM GUT STRUCK, ARIC.
YOU MUST FINISH THE BATTLE WITHOUT ME. PROMISE ME... YOU WILL LOOK AFTER MY FAMILY.

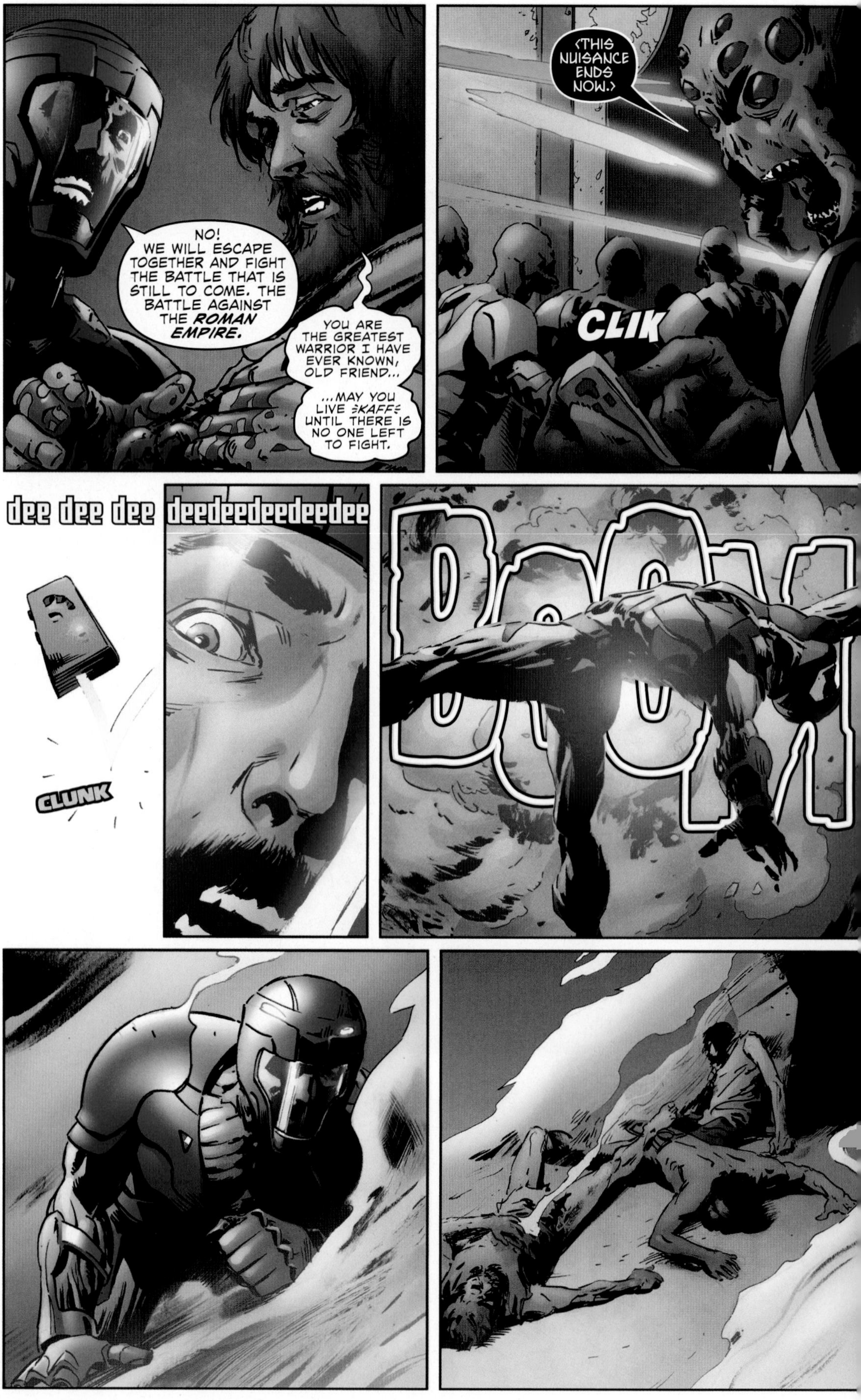
NO! WE WILL ESCAPE TOGETHER AND FIGHT THE BATTLE THAT IS STILL TO COME. THE BATTLE AGAINST THE *ROMAN EMPIRE.*
YOU ARE THE GREATEST WARRIOR I HAVE EVER KNOWN, OLD FRIEND...
...MAY YOU LIVE ≑KAFF≑ UNTIL THERE IS NO ONE LEFT TO FIGHT.
<THIS NUISANCE ENDS NOW.>
CLIK
dee dee dee deedeedeedeedee
CLUNK
BOOM

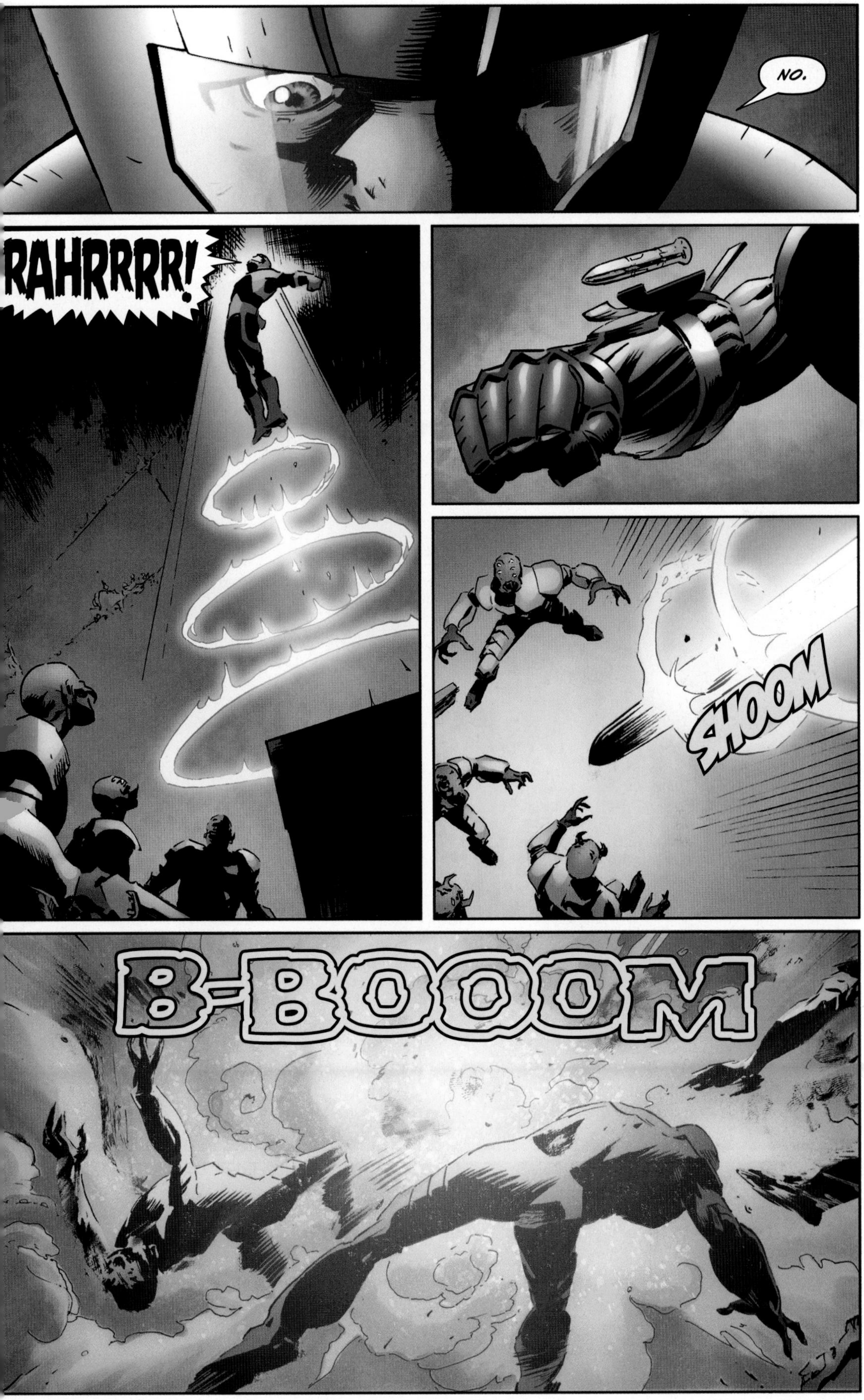
NO.
RAHRRRR!
SHOOM
B-BOOOM

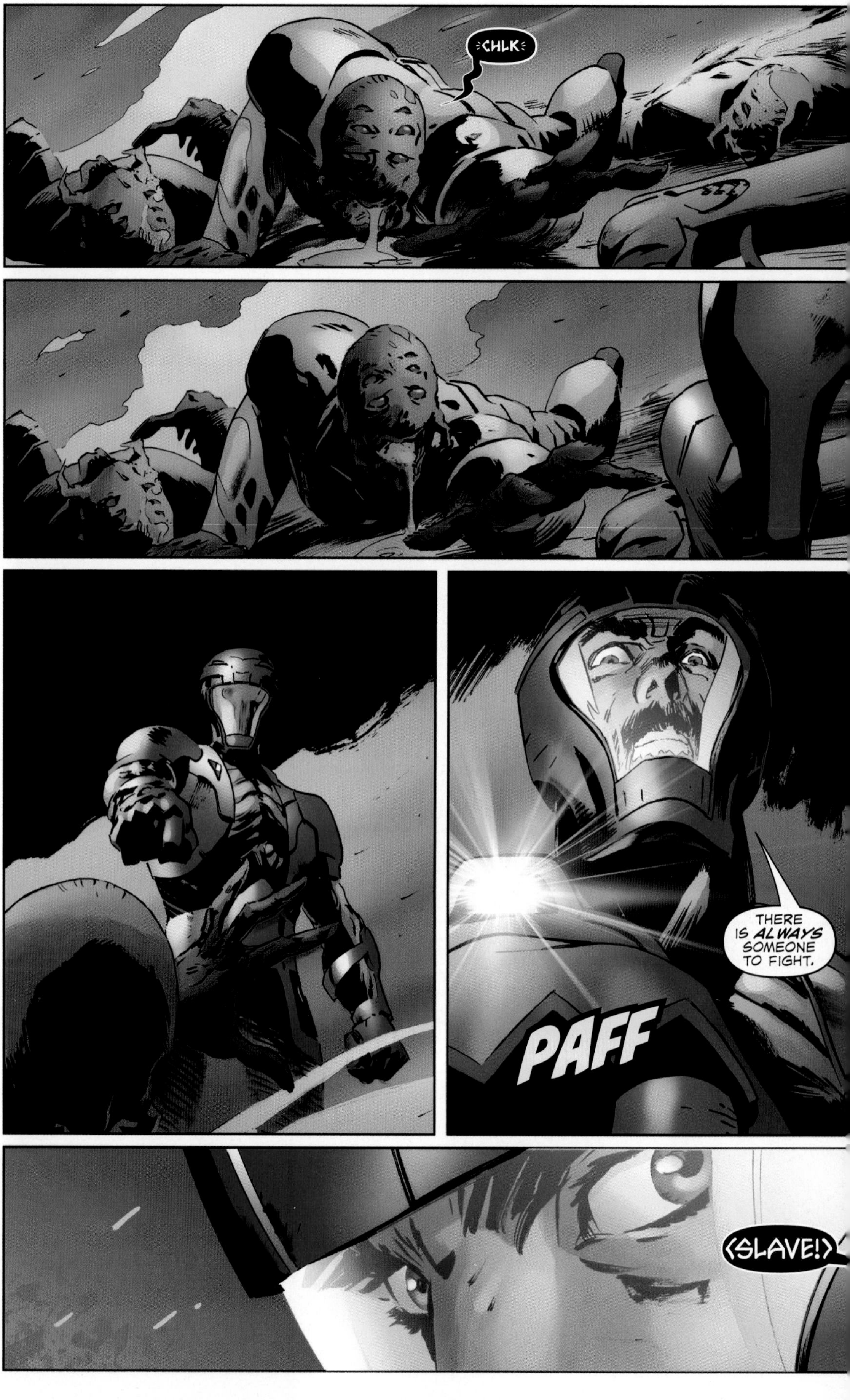
CHLK
THERE IS ALWAYS SOMEONE TO FIGHT.
PAFF
‹SLAVE!›

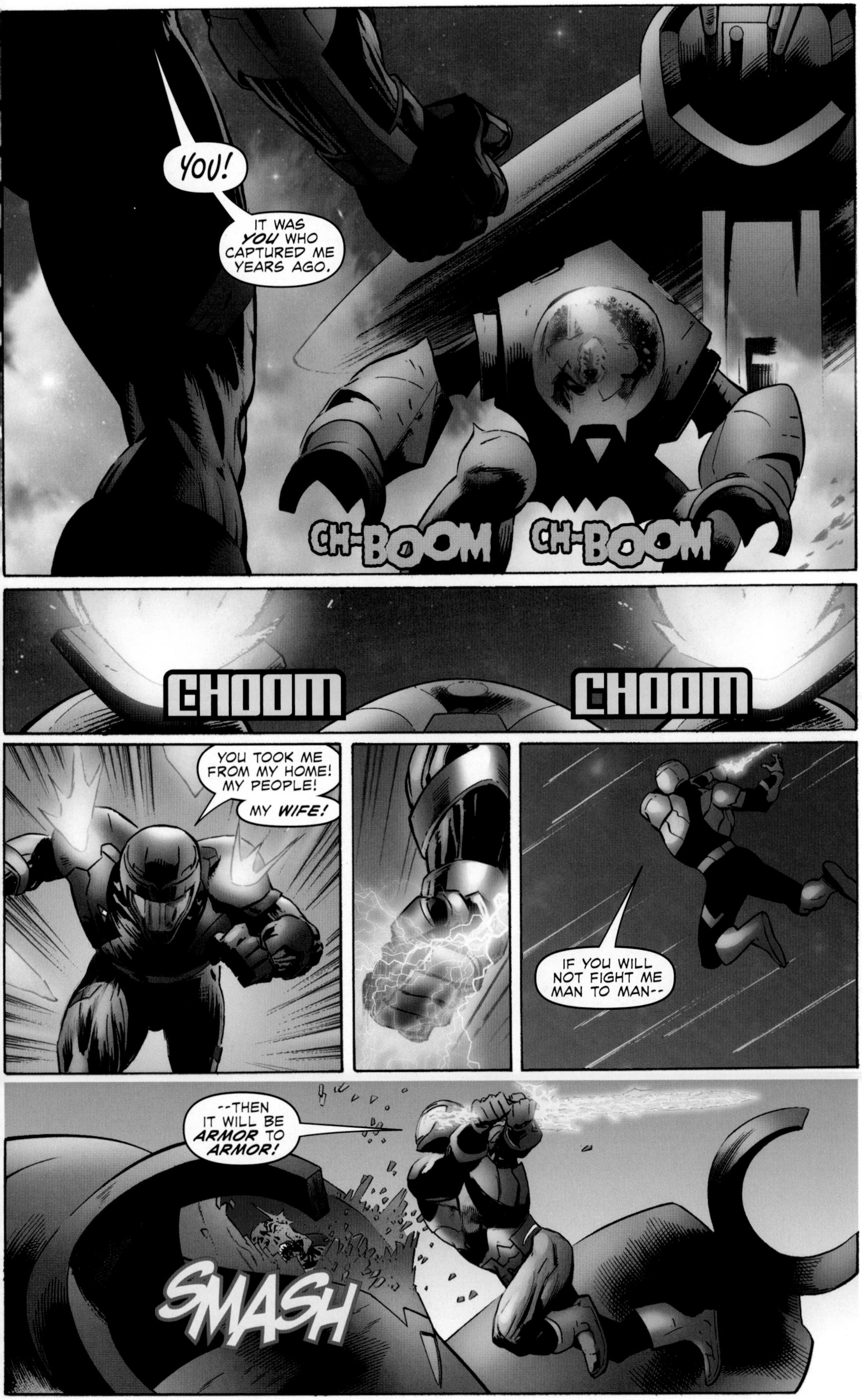

YOU!
IT WAS YOU WHO CAPTURED ME YEARS AGO.
CH-BOOM CH-BOOM
CHOOM
CHOOM
YOU TOOK ME FROM MY HOME! MY PEOPLE!
MY WIFE!
IF YOU WILL NOT FIGHT ME MAN TO MAN--
--THEN IT WILL BE ARMOR TO ARMOR!
SMASH

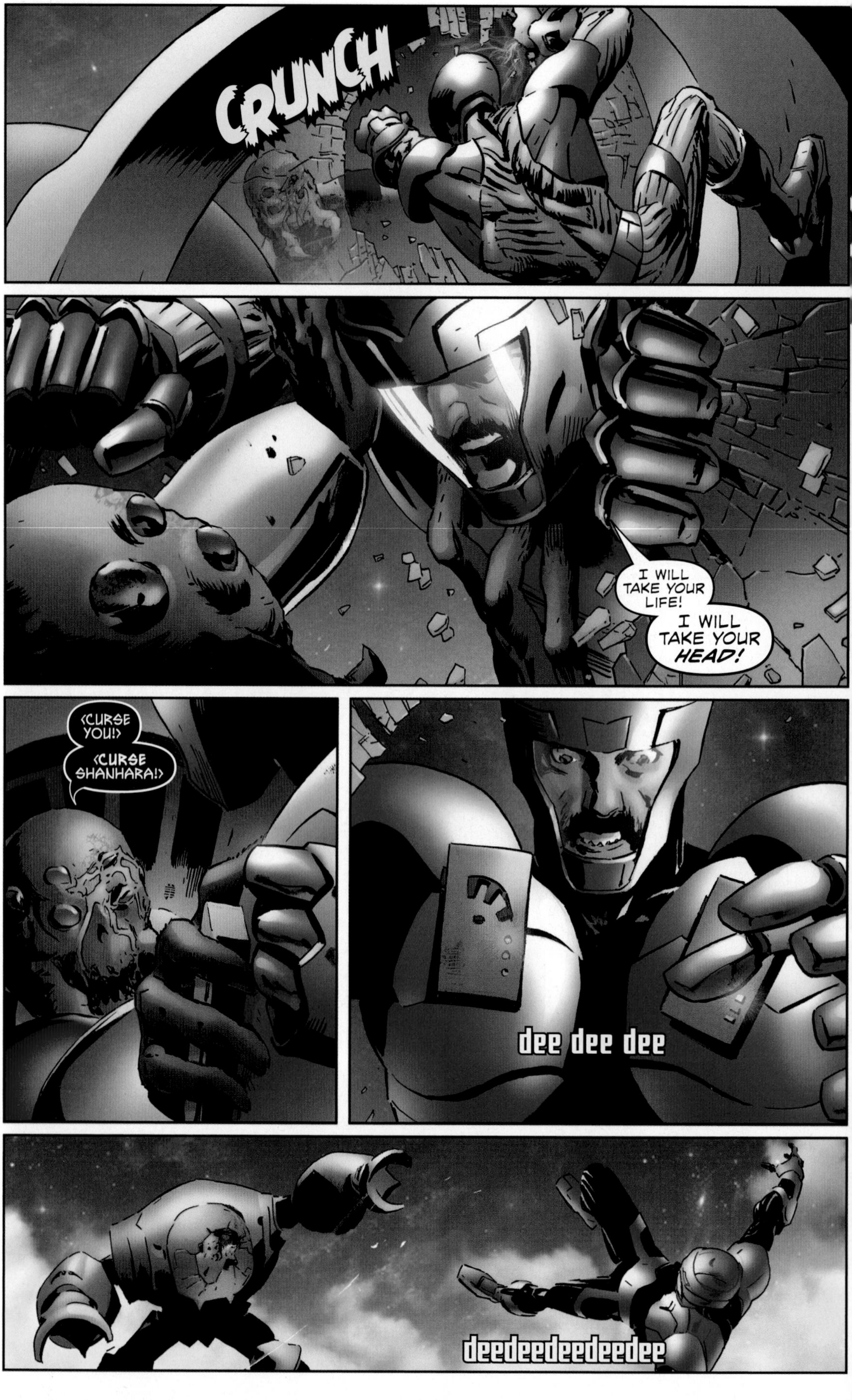
CRUNCH
I WILL TAKE YOUR LIFE!
I WILL TAKE YOUR HEAD!
‹CURSE YOU!›
‹CURSE SHANHARA!›
dee dee dee
deedeedeedeedee

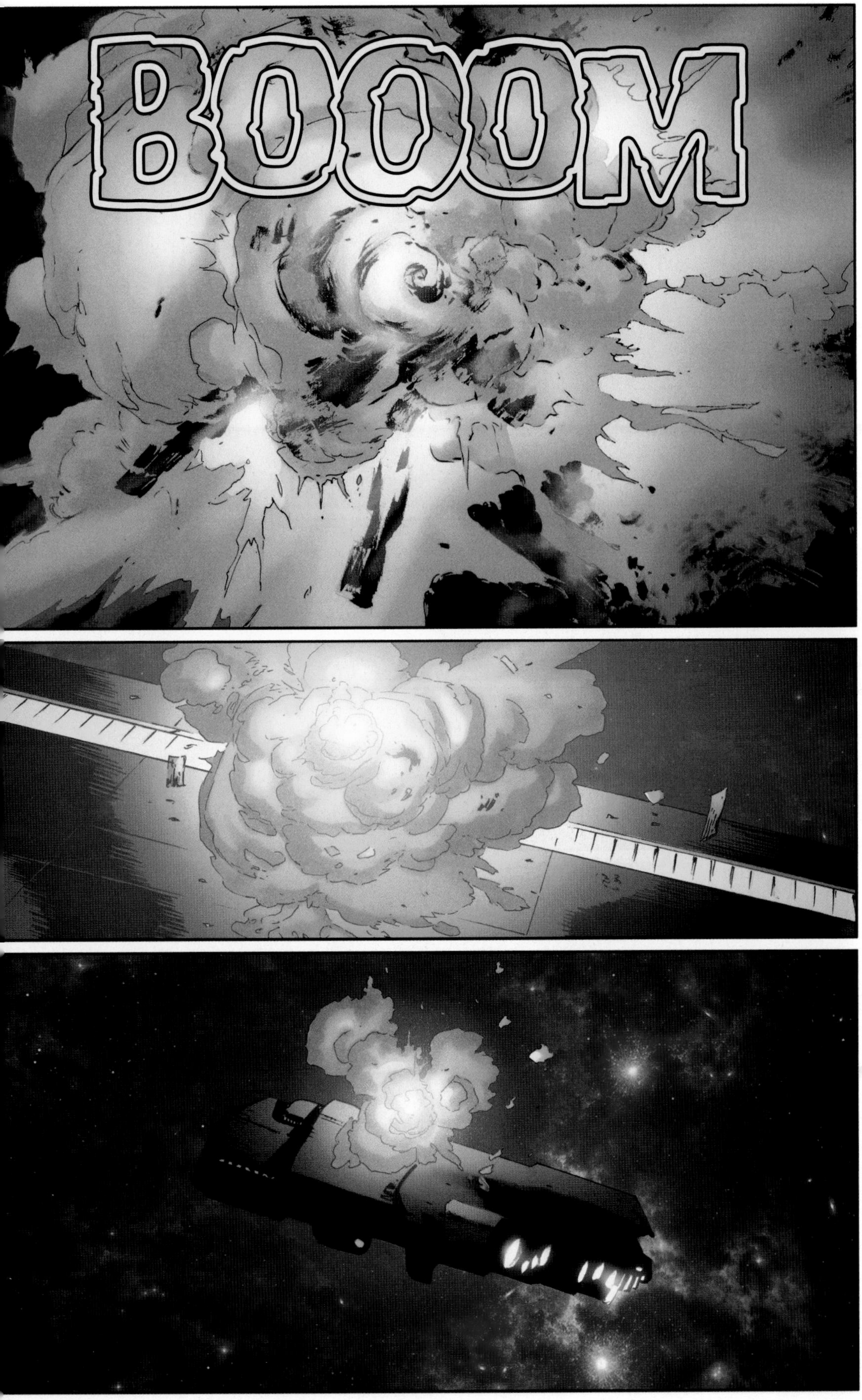
BOOOM

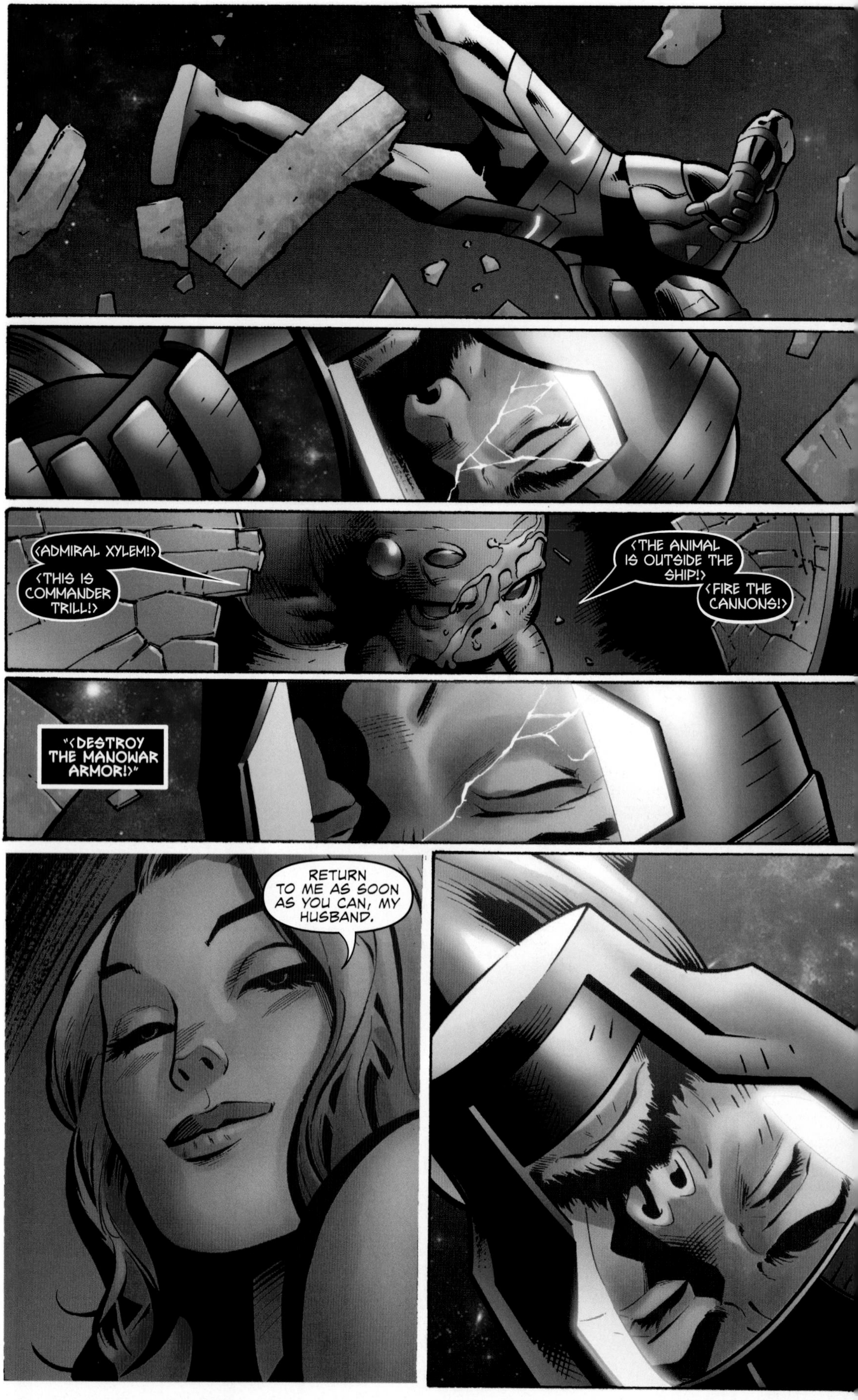

‹ADMIRAL XYLEM!›
‹THIS IS COMMANDER TRILL!›
‹THE ANIMAL IS OUTSIDE THE SHIP!›
‹FIRE THE CANNONS!›
"‹DESTROY THE MANOWAR ARMOR!›"
RETURN TO ME AS SOON AS YOU CAN, MY HUSBAND.

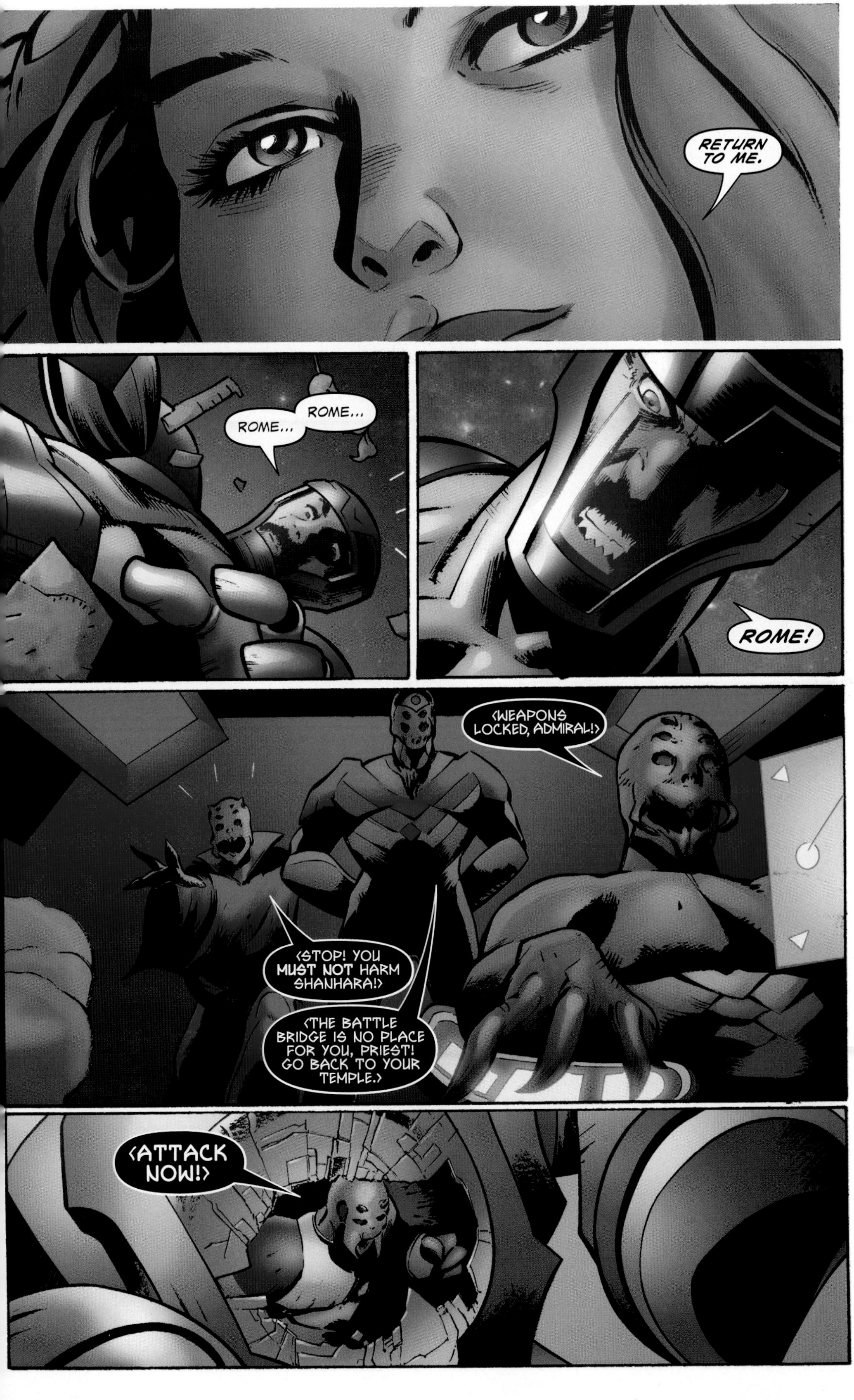
RETURN TO ME.
ROME...
ROME...
ROME!
‹WEAPONS LOCKED, ADMIRAL!›
‹STOP! YOU **MUST NOT** HARM SHANHARA!›
‹THE BATTLE BRIDGE IS NO PLACE FOR YOU, PRIEST! GO BACK TO YOUR TEMPLE.›
‹ATTACK NOW!›

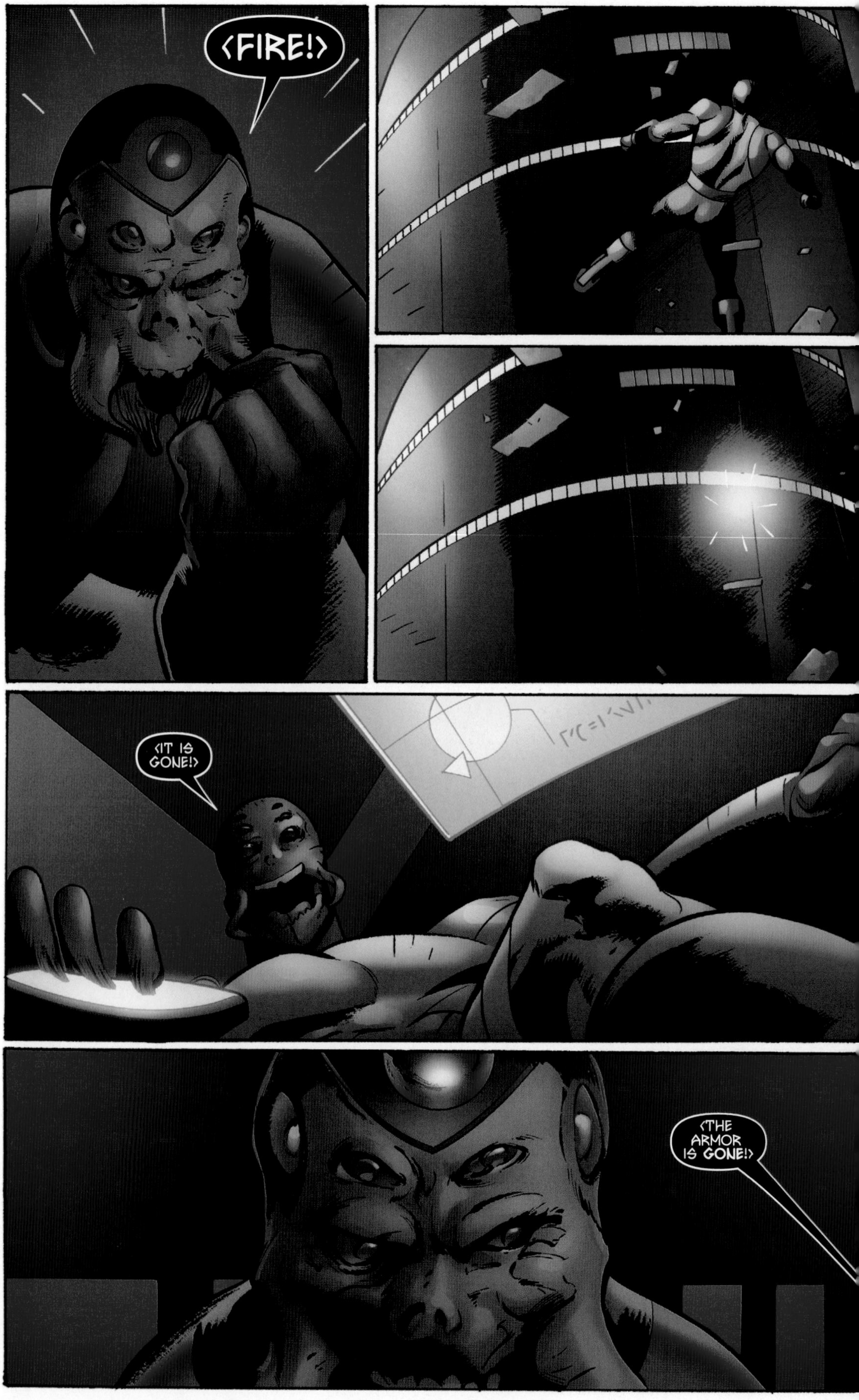
‹FIRE!›
‹IT IS GONE!›
‹THE ARMOR IS GONE!›

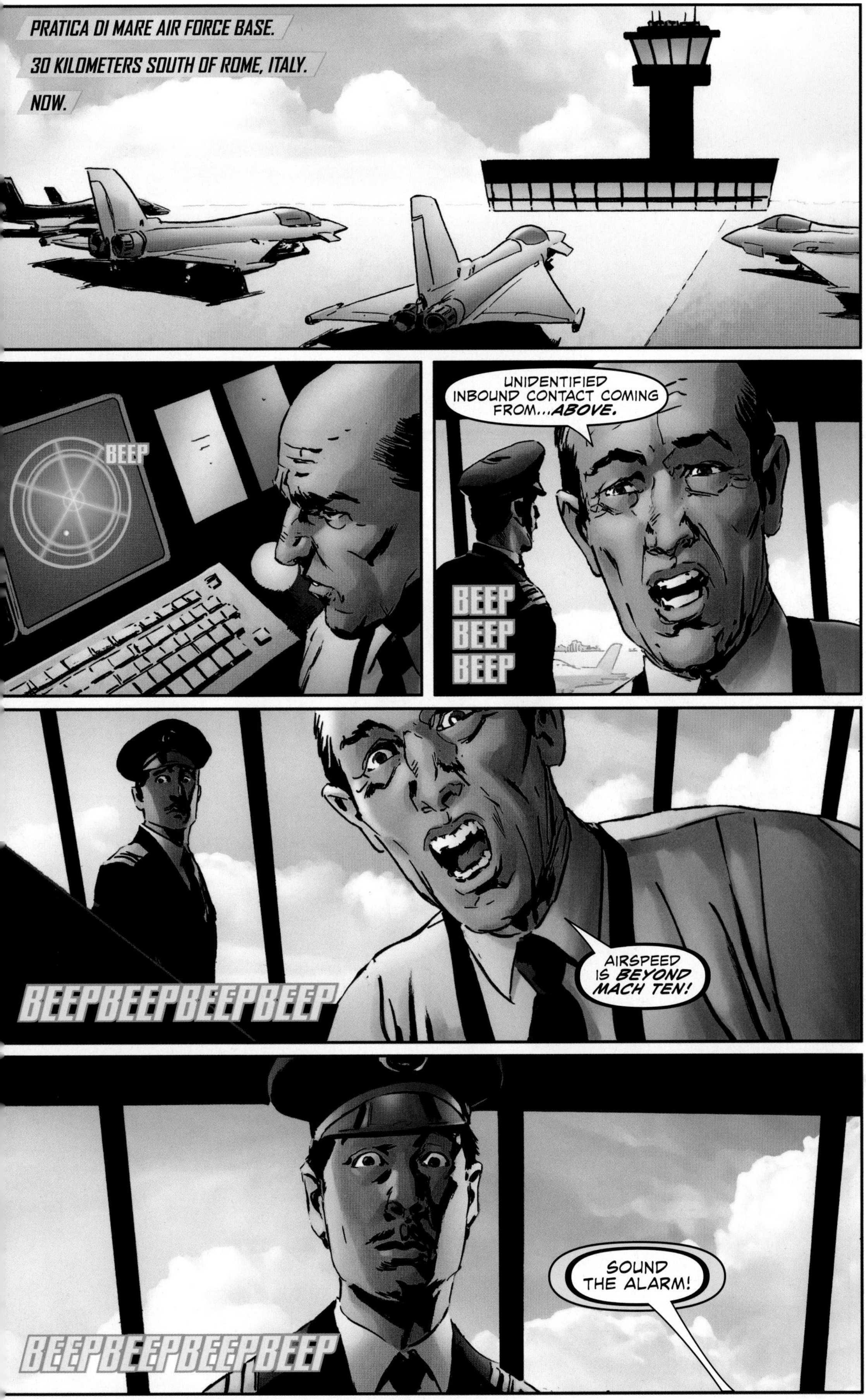
PRATICA DI MARE AIR FORCE BASE.
30 KILOMETERS SOUTH OF ROME, ITALY.
NOW.
BEEP
UNIDENTIFIED INBOUND CONTACT COMING FROM...ABOVE.
BEEP BEEP BEEP
AIRSPEED IS BEYOND MACH TEN!
BEEPBEEPBEEPBEEP
SOUND THE ALARM!
BEEPBEEPBEEPBEEP

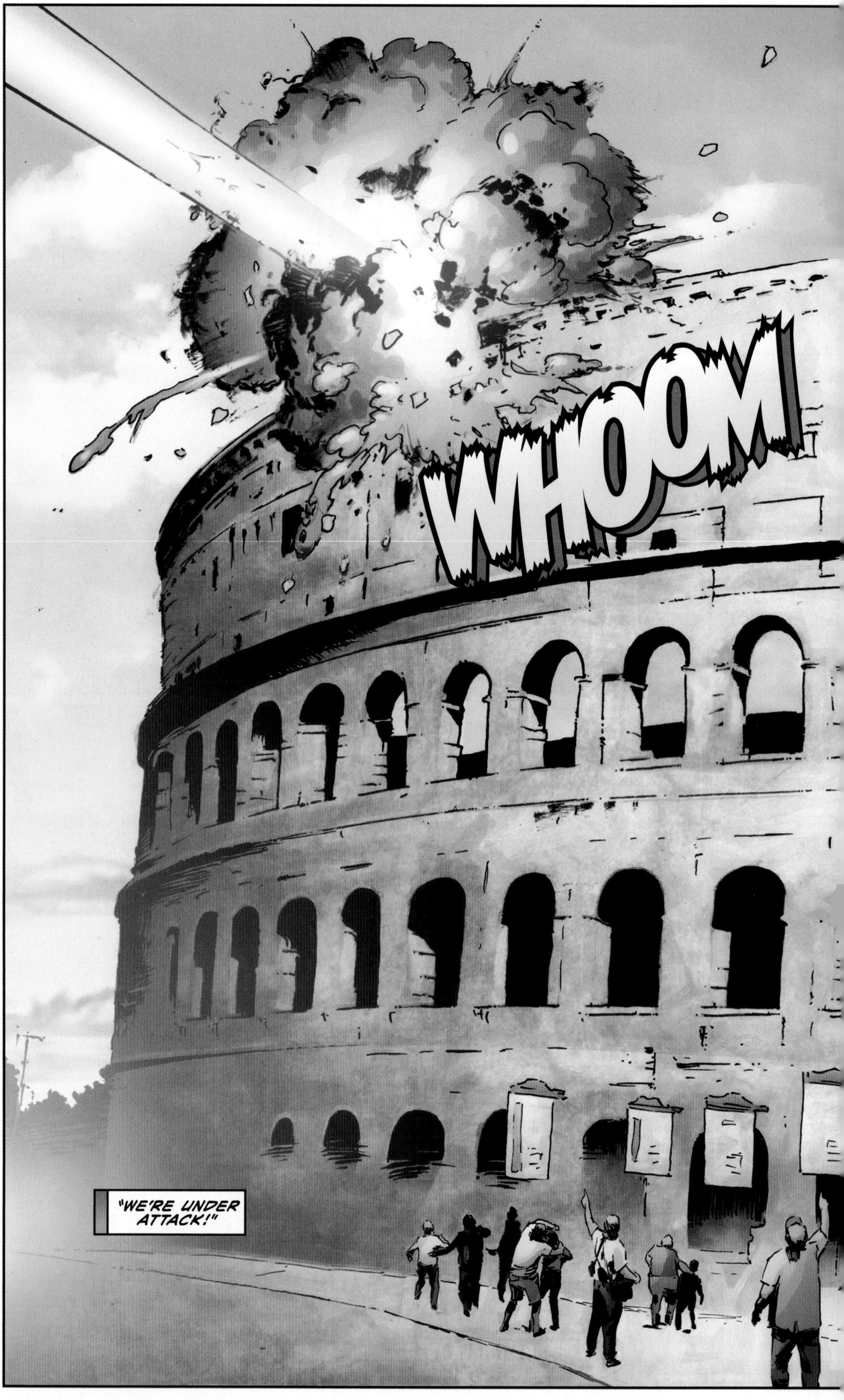
WHOOM
"WE'RE UNDER ATTACK!"

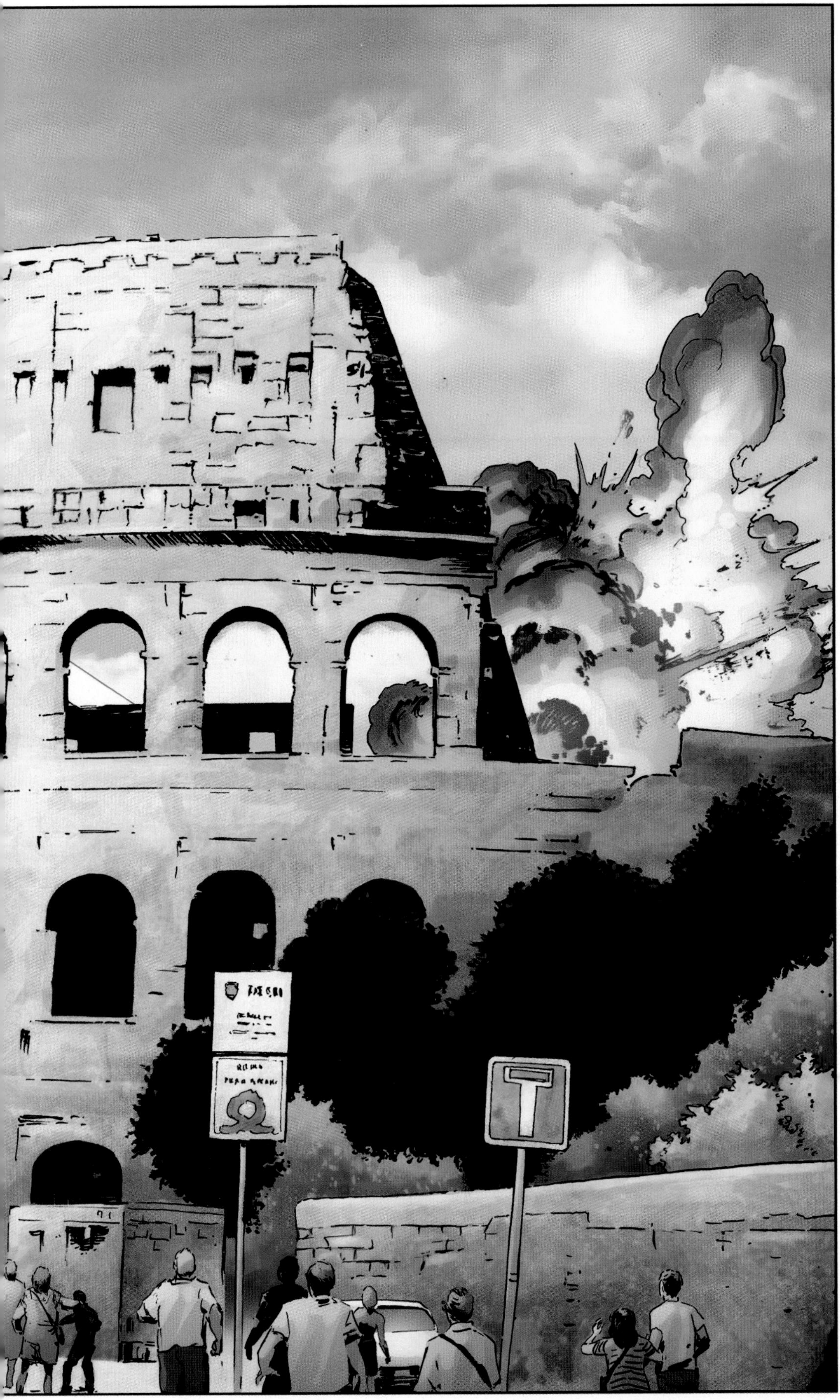

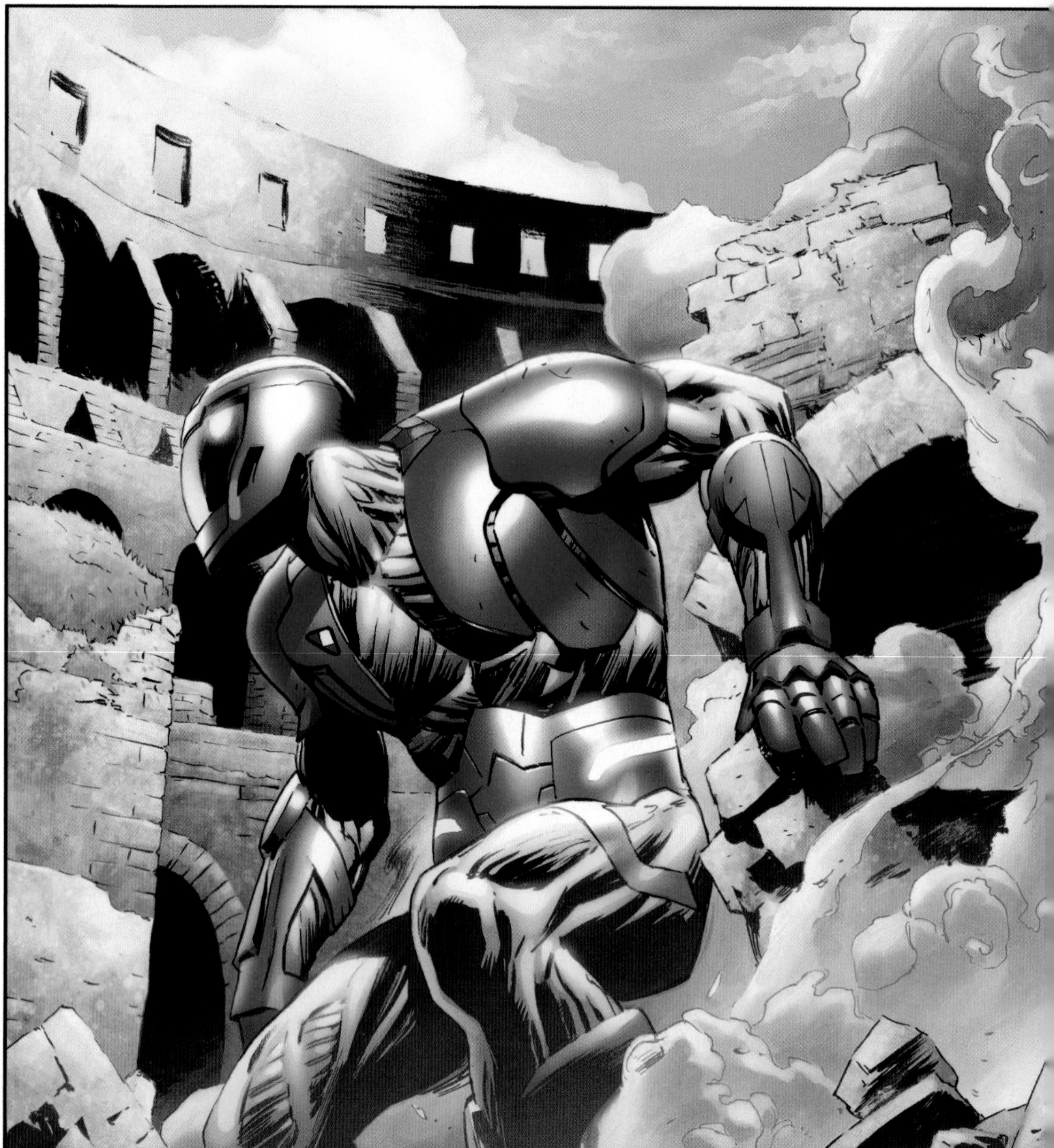
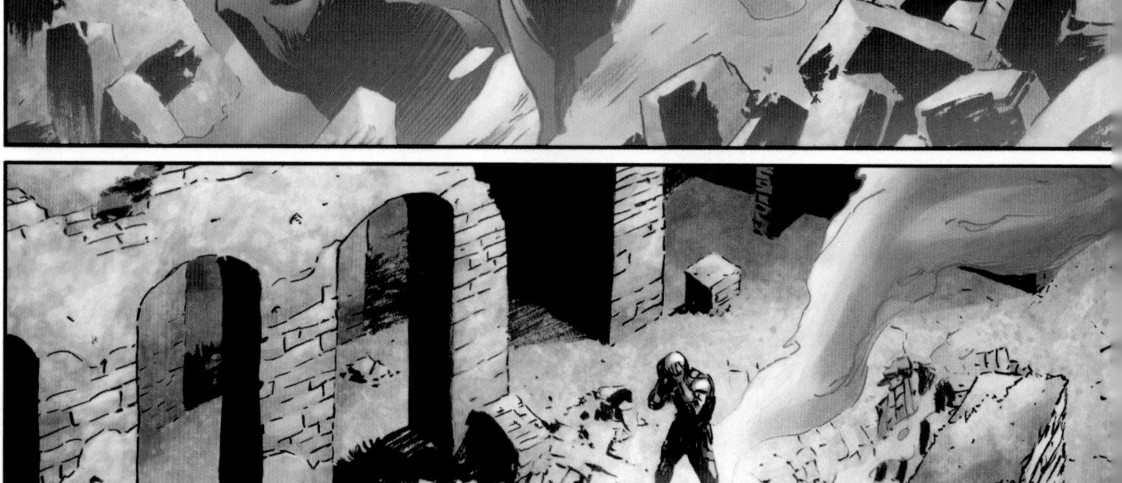

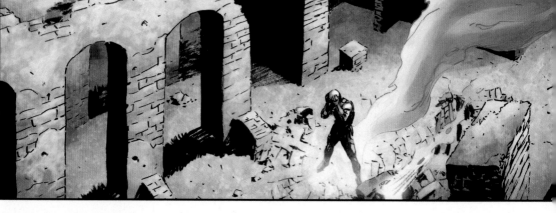

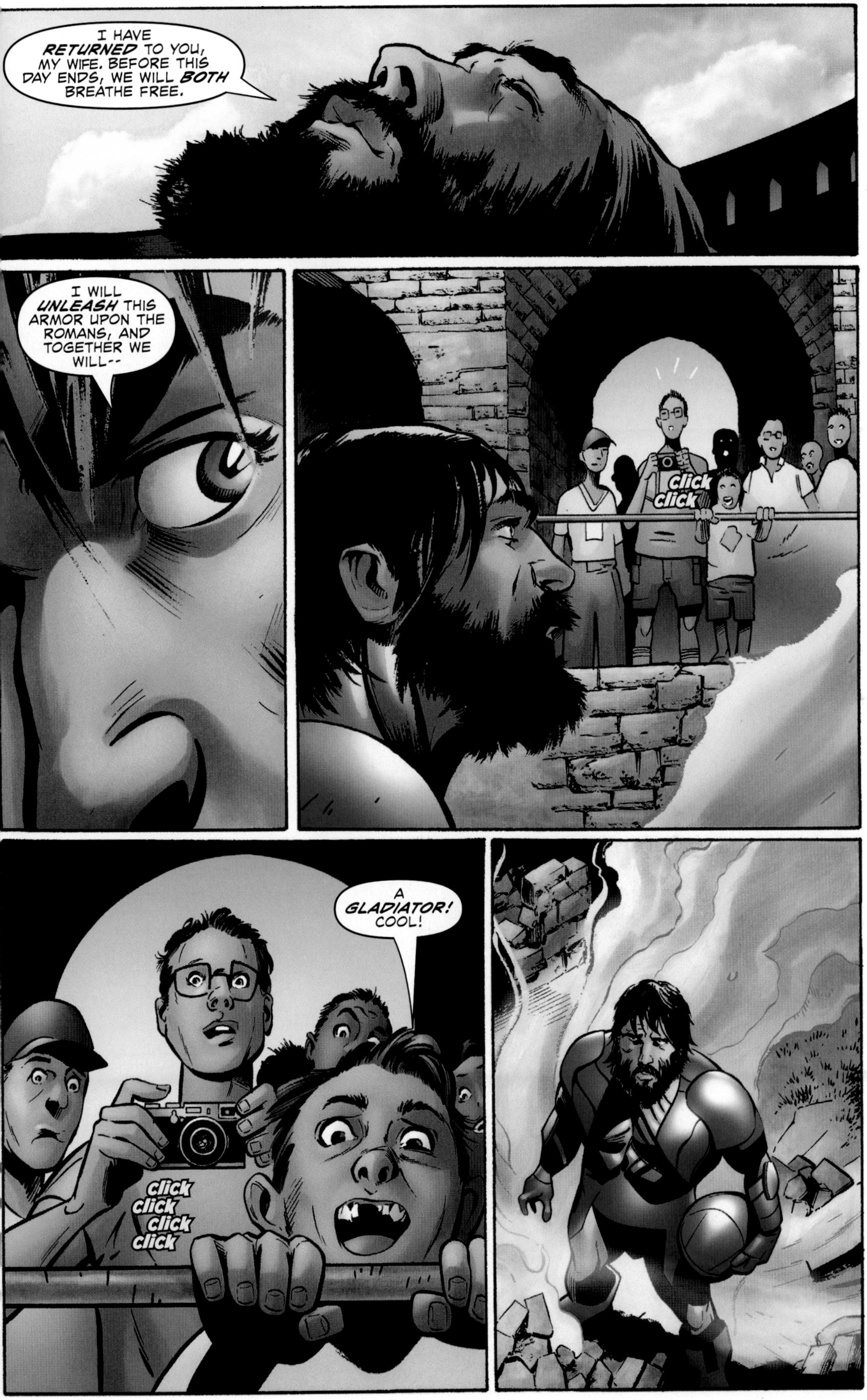
I HAVE RETURNED TO YOU, MY WIFE. BEFORE THIS DAY ENDS, WE WILL BOTH BREATHE FREE.
I WILL UNLEASH THIS ARMOR UPON THE ROMANS, AND TOGETHER WE WILL--
Click
Click
A GLADIATOR! COOL!
click
click
click
click

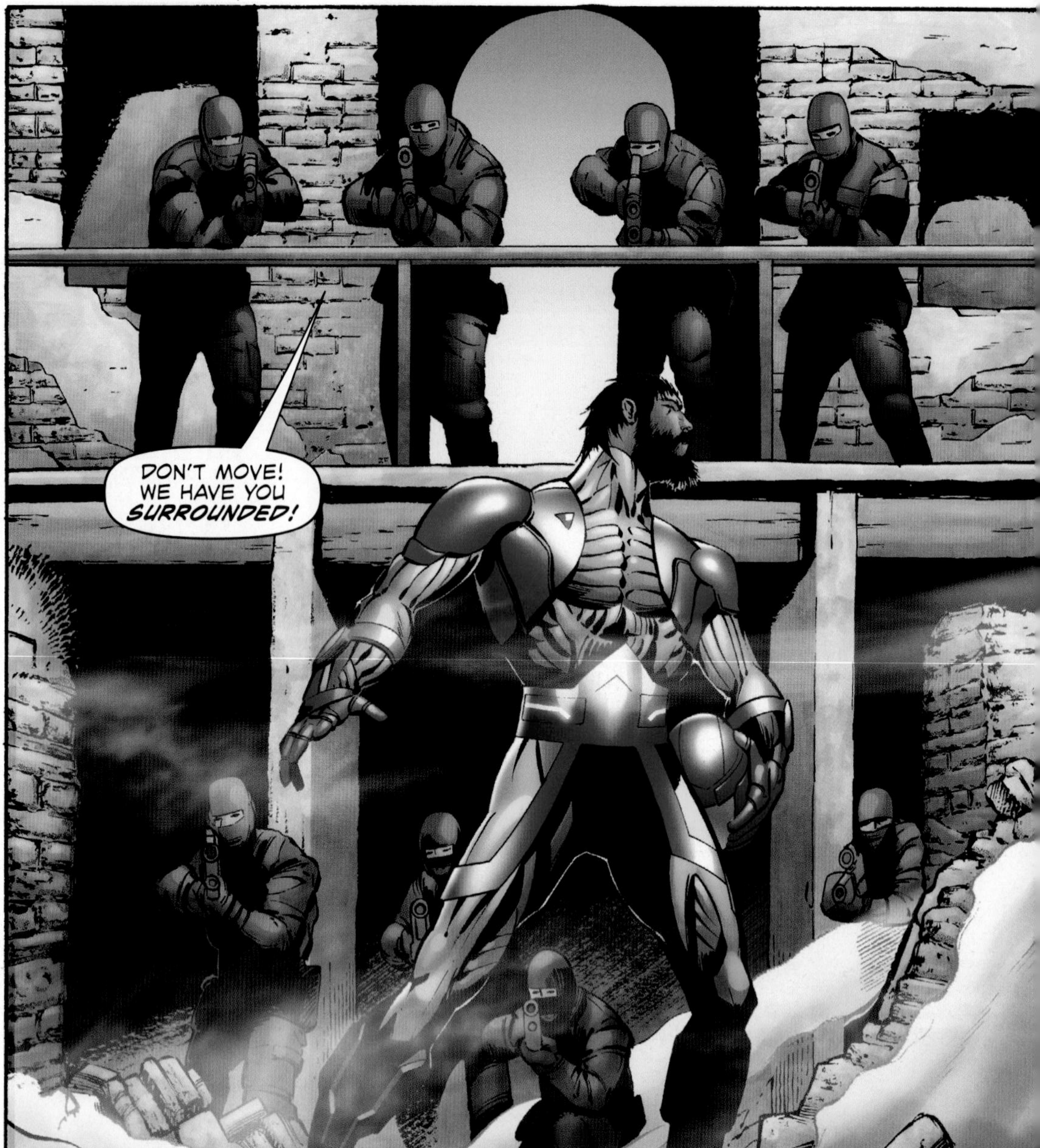
DON'T MOVE! WE HAVE YOU SURROUNDED!

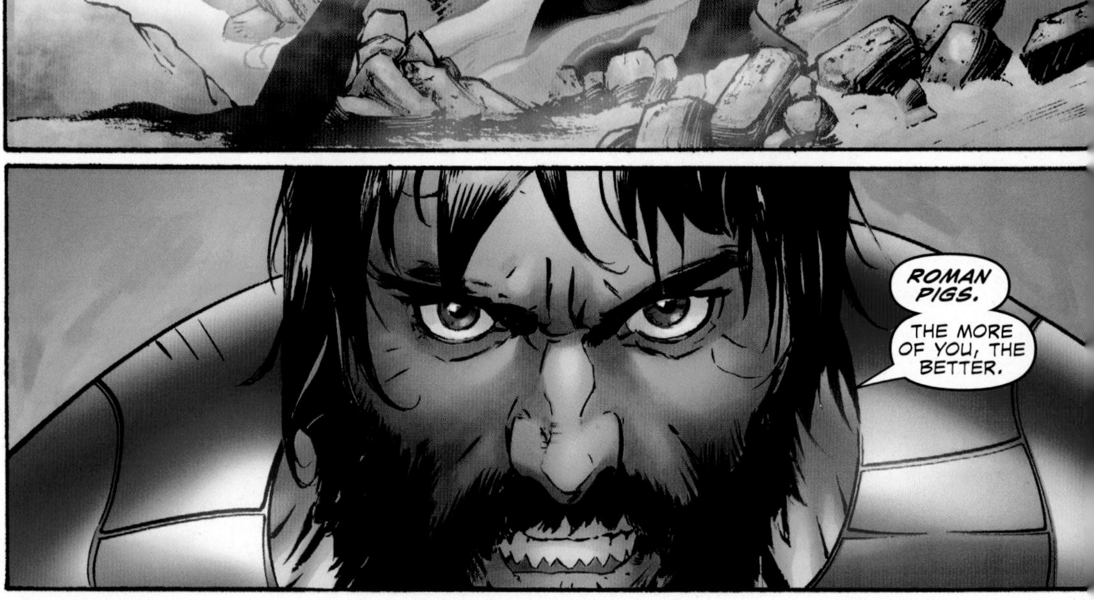
ROMAN PIGS.
THE MORE OF YOU, THE BETTER.

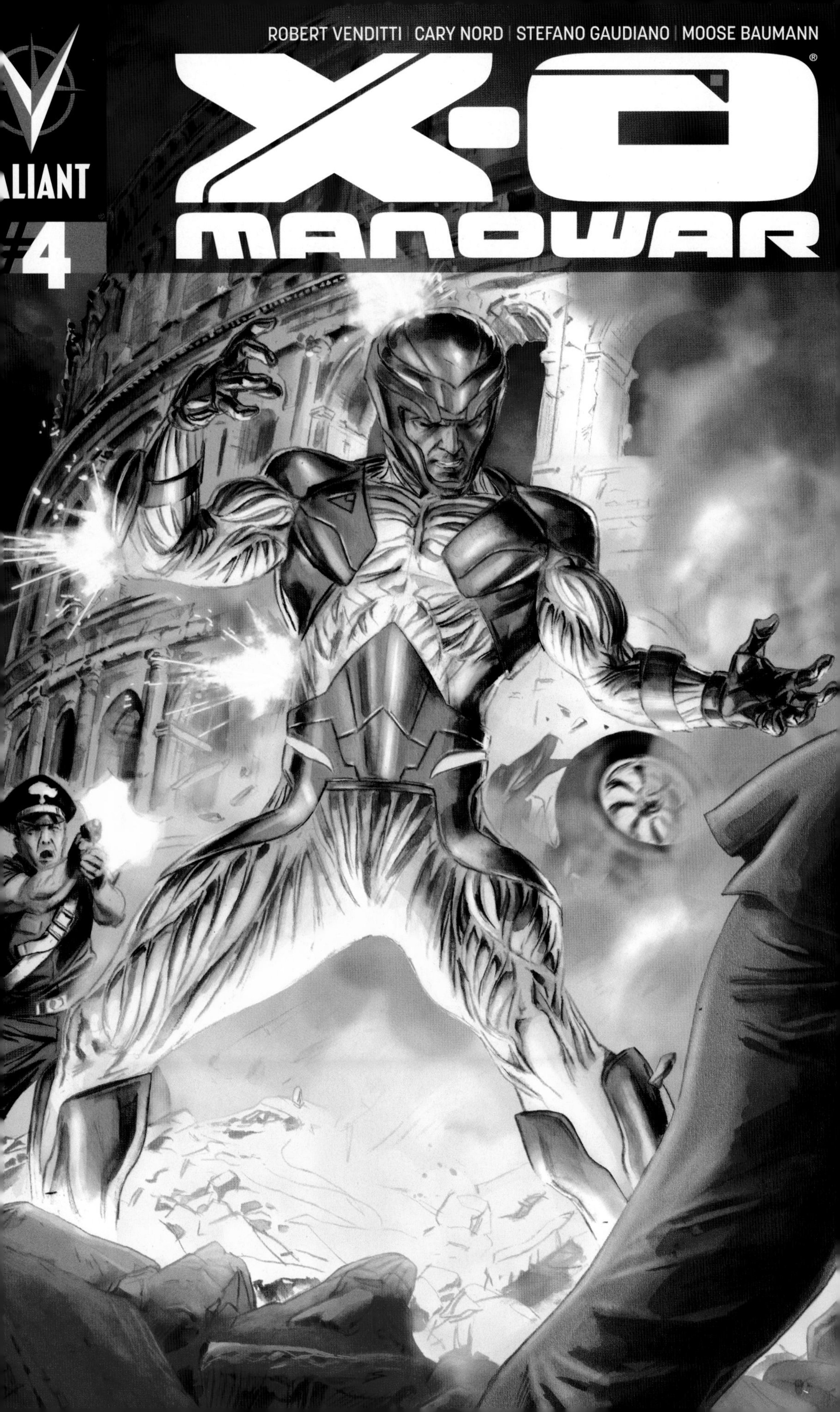
ROBERT VENDITTI | CARY NORD | STEFANO GAUDIANO | MOOSE BAUMANN
VALIANT
#4
X-O
MANOWAR

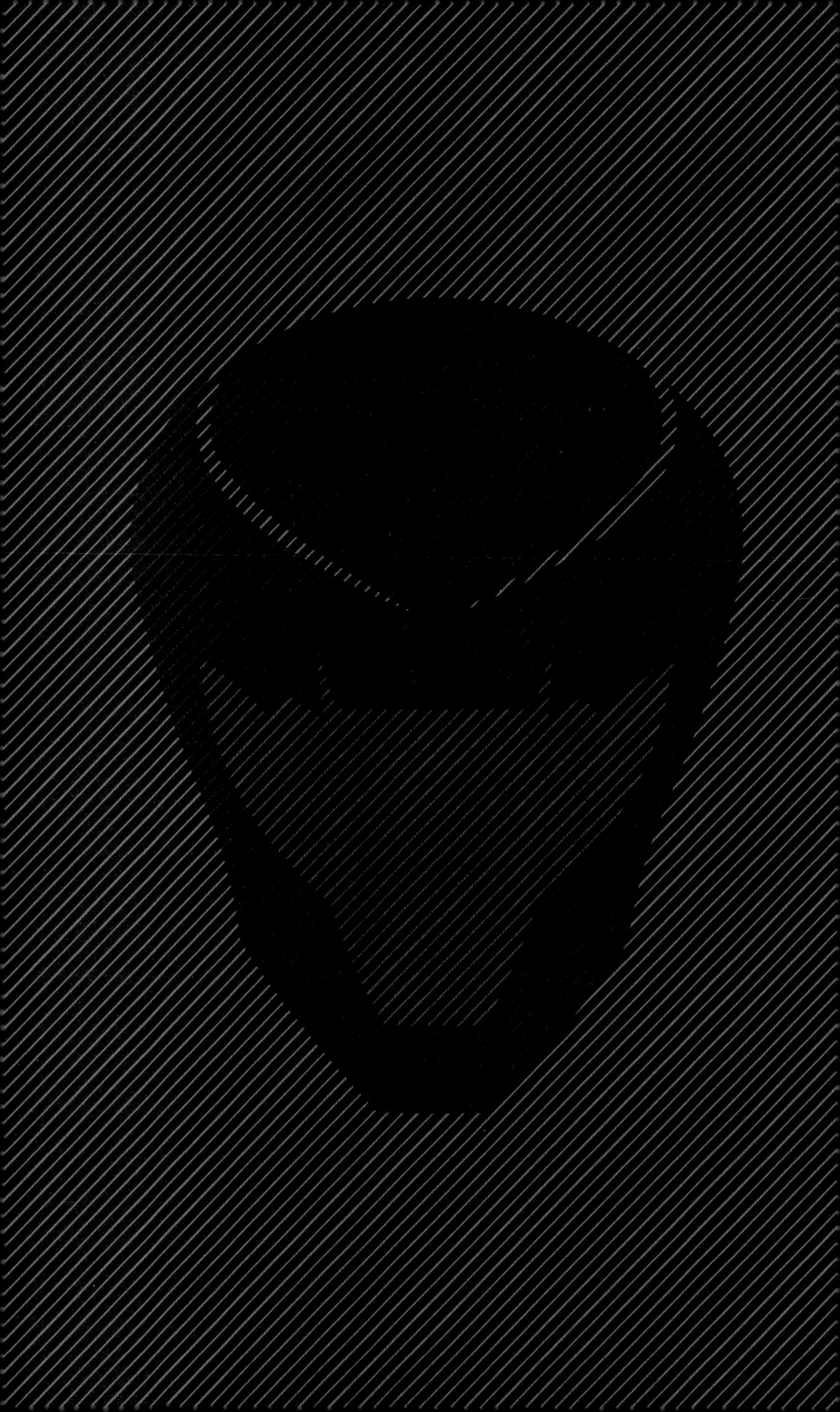

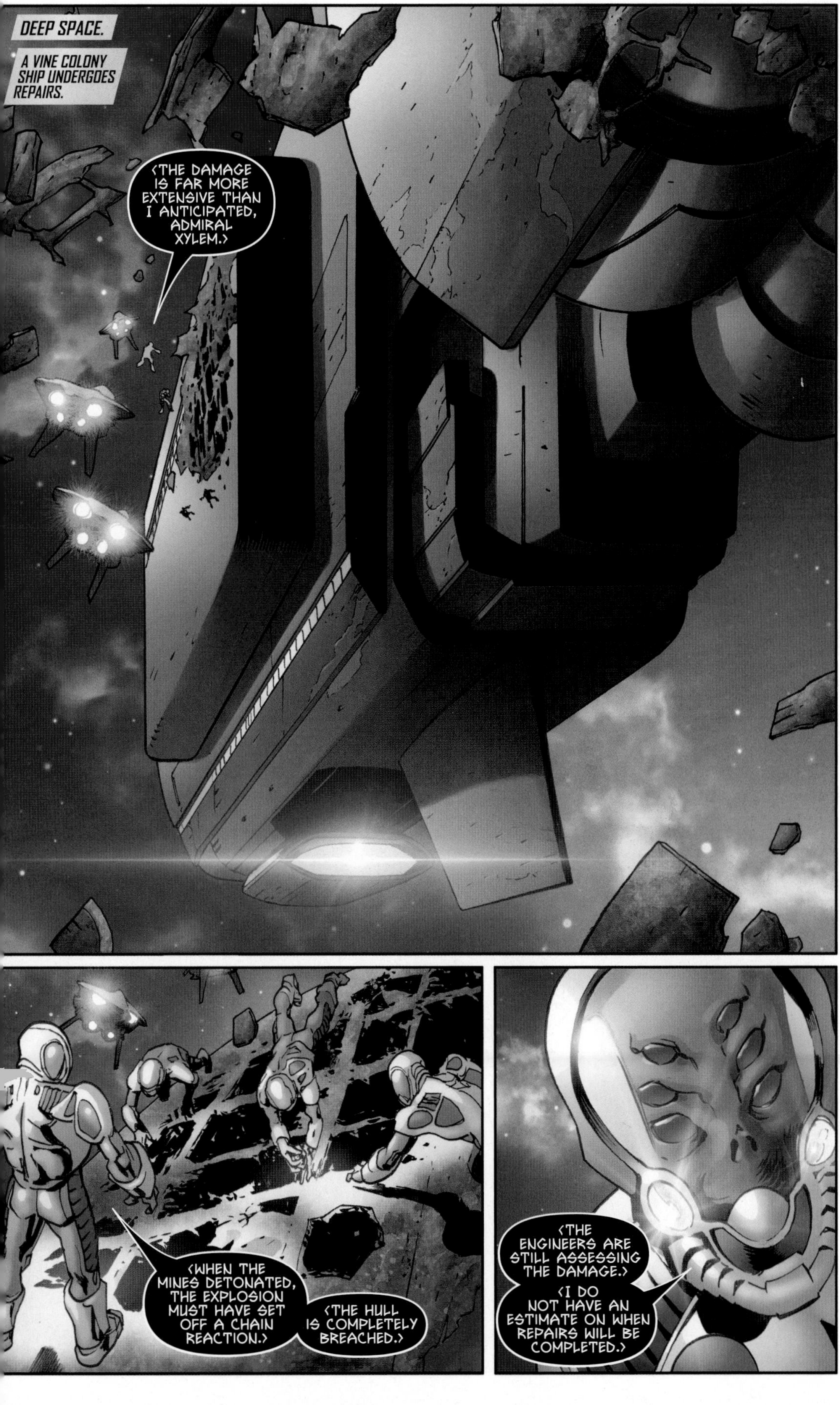
DEEP SPACE.
A VINE COLONY SHIP UNDERGOES REPAIRS.
‹THE DAMAGE IS FAR MORE EXTENSIVE THAN I ANTICIPATED, ADMIRAL XYLEM.›
‹WHEN THE MINES DETONATED, THE EXPLOSION MUST HAVE SET OFF A CHAIN REACTION.›
‹THE HULL IS COMPLETELY BREACHED.›
‹THE ENGINEERS ARE STILL ASSESSING THE DAMAGE.›
‹I DO NOT HAVE AN ESTIMATE ON WHEN REPAIRS WILL BE COMPLETED.›

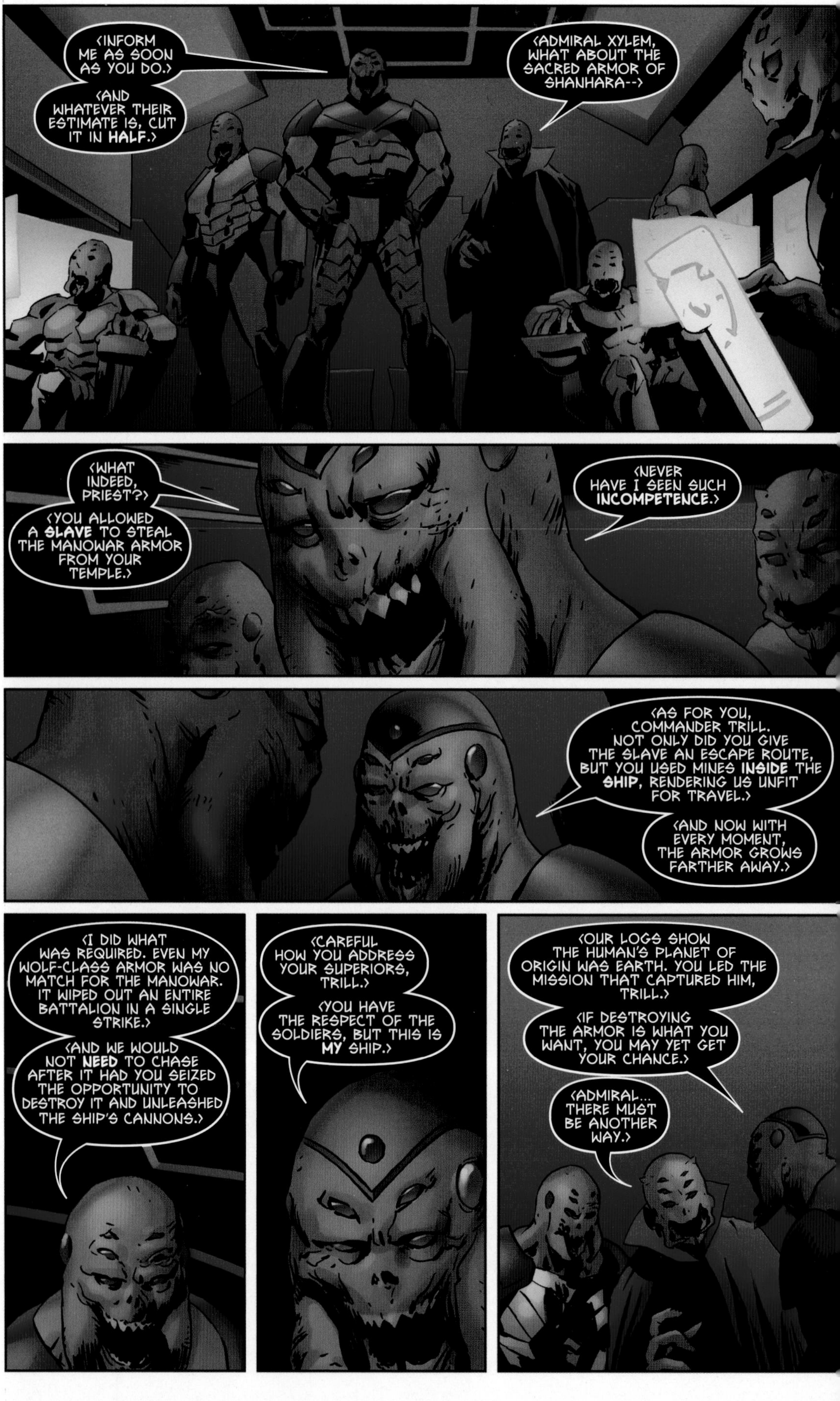
<INFORM ME AS SOON AS YOU DO.>
<AND WHATEVER THEIR ESTIMATE IS, CUT IT IN **HALF**.>
<ADMIRAL XYLEM, WHAT ABOUT THE SACRED ARMOR OF SHANHARA-->
<WHAT INDEED, PRIEST?>
<YOU ALLOWED A **SLAVE** TO STEAL THE MANOWAR ARMOR FROM YOUR TEMPLE.>
<NEVER HAVE I SEEN SUCH **INCOMPETENCE**.>
<AS FOR YOU, COMMANDER TRILL. NOT ONLY DID YOU GIVE THE SLAVE AN ESCAPE ROUTE, BUT YOU USED MINES **INSIDE** THE **SHIP**, RENDERING US UNFIT FOR TRAVEL.>
<AND NOW WITH EVERY MOMENT, THE ARMOR GROWS FARTHER AWAY.>
<I DID WHAT WAS REQUIRED. EVEN MY WOLF-CLASS ARMOR WAS NO MATCH FOR THE MANOWAR. IT WIPED OUT AN ENTIRE BATTALION IN A SINGLE STRIKE.>
<AND WE WOULD NOT **NEED** TO CHASE AFTER IT HAD YOU SEIZED THE OPPORTUNITY TO DESTROY IT AND UNLEASHED THE SHIP'S CANNONS.>
<CAREFUL HOW YOU ADDRESS YOUR SUPERIORS, TRILL.>
<YOU HAVE THE RESPECT OF THE SOLDIERS, BUT THIS IS **MY** SHIP.>
<OUR LOGS SHOW THE HUMAN'S PLANET OF ORIGIN WAS EARTH. YOU LED THE MISSION THAT CAPTURED HIM, TRILL.>
<IF DESTROYING THE ARMOR IS WHAT YOU WANT, YOU MAY YET GET YOUR CHANCE.>
<ADMIRAL... THERE MUST BE ANOTHER WAY.>

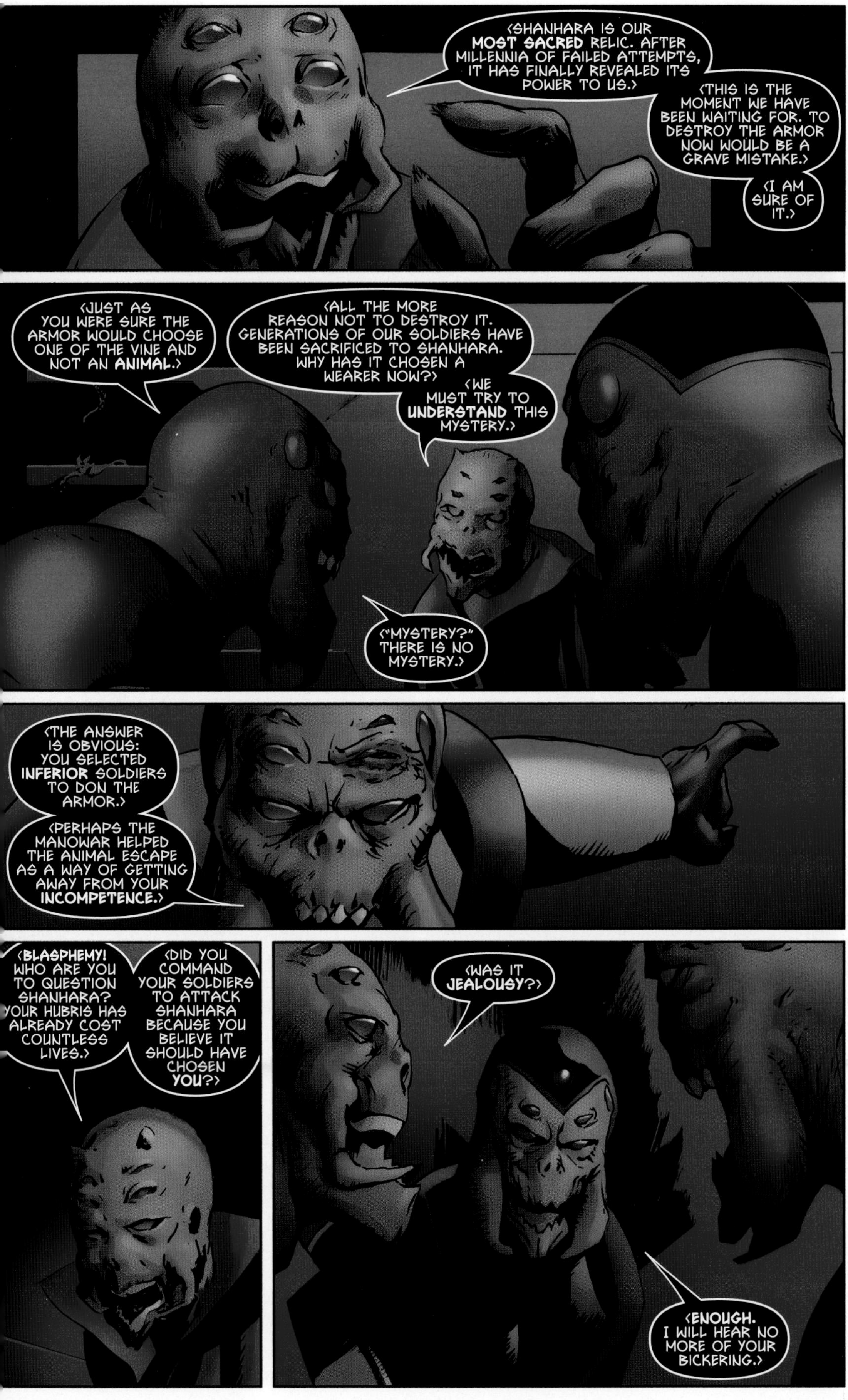

‹SHANHARA IS OUR MOST SACRED RELIC. AFTER MILLENNIA OF FAILED ATTEMPTS, IT HAS FINALLY REVEALED ITS POWER TO US.›
‹THIS IS THE MOMENT WE HAVE BEEN WAITING FOR. TO DESTROY THE ARMOR NOW WOULD BE A GRAVE MISTAKE.›
‹I AM SURE OF IT.›
‹JUST AS YOU WERE SURE THE ARMOR WOULD CHOOSE ONE OF THE VINE AND NOT AN ANIMAL.›
‹ALL THE MORE REASON NOT TO DESTROY IT. GENERATIONS OF OUR SOLDIERS HAVE BEEN SACRIFICED TO SHANHARA. WHY HAS IT CHOSEN A WEARER NOW?›
‹WE MUST TRY TO UNDERSTAND THIS MYSTERY.›
‹"MYSTERY?" THERE IS NO MYSTERY.›
‹THE ANSWER IS OBVIOUS: YOU SELECTED INFERIOR SOLDIERS TO DON THE ARMOR.›
‹PERHAPS THE MANOWAR HELPED THE ANIMAL ESCAPE AS A WAY OF GETTING AWAY FROM YOUR INCOMPETENCE.›
‹BLASPHEMY! WHO ARE YOU TO QUESTION SHANHARA? YOUR HUBRIS HAS ALREADY COST COUNTLESS LIVES.›
‹DID YOU COMMAND YOUR SOLDIERS TO ATTACK SHANHARA BECAUSE YOU BELIEVE IT SHOULD HAVE CHOSEN YOU?›
‹WAS IT JEALOUSY?›
‹ENOUGH. I WILL HEAR NO MORE OF YOUR BICKERING.›

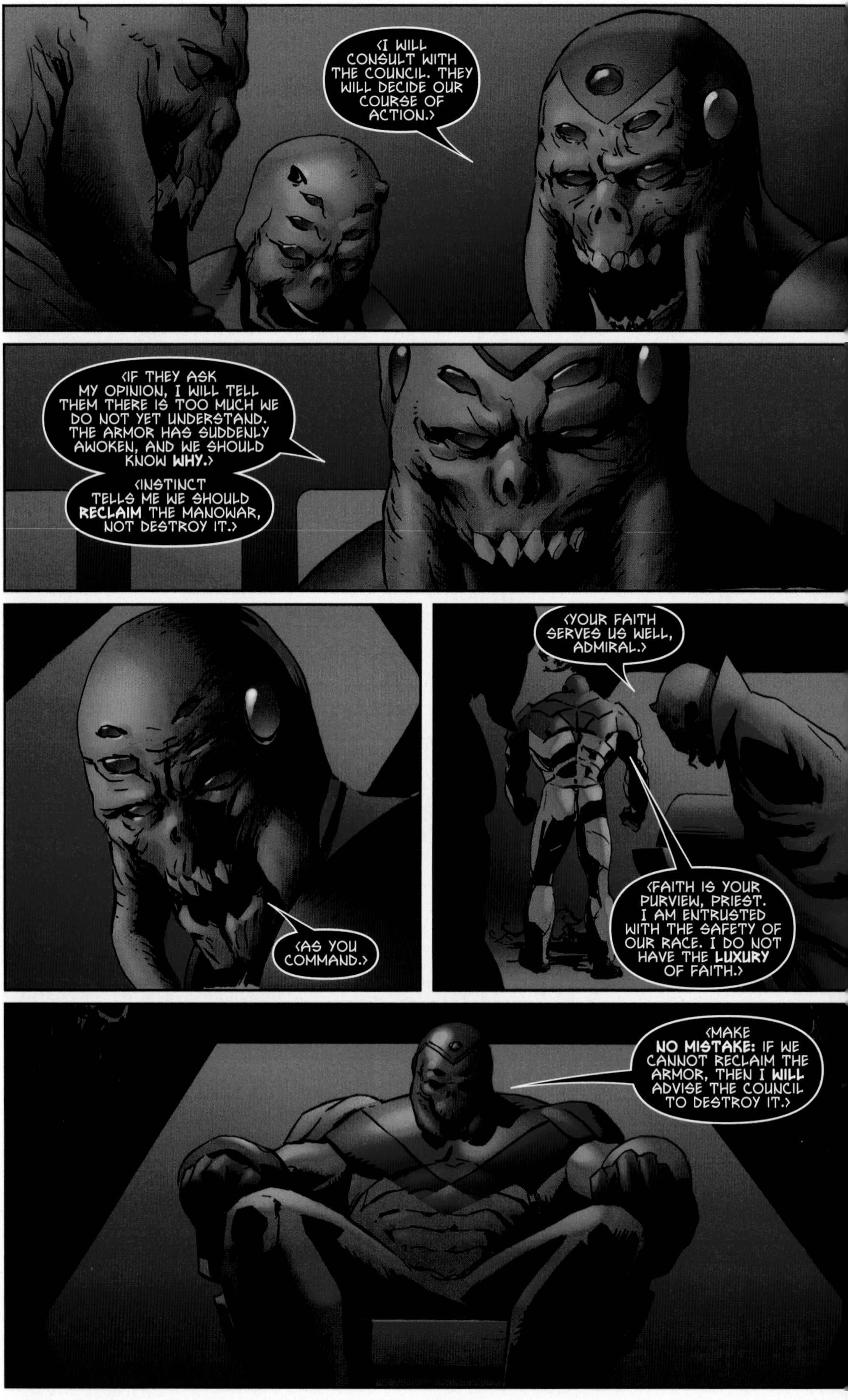
<I WILL CONSULT WITH THE COUNCIL. THEY WILL DECIDE OUR COURSE OF ACTION.>
<IF THEY ASK MY OPINION, I WILL TELL THEM THERE IS TOO MUCH WE DO NOT YET UNDERSTAND. THE ARMOR HAS SUDDENLY AWOKEN, AND WE SHOULD KNOW **WHY.**>
<INSTINCT TELLS ME WE SHOULD **RECLAIM** THE MANOWAR, NOT DESTROY IT.>
<AS YOU COMMAND.>
<YOUR FAITH SERVES US WELL, ADMIRAL.>
<FAITH IS YOUR PURVIEW, PRIEST. I AM ENTRUSTED WITH THE SAFETY OF OUR RACE. I DO NOT HAVE THE **LUXURY** OF FAITH.>
<MAKE **NO MISTAKE:** IF WE CANNOT RECLAIM THE ARMOR, THEN I **WILL** ADVISE THE COUNCIL TO DESTROY IT.>

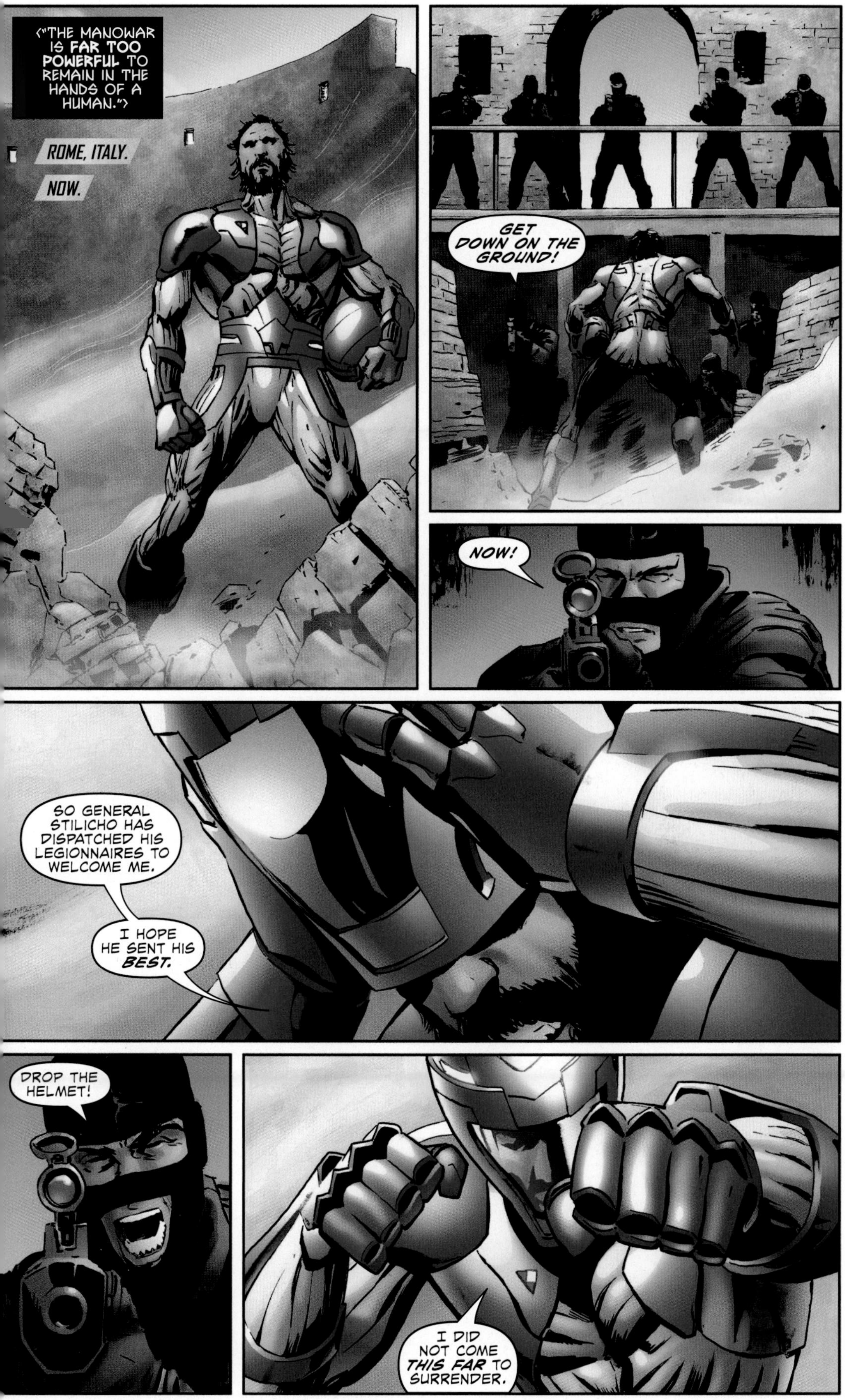

<"THE MANOWAR IS FAR TOO POWERFUL TO REMAIN IN THE HANDS OF A HUMAN.">
ROME, ITALY.
NOW.
GET DOWN ON THE GROUND!
NOW!
SO GENERAL STILICHO HAS DISPATCHED HIS LEGIONNAIRES TO WELCOME ME.
I HOPE HE SENT HIS BEST.
DROP THE HELMET!
I DID NOT COME THIS FAR TO SURRENDER.

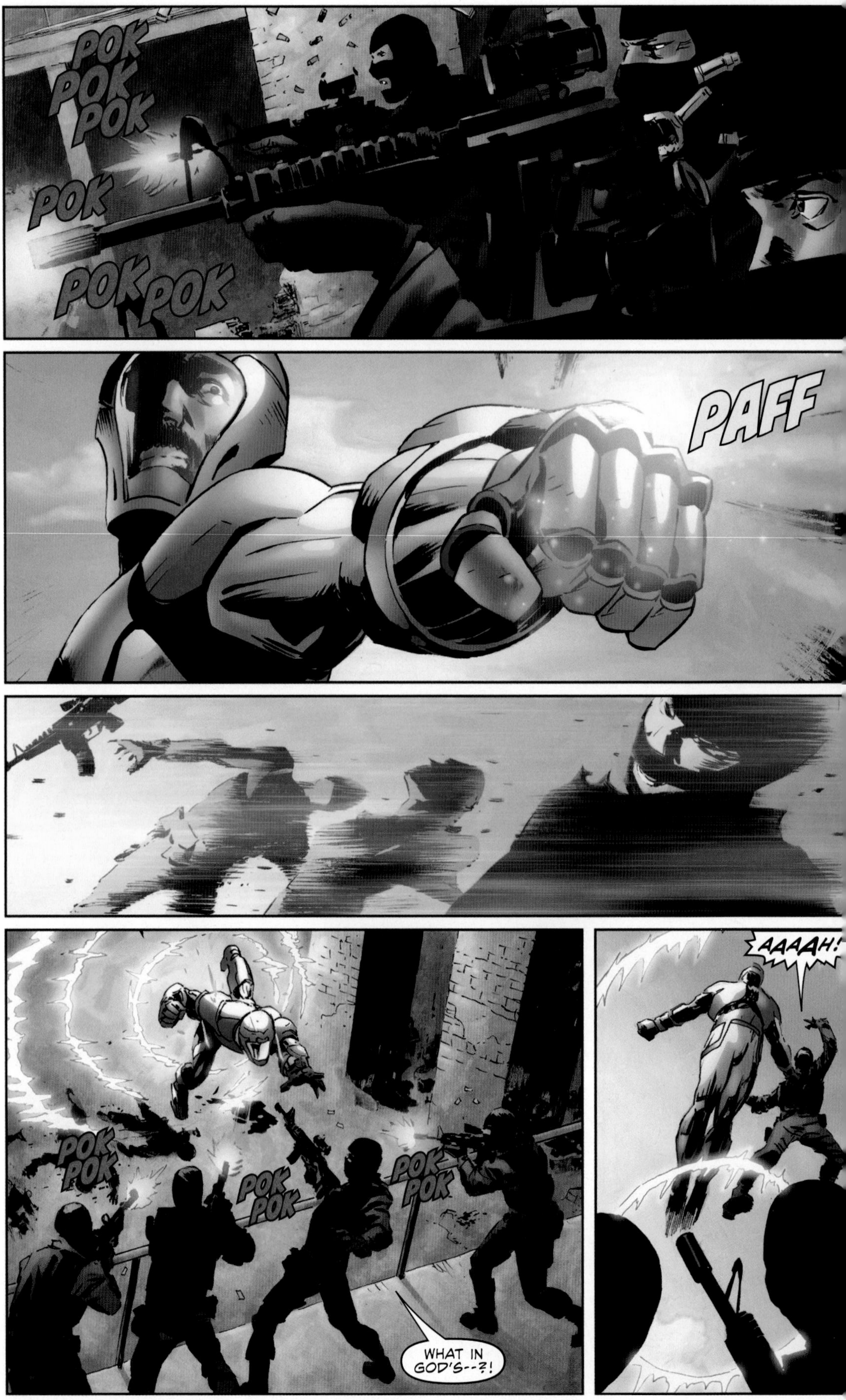
POK
POK
POK
POK
POK POK
PAFF
POK
POK
POK
POK
POK
POK
WHAT IN GOD'S--?!
AAAAH!

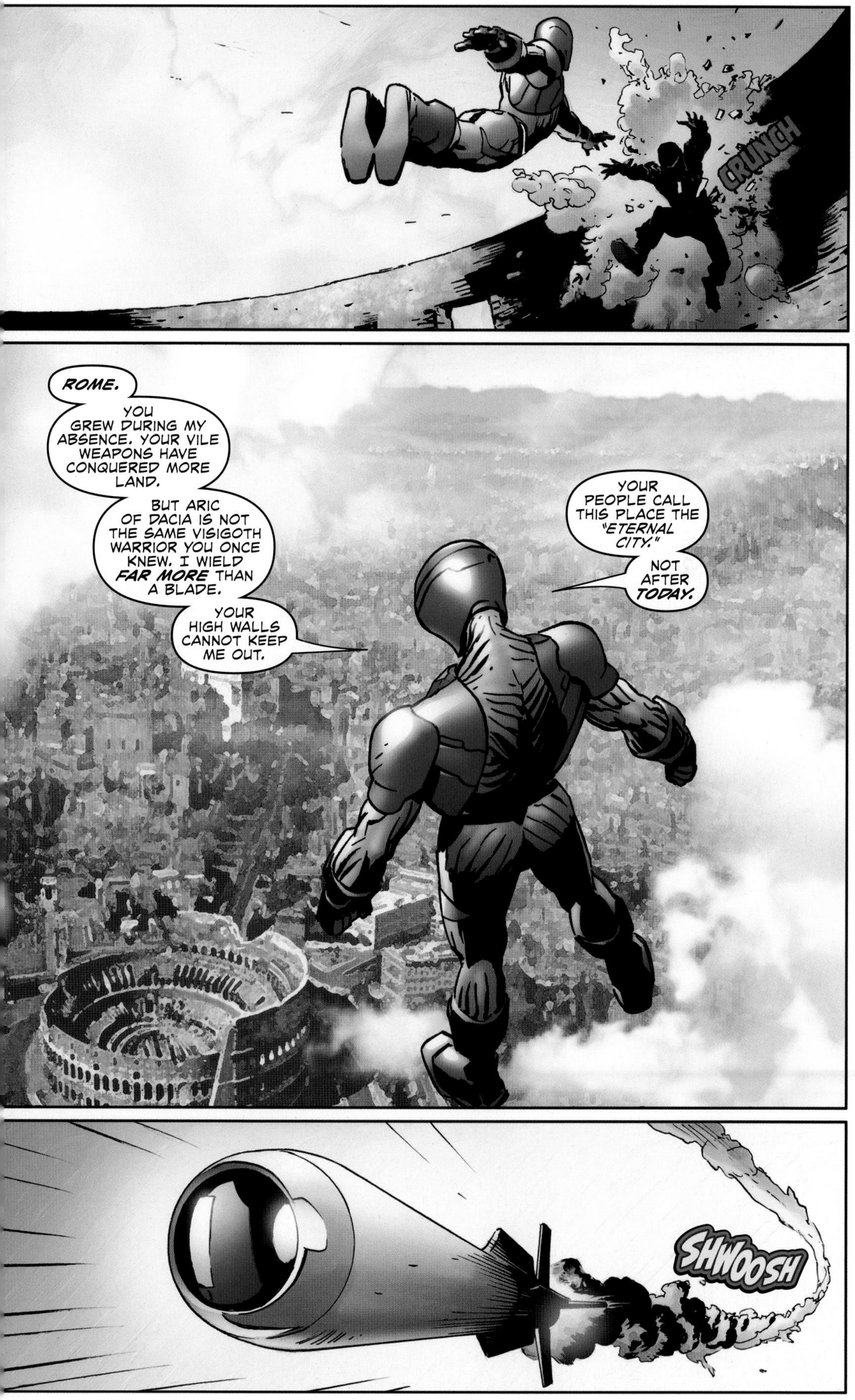
CRUNCH
ROME.
YOU GREW DURING MY ABSENCE. YOUR VILE WEAPONS HAVE CONQUERED MORE LAND.
BUT ARIC OF DACIA IS NOT THE SAME VISIGOTH WARRIOR YOU ONCE KNEW. I WIELD FAR MORE THAN A BLADE.
YOUR HIGH WALLS CANNOT KEEP ME OUT.
YOUR PEOPLE CALL THIS PLACE THE "ETERNAL CITY."
NOT AFTER TODAY.
SHWOOSH

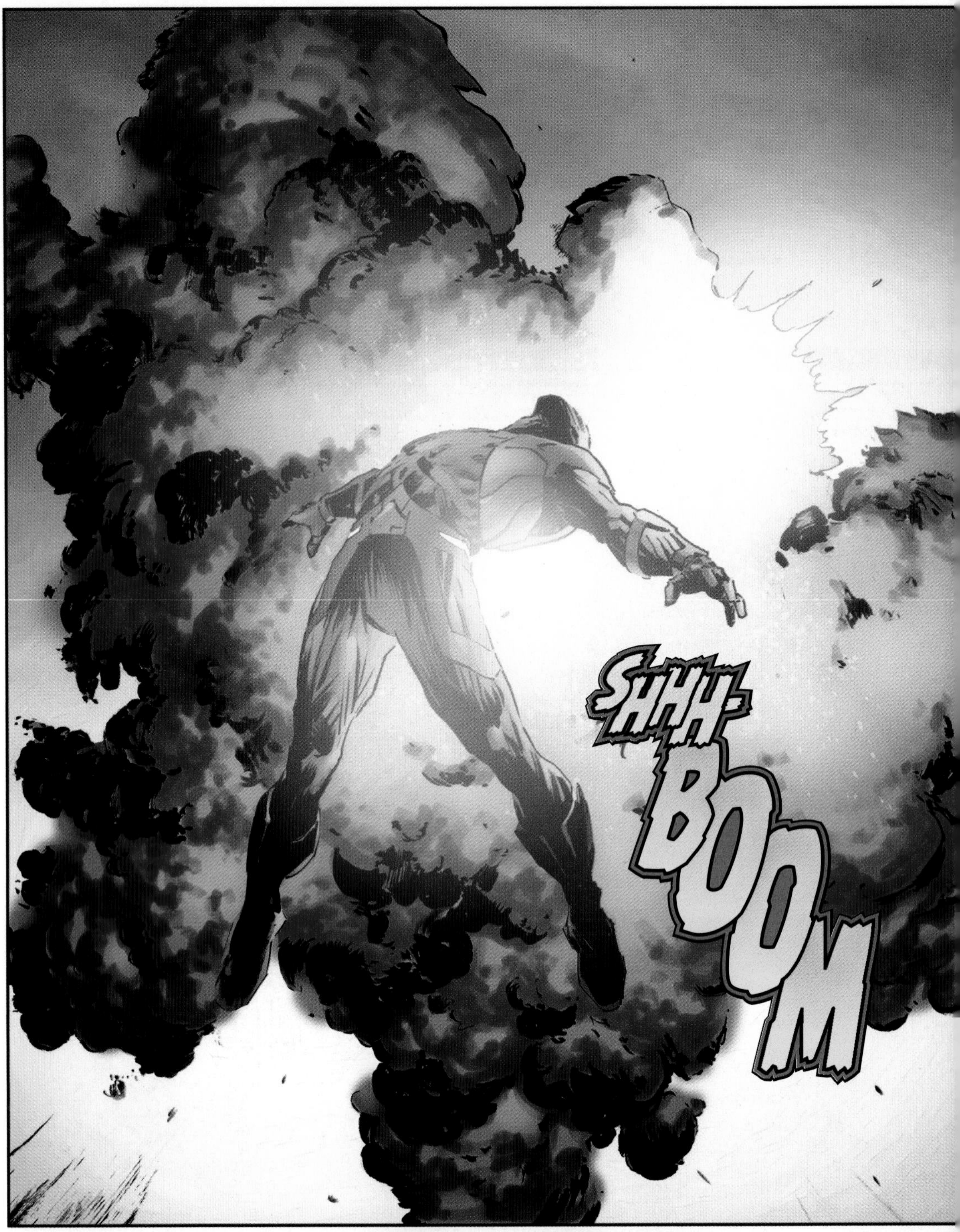
SHHH-BOOM

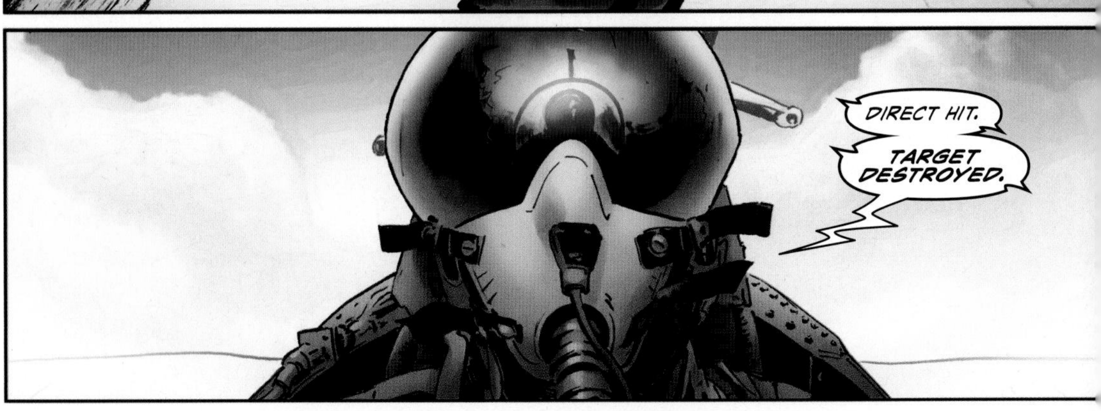
DIRECT HIT.
TARGET DESTROYED.

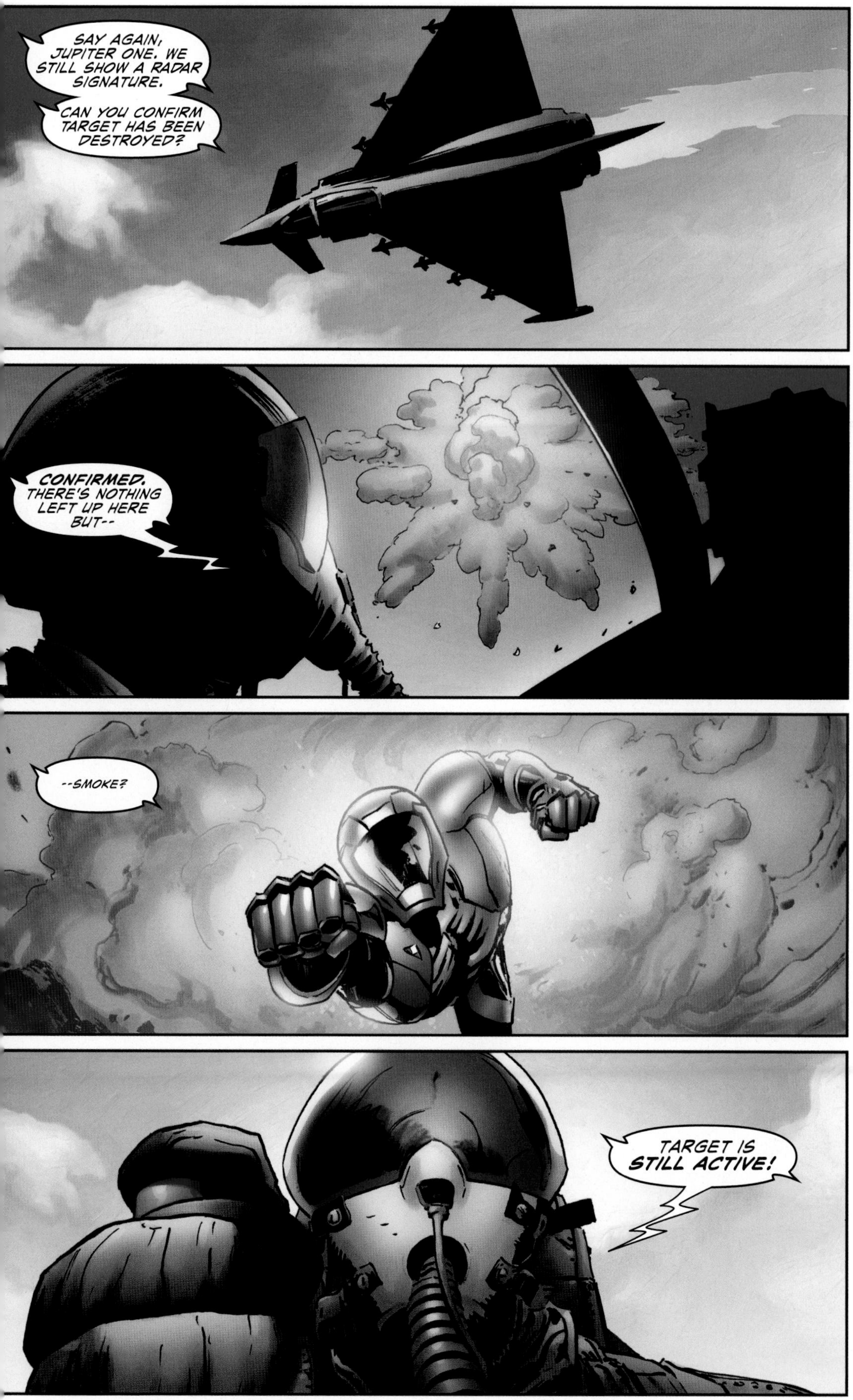
SAY AGAIN, JUPITER ONE. WE STILL SHOW A RADAR SIGNATURE.
CAN YOU CONFIRM TARGET HAS BEEN DESTROYED?
CONFIRMED. THERE'S NOTHING LEFT UP HERE BUT--
--SMOKE?
TARGET IS STILL ACTIVE!

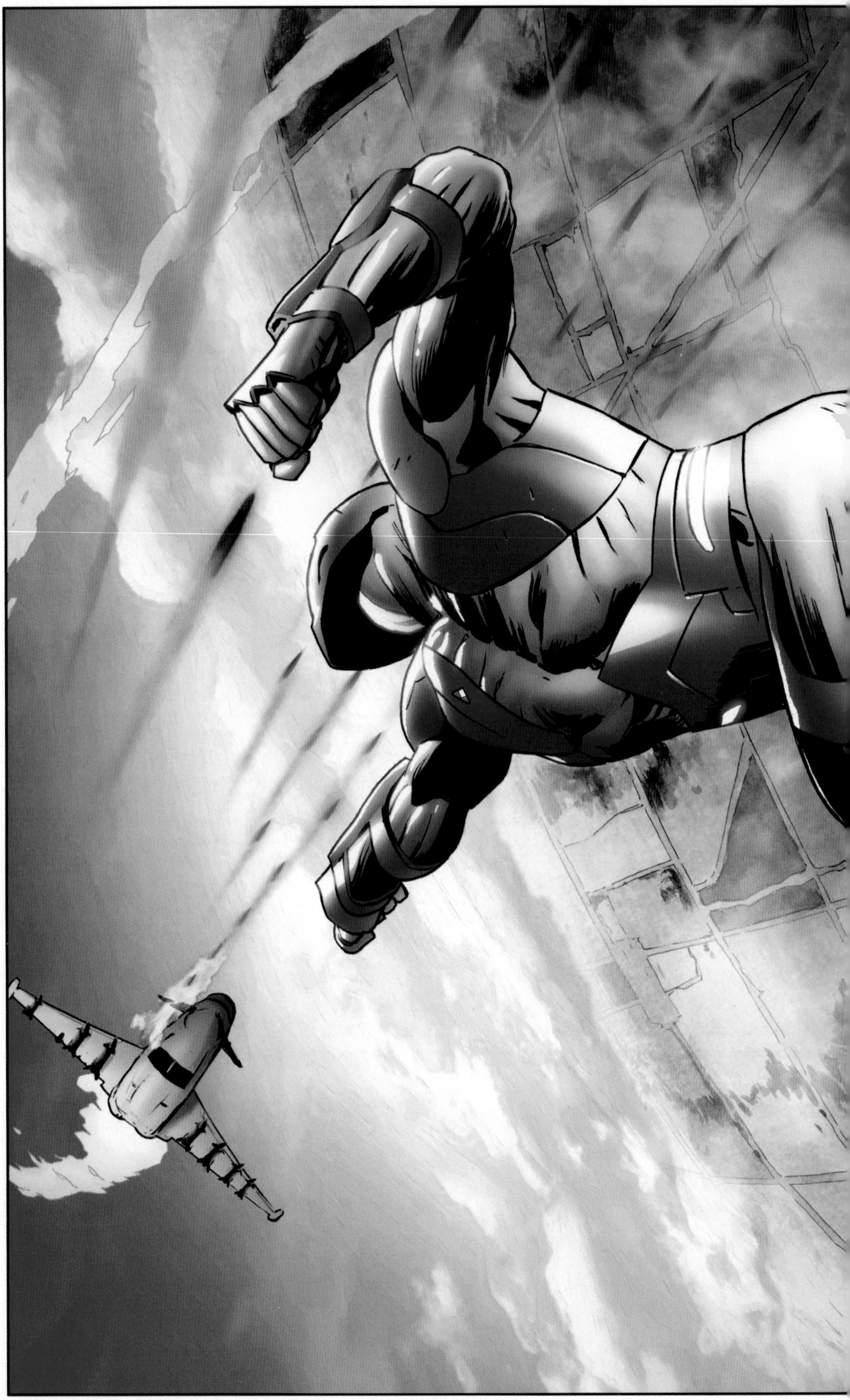

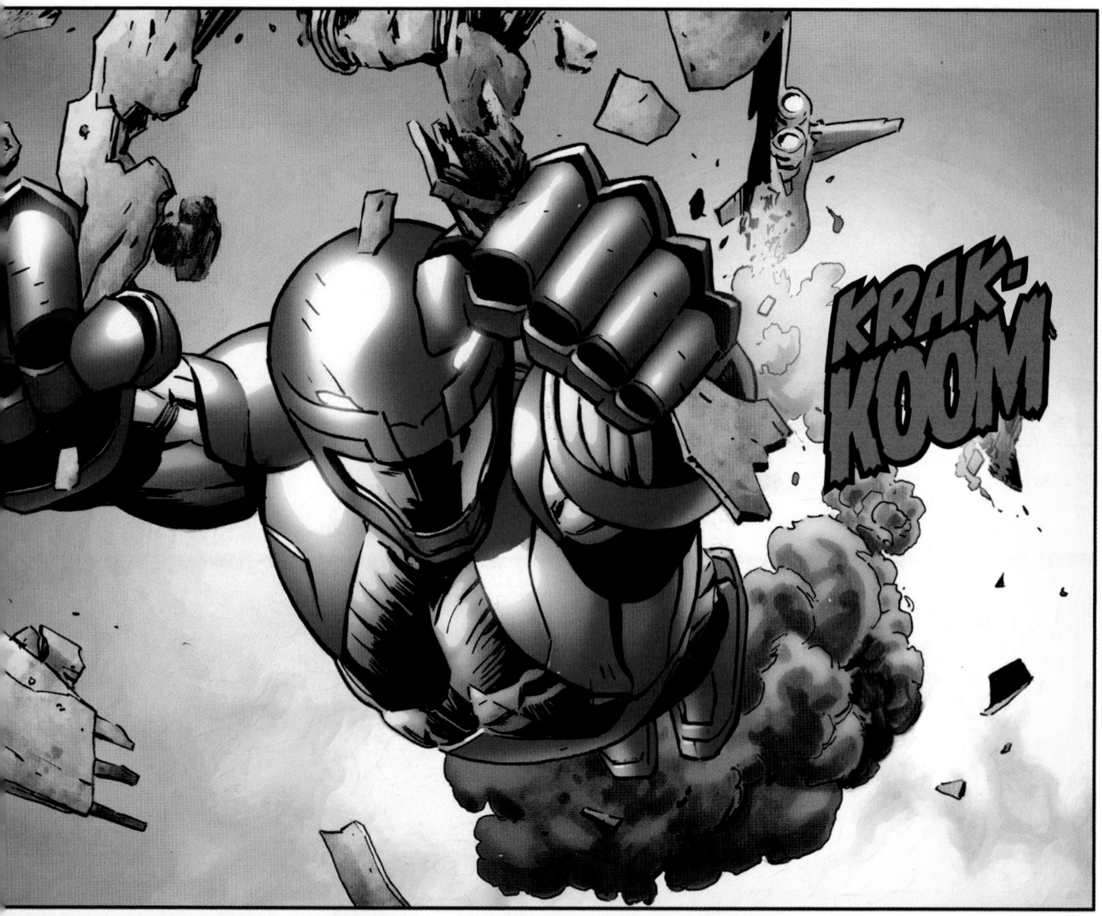
KRAK-KOOM

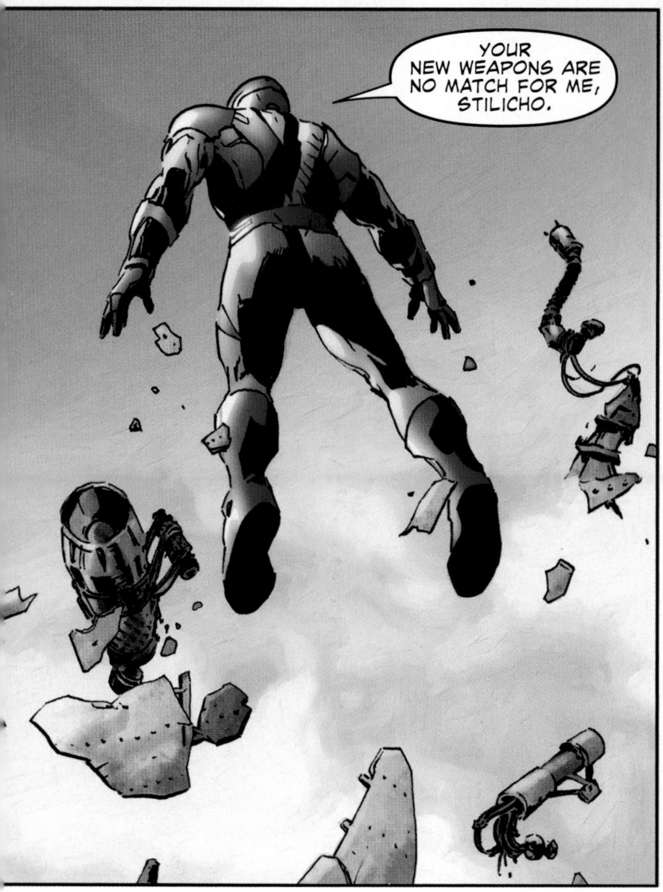
YOUR NEW WEAPONS ARE NO MATCH FOR ME, STILICHO.

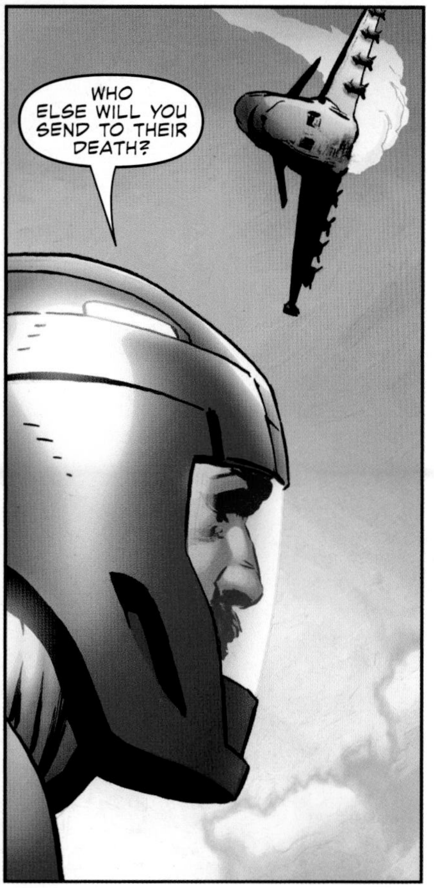
WHO ELSE WILL YOU SEND TO THEIR DEATH?

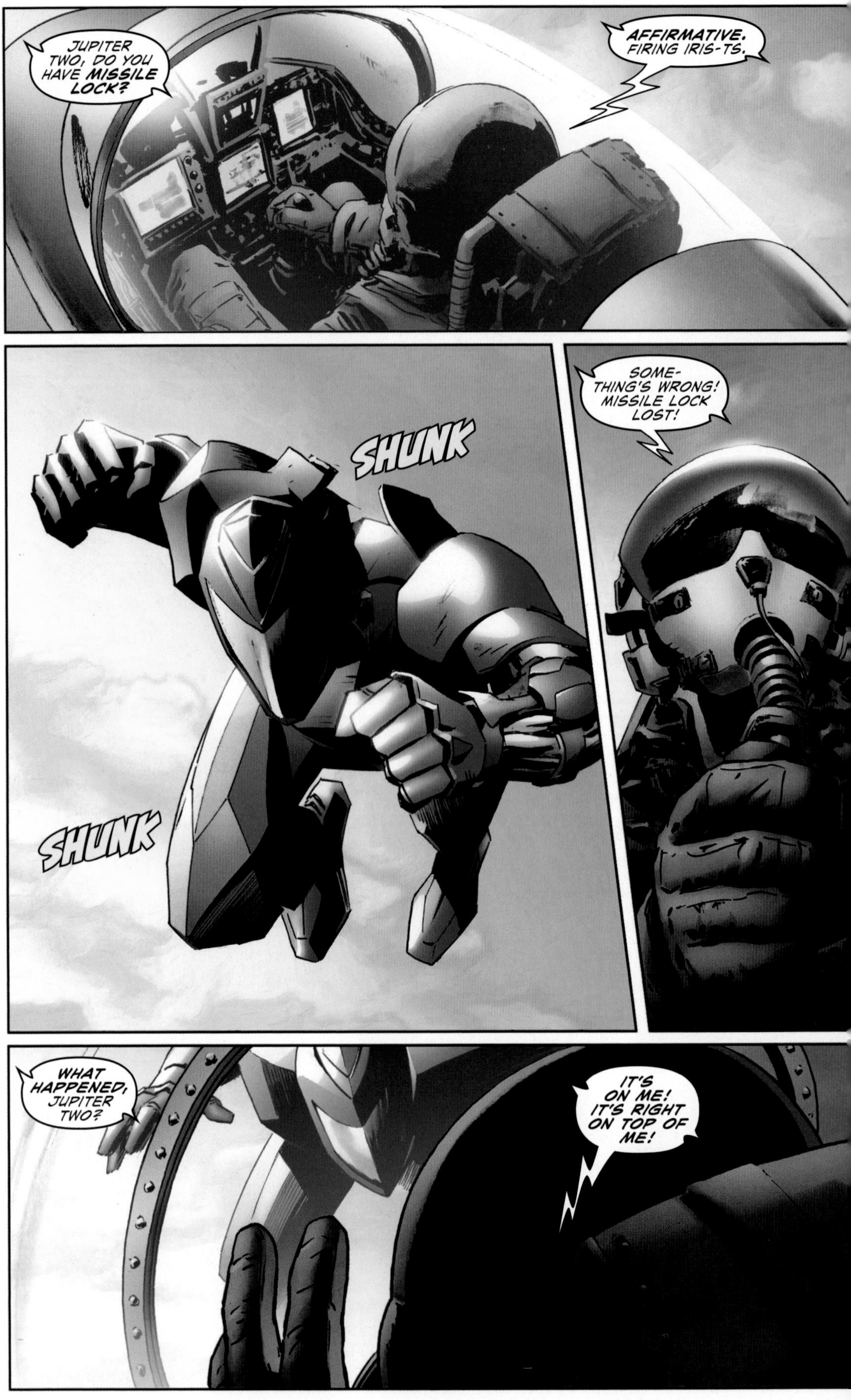
JUPITER TWO, DO YOU HAVE MISSILE LOCK?
AFFIRMATIVE. FIRING IRIS-TS.
SHUNK
SHUNK
SOME-THING'S WRONG! MISSILE LOCK LOST!
WHAT HAPPENED, JUPITER TWO?
IT'S ON ME! IT'S RIGHT ON TOP OF ME!

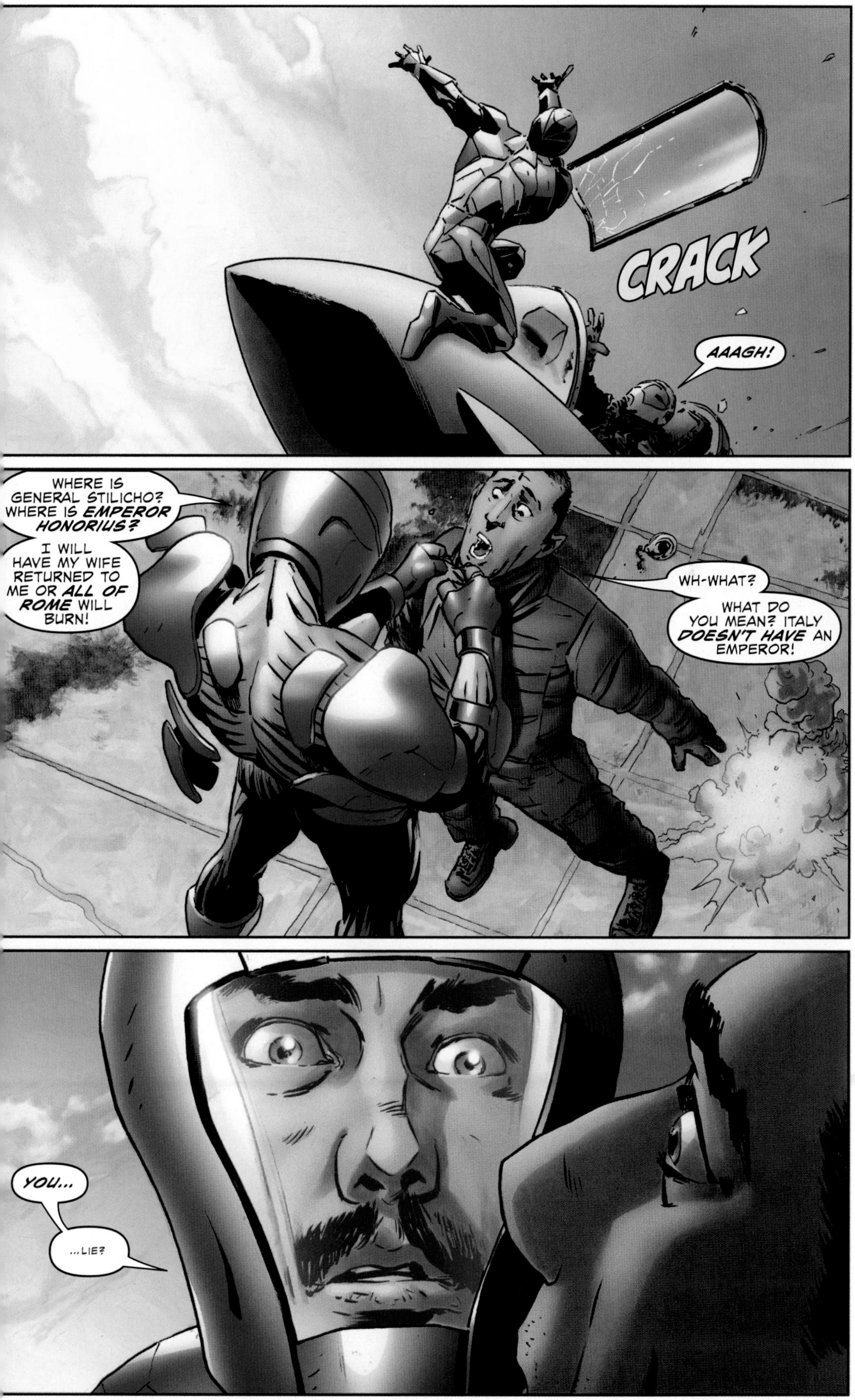
CRACK
AAAGH!
WHERE IS GENERAL STILICHO? WHERE IS EMPEROR HONORIUS?
I WILL HAVE MY WIFE RETURNED TO ME OR ALL OF ROME WILL BURN!
WH-WHAT?
WHAT DO YOU MEAN? ITALY DOESN'T HAVE AN EMPEROR!
YOU...
...LIE?

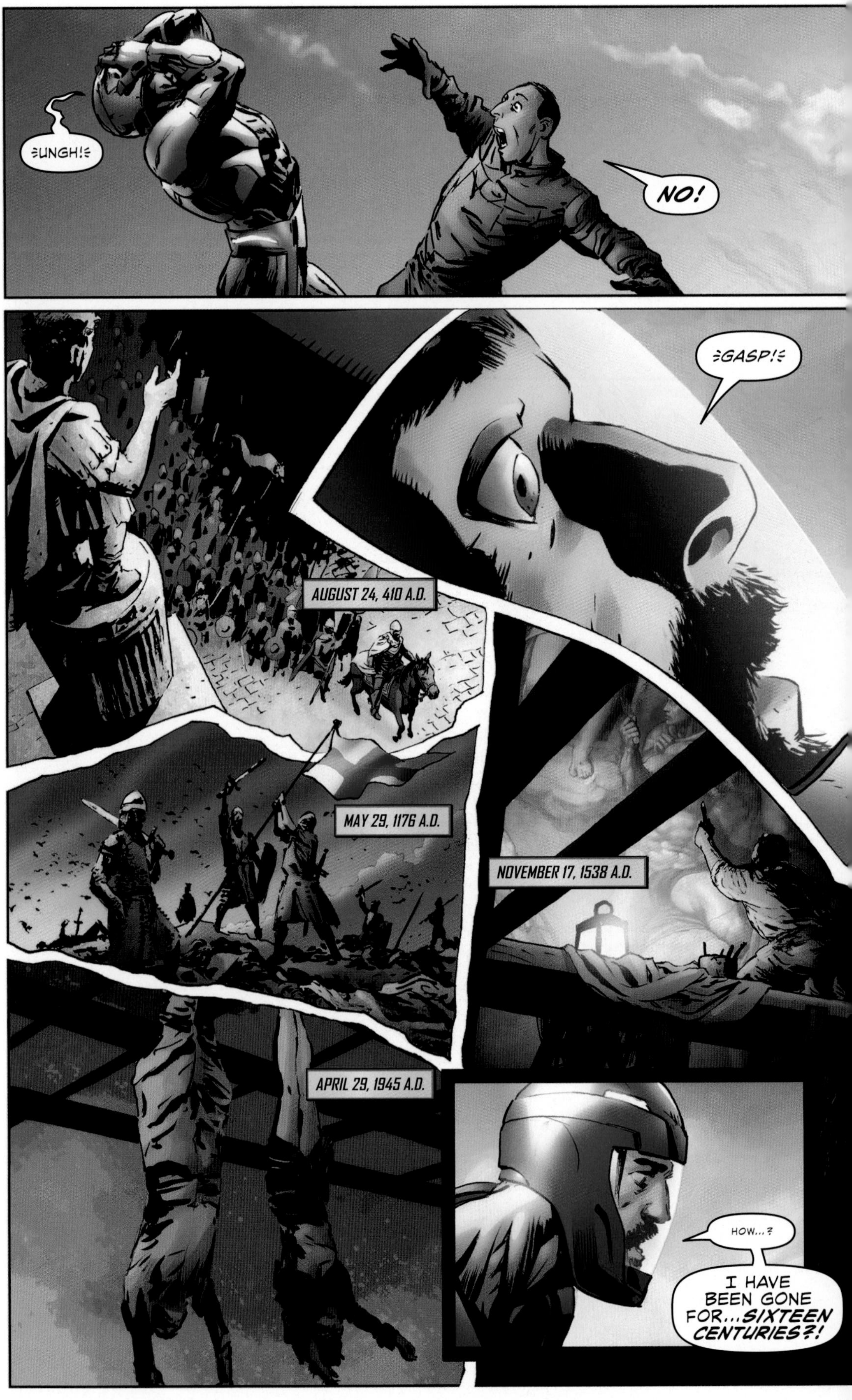
UNGH!
NO!
GASP!
AUGUST 24, 410 A.D.
MAY 29, 1176 A.D.
NOVEMBER 17, 1538 A.D.
APRIL 29, 1945 A.D.
HOW...?
I HAVE BEEN GONE FOR...SIXTEEN CENTURIES?!

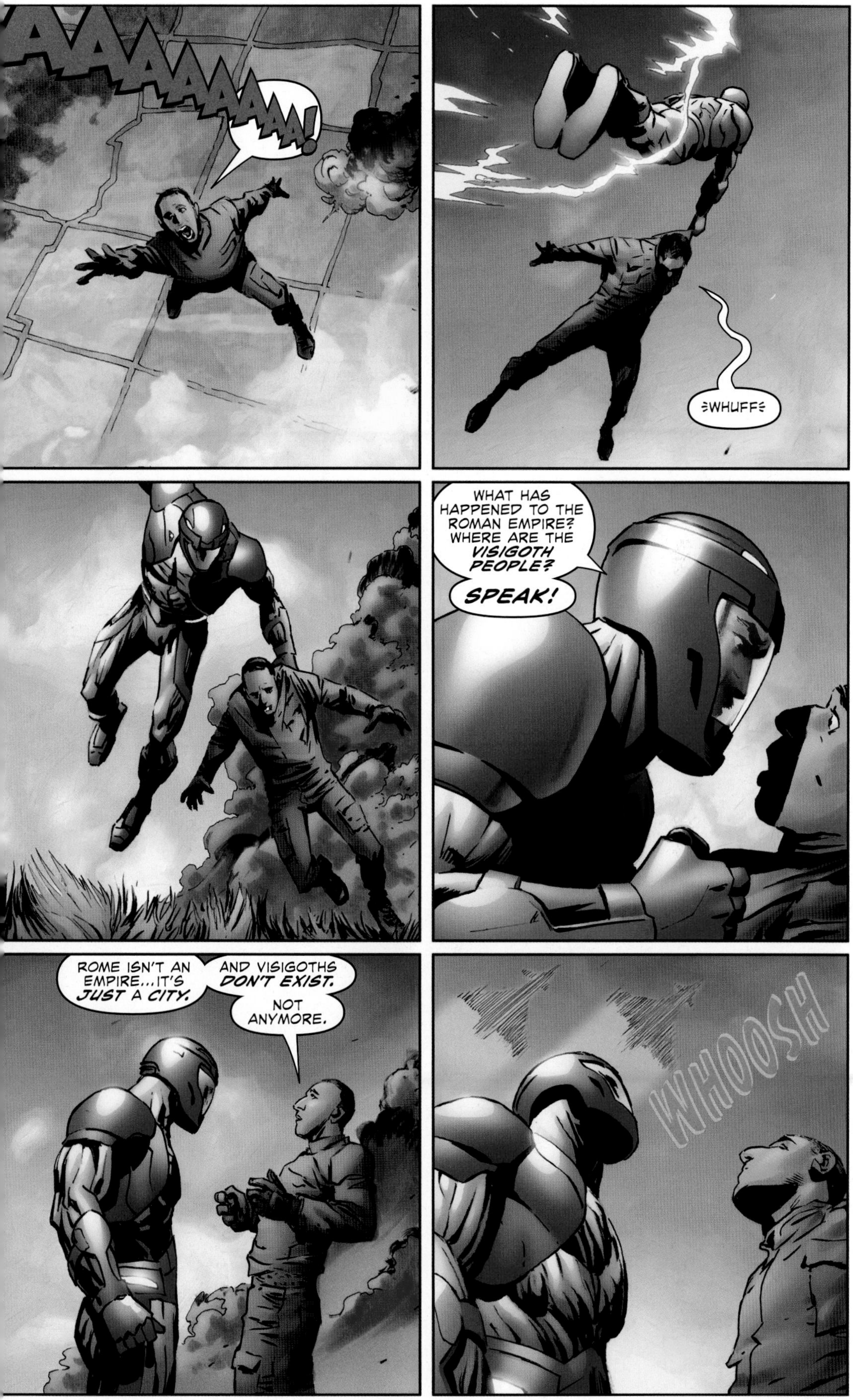
AAAAAAAAAAAA!
WHUFF
WHAT HAS HAPPENED TO THE ROMAN EMPIRE? WHERE ARE THE VISIGOTH PEOPLE?
SPEAK!
ROME ISN'T AN EMPIRE...IT'S JUST A CITY.
AND VISIGOTHS DON'T EXIST.
NOT ANYMORE.
WHOOSH

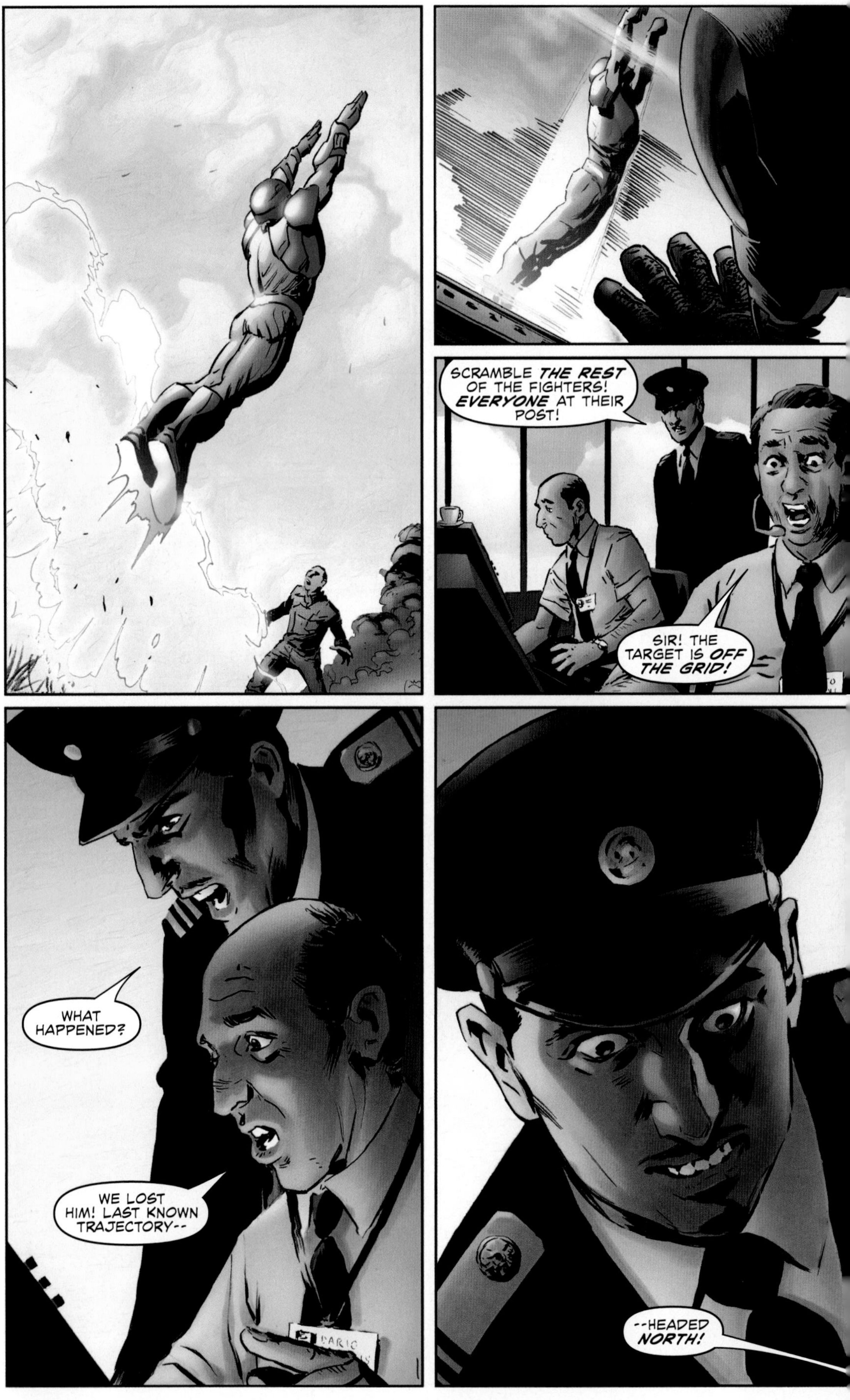
SCRAMBLE THE REST OF THE FIGHTERS! EVERYONE AT THEIR POST!
SIR! THE TARGET IS OFF THE GRID!
WHAT HAPPENED?
WE LOST HIM! LAST KNOWN TRAJECTORY--
--HEADED NORTH!

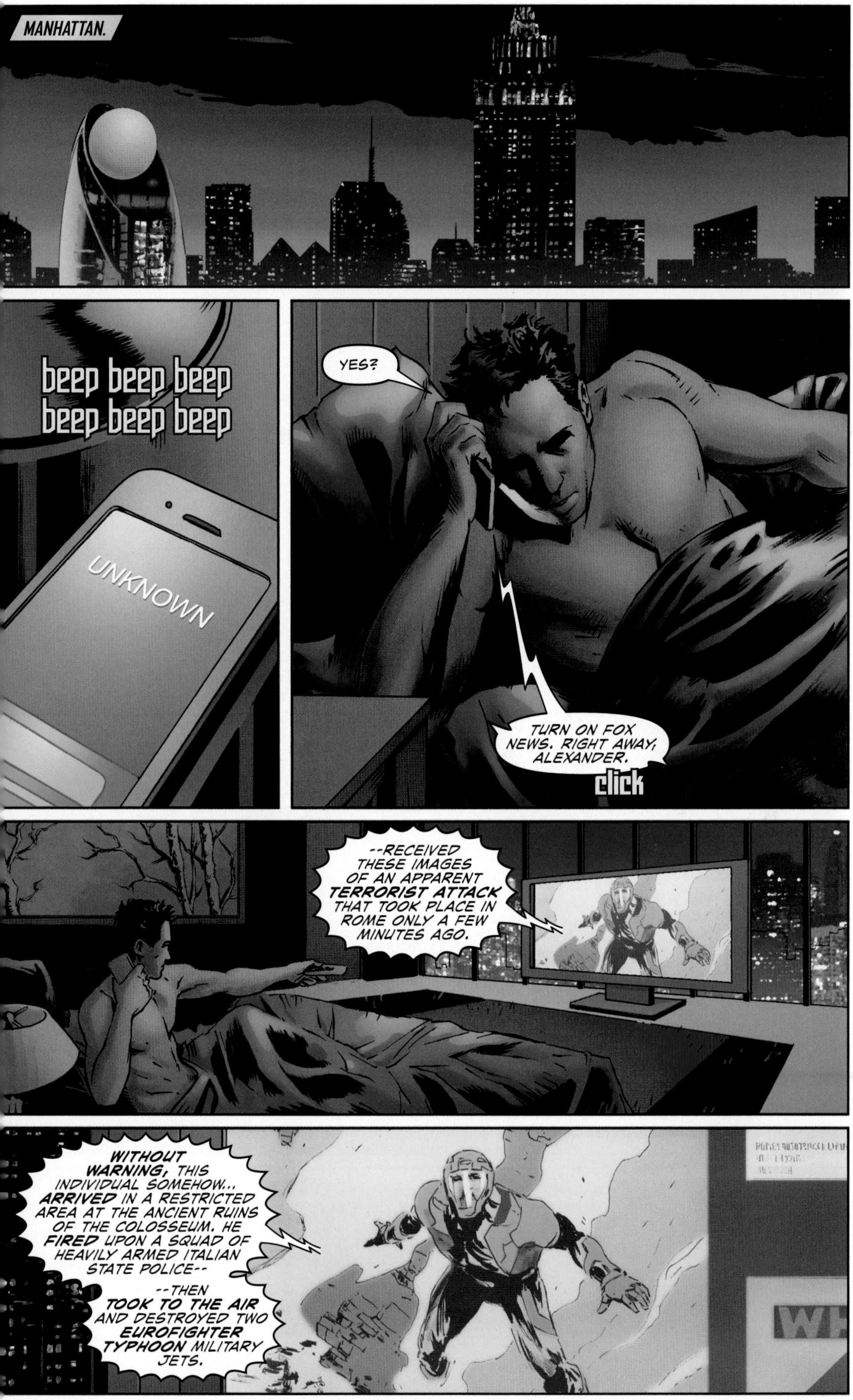

MANHATTAN.
beep beep beep
beep beep beep
UNKNOWN
YES?
TURN ON FOX NEWS. RIGHT AWAY, ALEXANDER.
click
--RECEIVED THESE IMAGES OF AN APPARENT TERRORIST ATTACK THAT TOOK PLACE IN ROME ONLY A FEW MINUTES AGO.
WITHOUT WARNING, THIS INDIVIDUAL SOMEHOW... ARRIVED IN A RESTRICTED AREA AT THE ANCIENT RUINS OF THE COLOSSEUM. HE FIRED UPON A SQUAD OF HEAVILY ARMED ITALIAN STATE POLICE--
--THEN TOOK TO THE AIR AND DESTROYED TWO EUROFIGHTER TYPHOON MILITARY JETS.

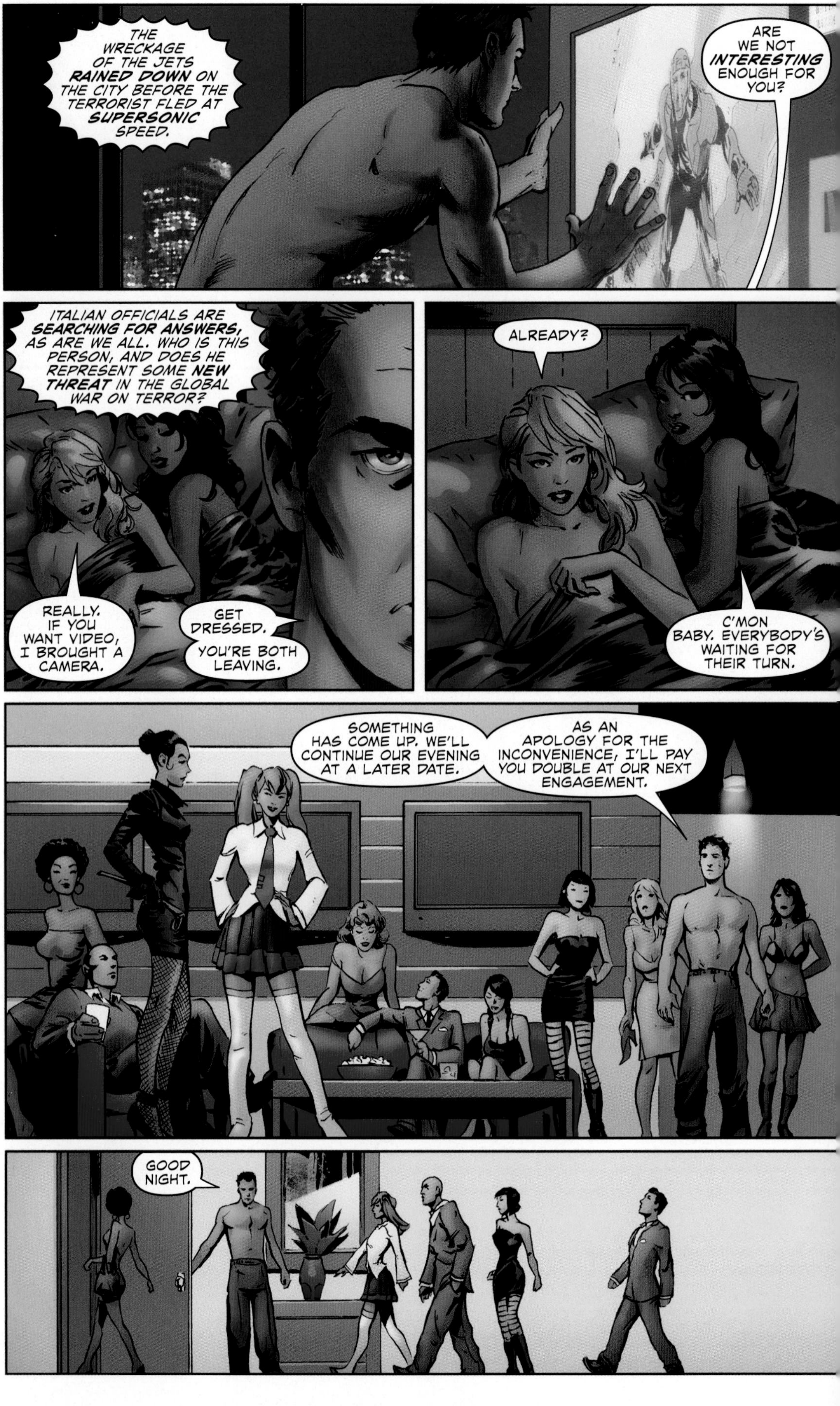
THE WRECKAGE OF THE JETS RAINED DOWN ON THE CITY BEFORE THE TERRORIST FLED AT SUPERSONIC SPEED.
ARE WE NOT INTERESTING ENOUGH FOR YOU?
ITALIAN OFFICIALS ARE SEARCHING FOR ANSWERS, AS ARE WE ALL. WHO IS THIS PERSON, AND DOES HE REPRESENT SOME NEW THREAT IN THE GLOBAL WAR ON TERROR?
REALLY. IF YOU WANT VIDEO, I BROUGHT A CAMERA.
GET DRESSED.
YOU'RE BOTH LEAVING.
ALREADY?
C'MON BABY. EVERYBODY'S WAITING FOR THEIR TURN.
SOMETHING HAS COME UP. WE'LL CONTINUE OUR EVENING AT A LATER DATE.
AS AN APOLOGY FOR THE INCONVENIENCE, I'LL PAY YOU DOUBLE AT OUR NEXT ENGAGEMENT.
GOOD NIGHT.

AN UNPROVOKED ATTACK IN THE *HEART* OF ONE OF THE WORLD'S MOST CHERISHED CITIES.

CIVILIANS *RUNNING* FOR THEIR LIVES. *SCREAMING* IN TERROR.

NO WORD ON THE *NUMBER OF* FATALITIES--

--BUT IT COULD BE AS HIGH AS A DOZEN, INCLUDING THE PILOT OF THIS *DOWNED FIGHTER JET.*

click

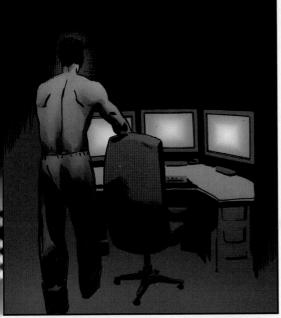

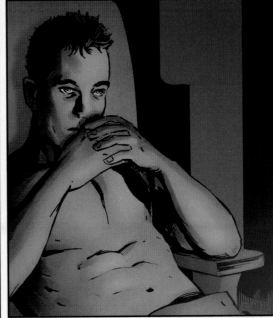

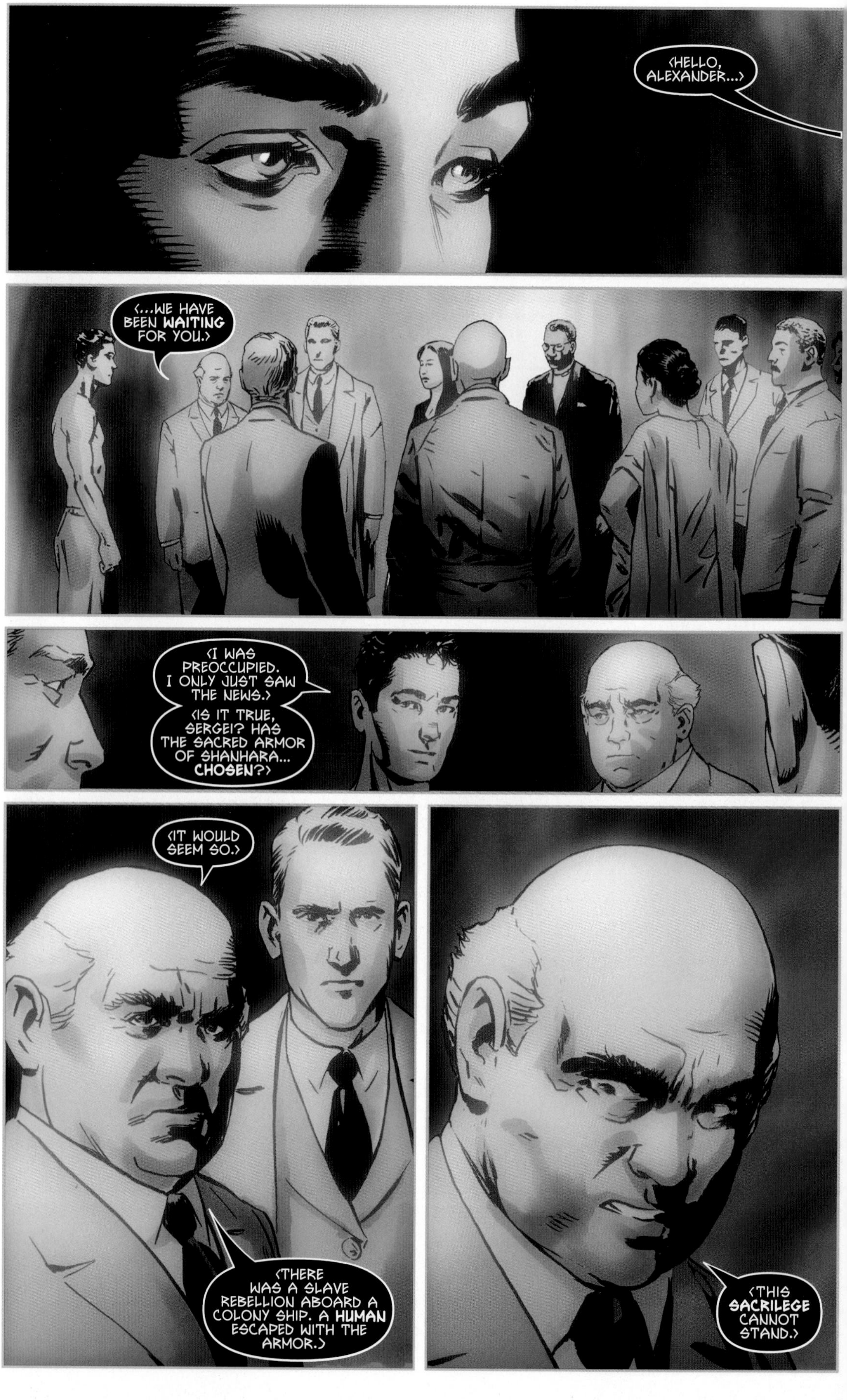
‹HELLO, ALEXANDER...›
‹...WE HAVE BEEN WAITING FOR YOU.›
‹I WAS PREOCCUPIED. I ONLY JUST SAW THE NEWS.›
‹IS IT TRUE, SERGEI? HAS THE SACRED ARMOR OF SHANHARA... CHOSEN?›
‹IT WOULD SEEM SO.›
‹THERE WAS A SLAVE REBELLION ABOARD A COLONY SHIP. A HUMAN ESCAPED WITH THE ARMOR.›
‹THIS SACRILEGE CANNOT STAND.›

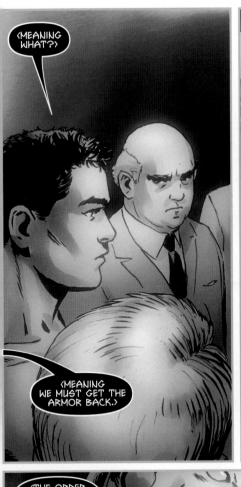

‹MEANING
WHAT?›

‹MEANING
WE MUST GET THE
ARMOR BACK.›

‹INVASION IS
IMMINENT. MY FLEET
WILL SOON TRAVEL
TO EARTH.›

‹A FLEET,
ADMIRAL?
COMING
HERE?›

‹THE ORDER
COMES DIRECTLY
FROM THE
COUNCIL.›

‹THE HUMANS
HAVE SEEN WHAT THE
ARMOR CAN DO. HOW LONG
BEFORE THEY START ASKING
WHERE IT CAME FROM?
WHY IT IS SUDDENLY
AMONG THEM?›

‹THE COUNCIL
HAS COMMANDED THAT
YOU USE YOUR INFLUENCE ON
EARTH TO RECLAIM THE ARMOR
AHEAD OF MY ARRIVAL.›

‹ONE OF YOU
MUST LEAD THE
EFFORT. WHO WILL
VOLUNTEER?›

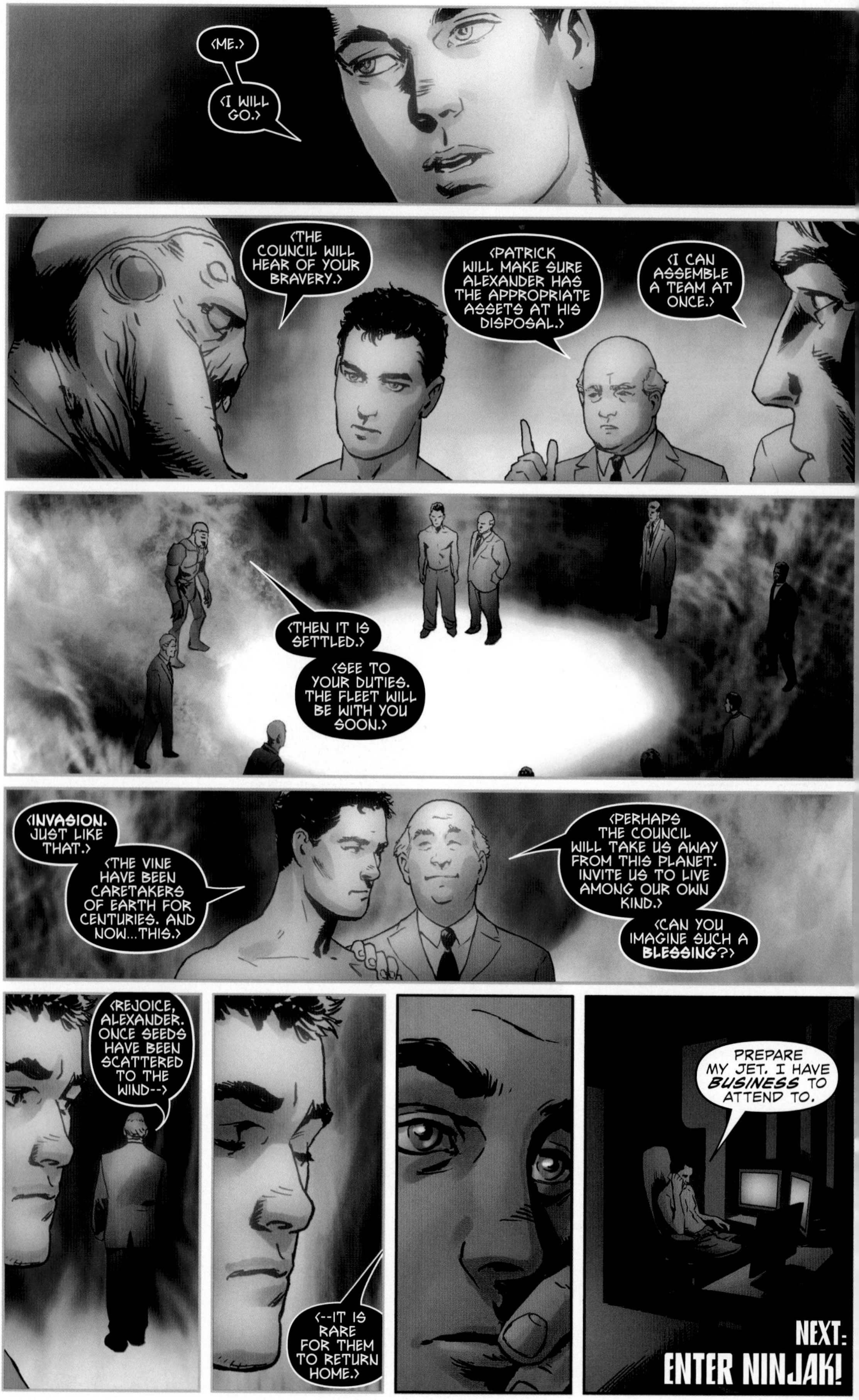

‹ME.›
‹I WILL GO.›
‹THE COUNCIL WILL HEAR OF YOUR BRAVERY.›
‹PATRICK WILL MAKE SURE ALEXANDER HAS THE APPROPRIATE ASSETS AT HIS DISPOSAL.›
‹I CAN ASSEMBLE A TEAM AT ONCE.›
‹THEN IT IS SETTLED.›
‹SEE TO YOUR DUTIES. THE FLEET WILL BE WITH YOU SOON.›
‹INVASION. JUST LIKE THAT.›
‹THE VINE HAVE BEEN CARETAKERS OF EARTH FOR CENTURIES. AND NOW...THIS.›
‹PERHAPS THE COUNCIL WILL TAKE US AWAY FROM THIS PLANET. INVITE US TO LIVE AMONG OUR OWN KIND.›
‹CAN YOU IMAGINE SUCH A BLESSING?›
‹REJOICE, ALEXANDER. ONCE SEEDS HAVE BEEN SCATTERED TO THE WIND--›
‹--IT IS RARE FOR THEM TO RETURN HOME.›
PREPARE MY JET. I HAVE BUSINESS TO ATTEND TO.
NEXT: ENTER NINJAK!

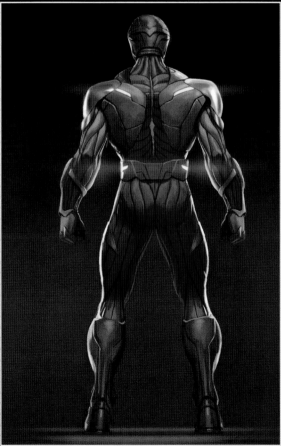

X-O MANOWAR
Final design by
JELENA KEVIC-DJURDJEVIC

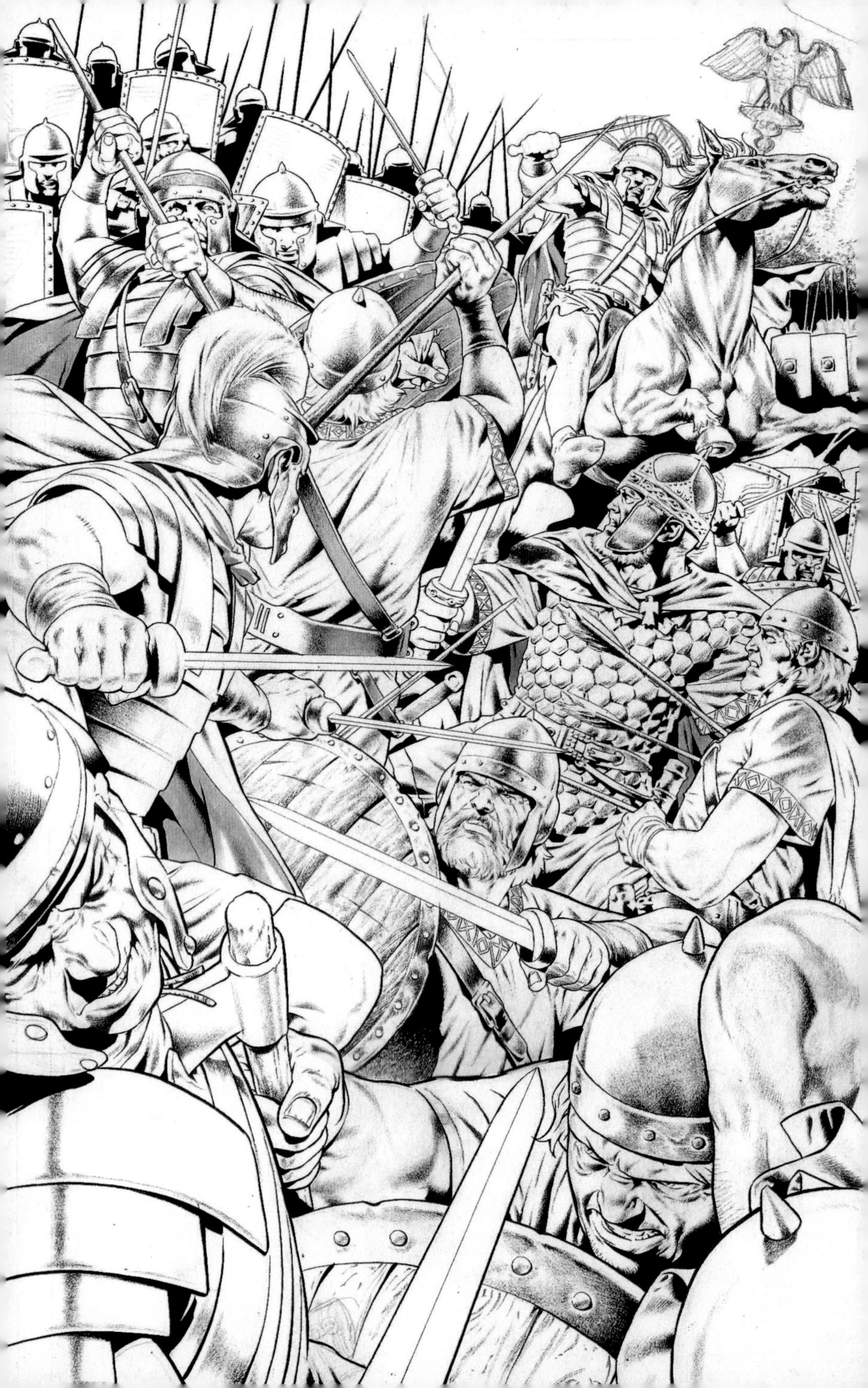

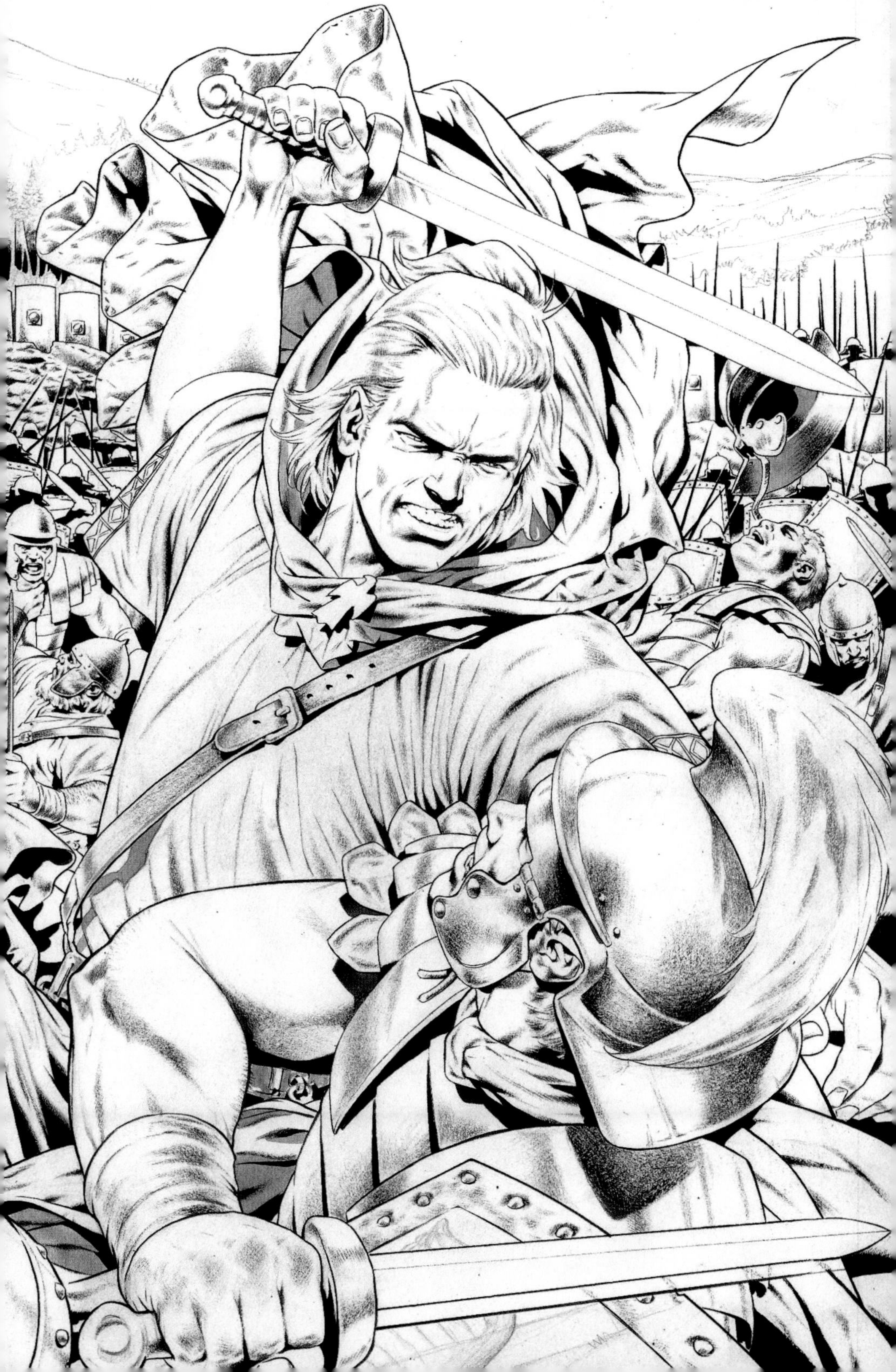

X-O MANOWAR #1 PULLBOX EXCLUSIVE VARIANT
Cover pencils by CARY NORD

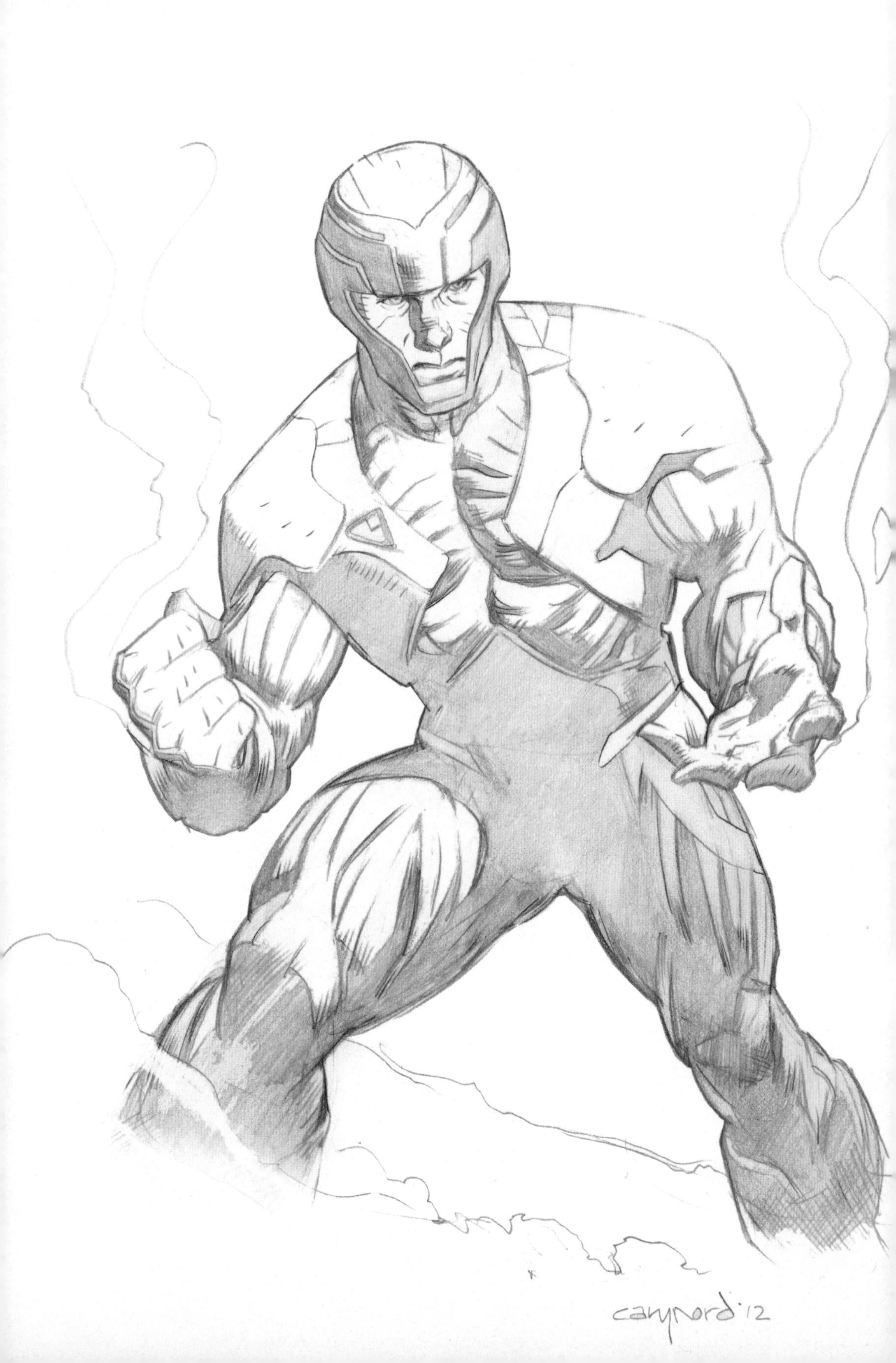
carynord '12

X-O MANOWAR #1 PULLBOX EXCLUSIVE VARIANT
Cover by CARY NORD and STEFANO GAUDIANO
with IAN HANNIN

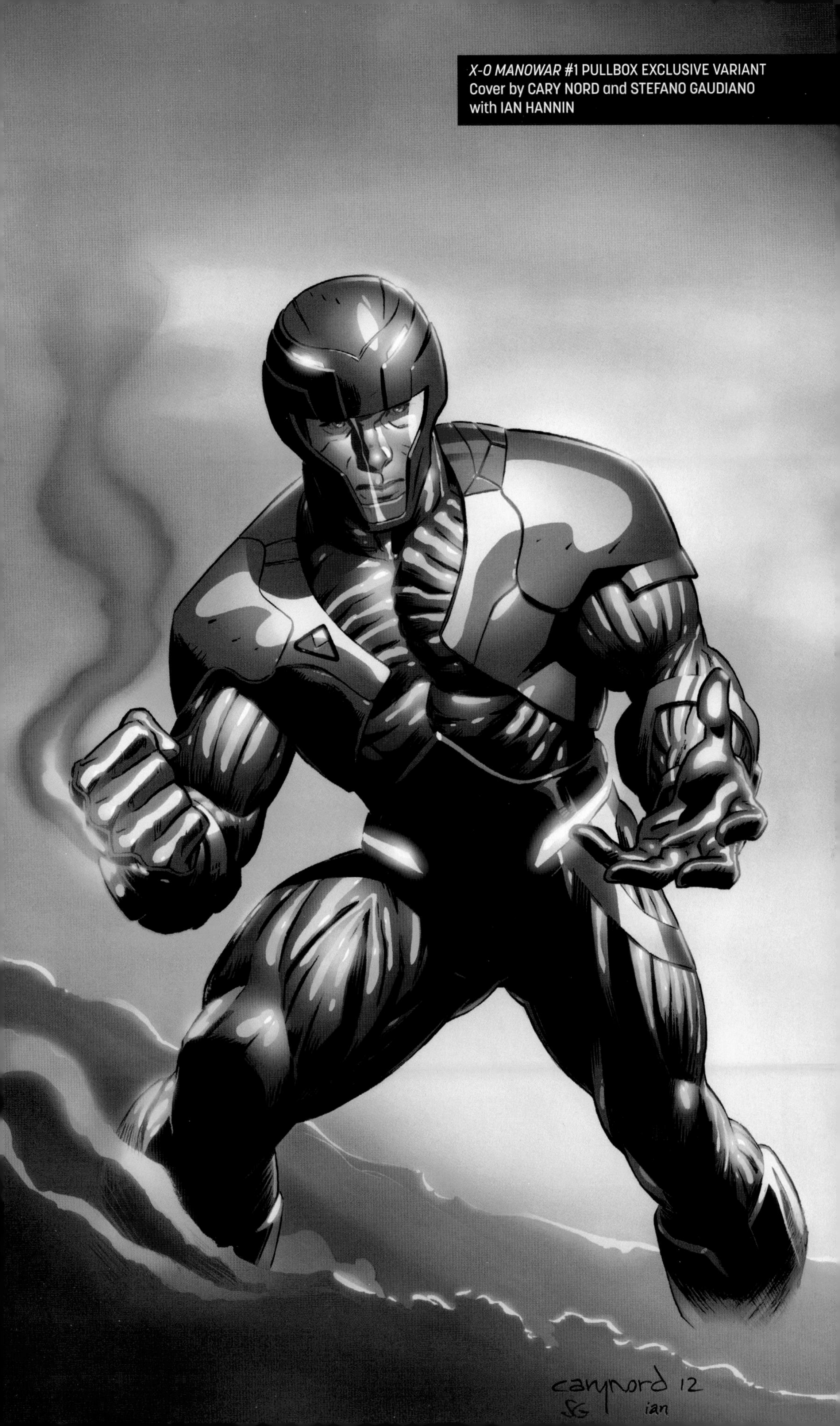

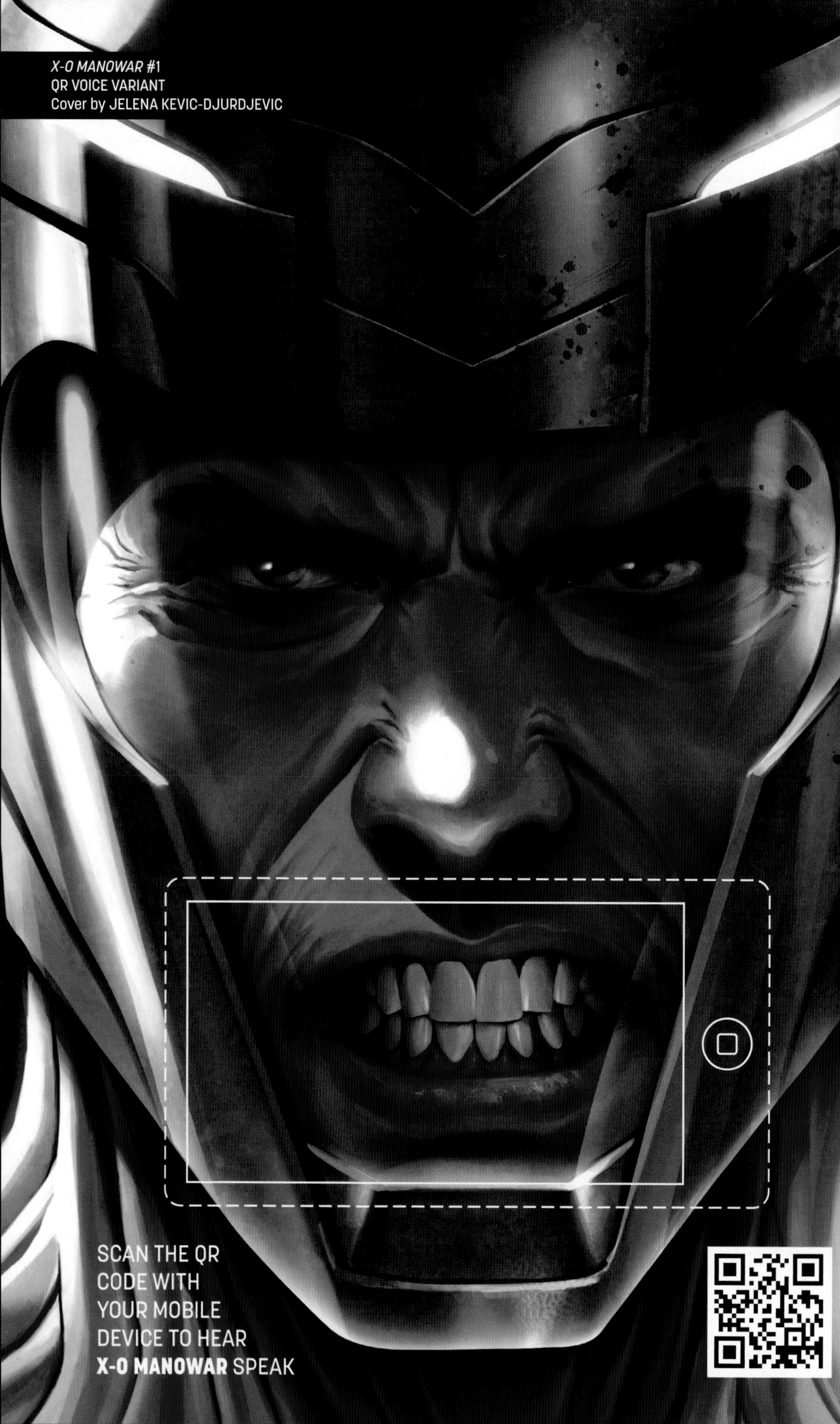
SCAN THE QR
CODE WITH
YOUR MOBILE
DEVICE TO HEAR
X-O MANOWAR SPEAK

X-O MANOWAR #1
QR VOICE VARIANT
Cover by JELENA KEVIC-DJURDJEVIC

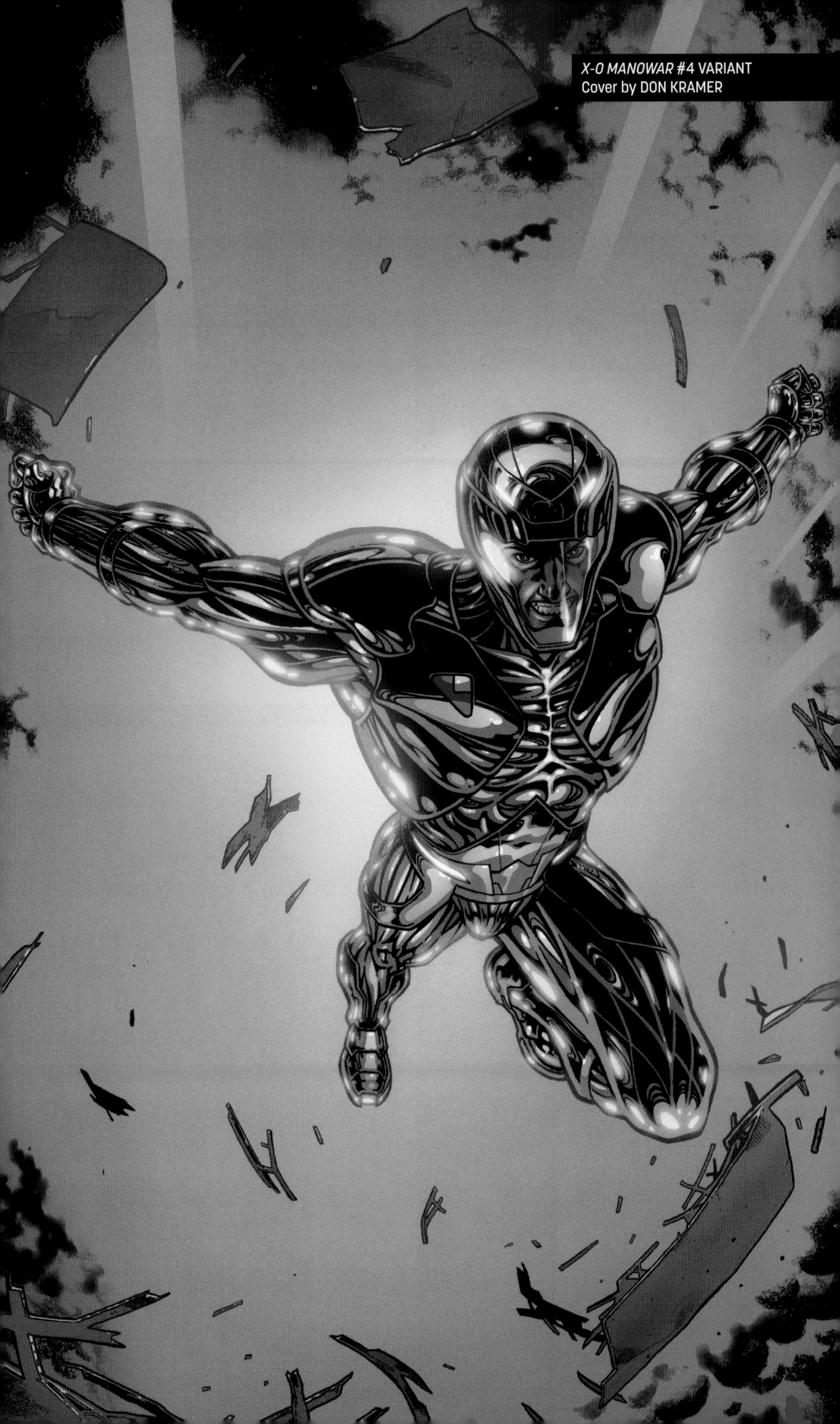

X-O MANOWAR #4 VARIANT
Cover by DON KRAMER

X-O MANOWAR
Designs by TREVOR HAIRSINE

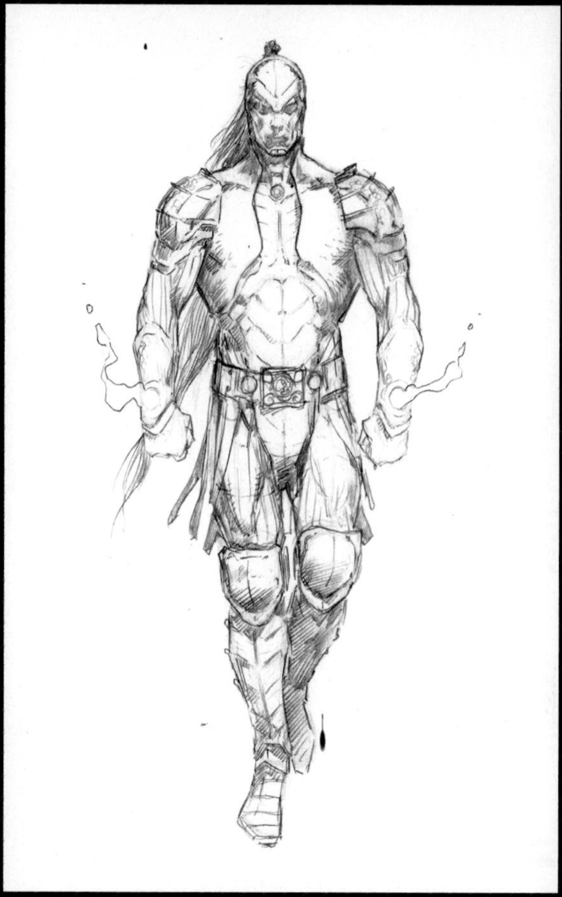

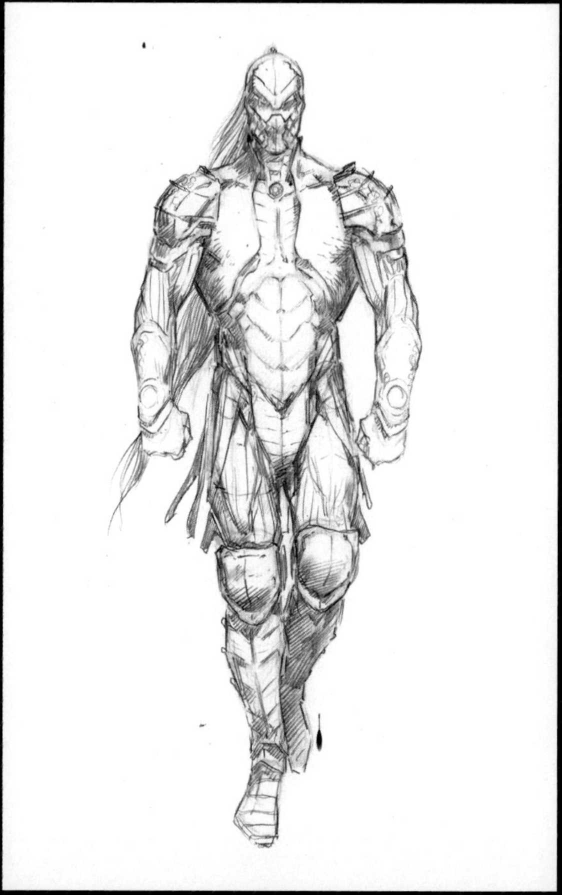

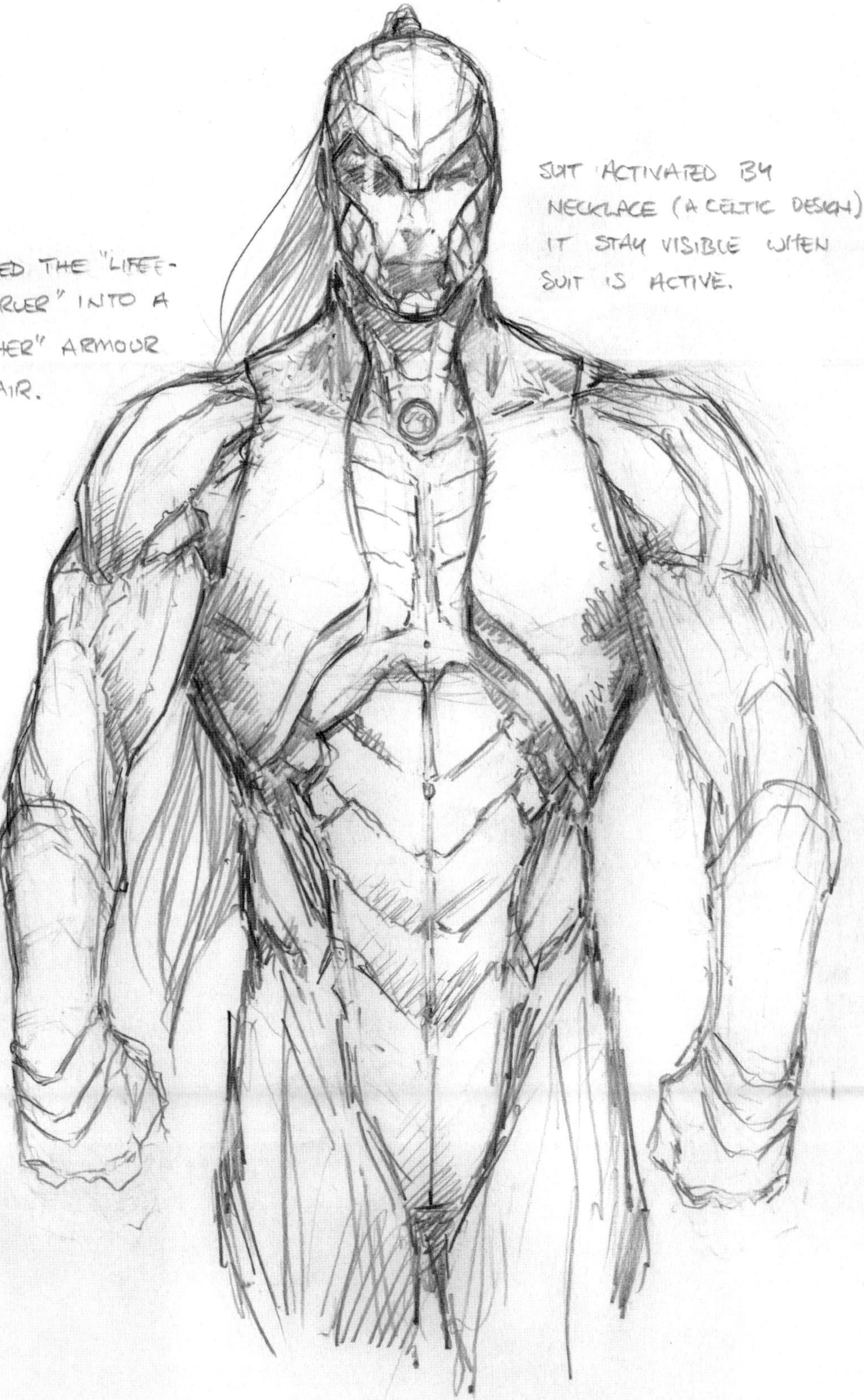
"PONY TAIL" TAKEN FROM CELTIC HELMET DESIGN
SUIT ACTIVATED BY NECKLACE (A CELTIC DESIGN) IT STAY VISIBLE WHEN SUIT IS ACTIVE.
SHAPED THE "LIFE-PRESERVER" INTO A "LEATHER" ARMOUR AFFAIR.

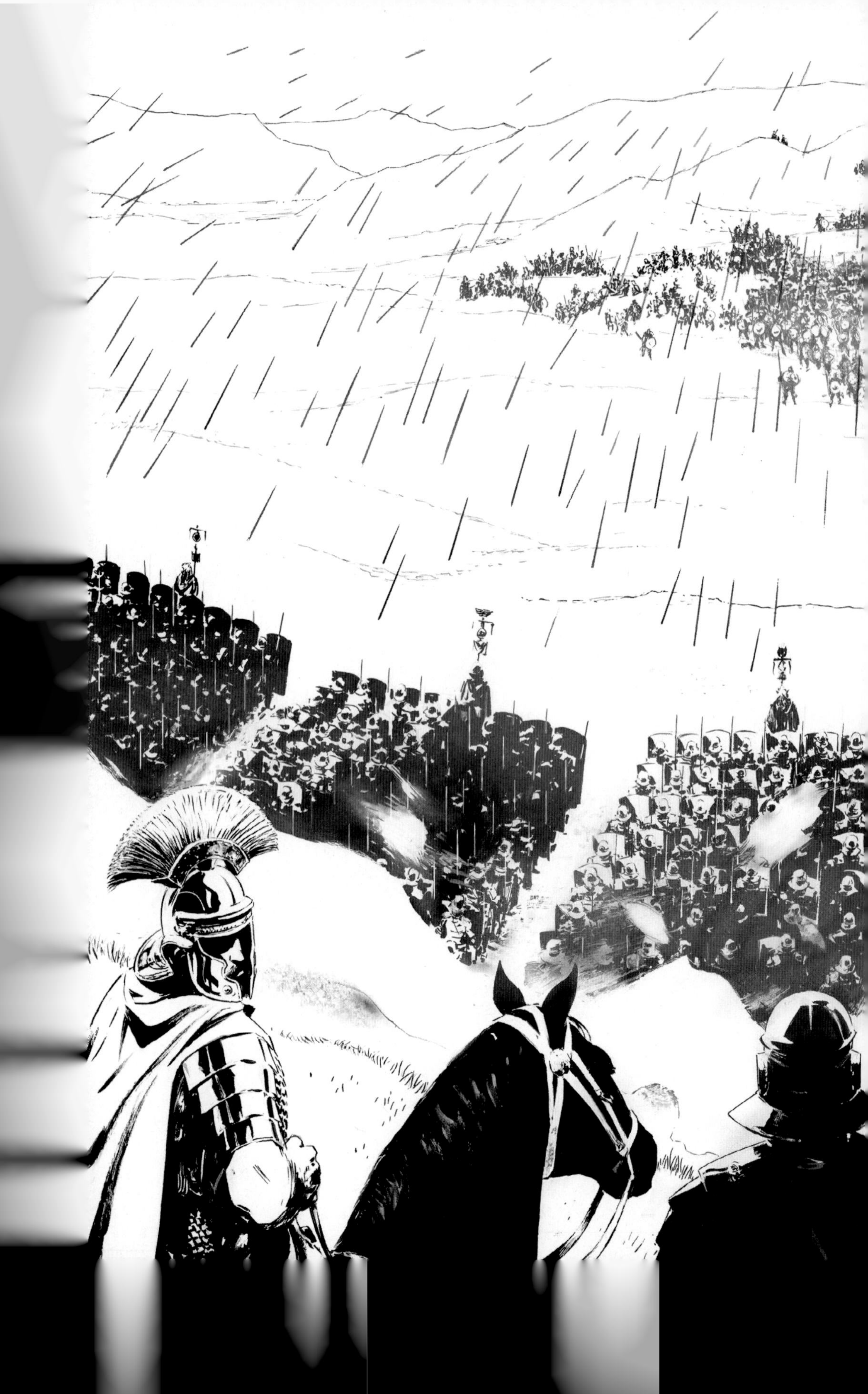

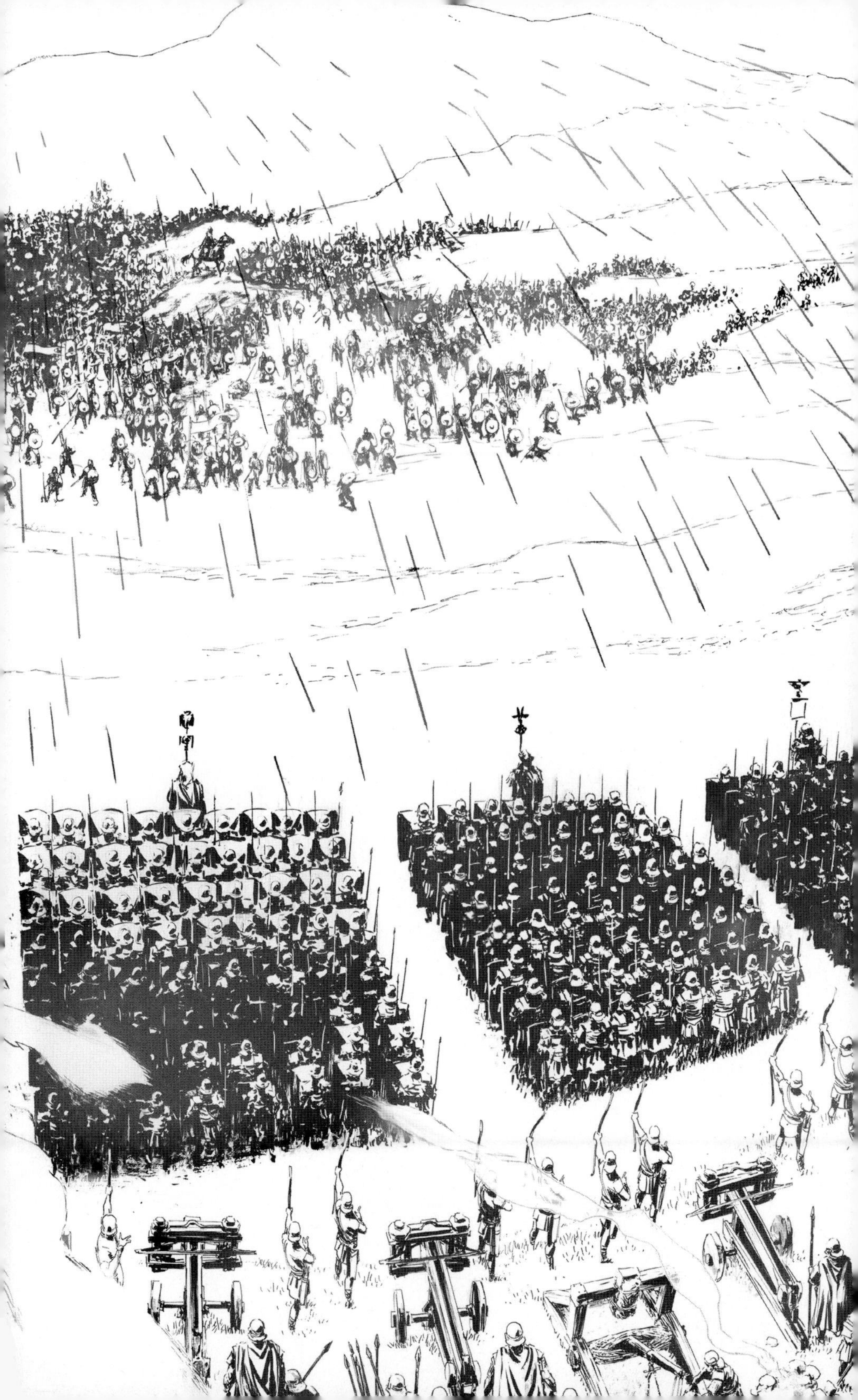

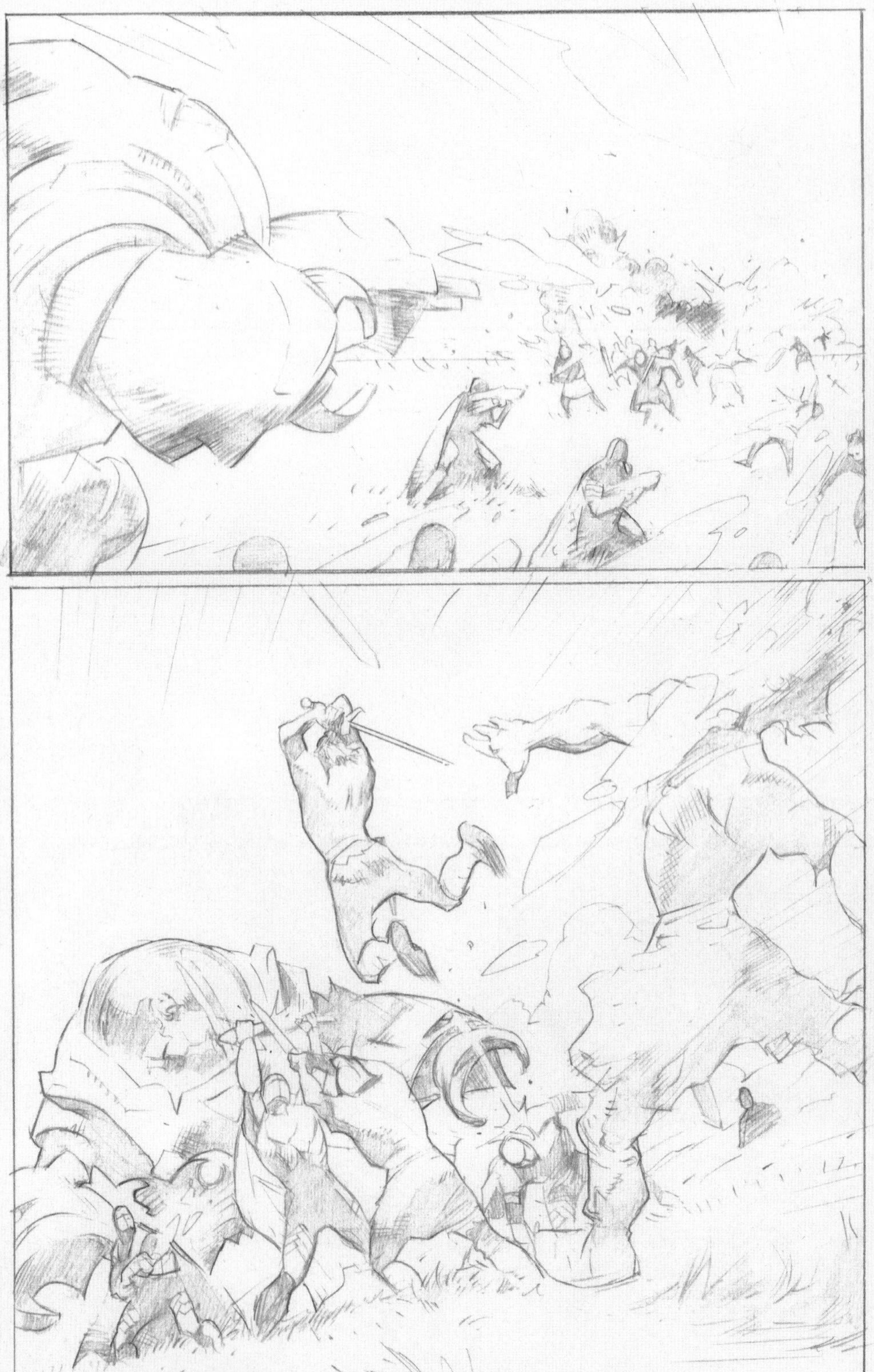

X-O MANOWAR #1, p. 17
Pencils by CARY NORD
Inks (facing) by STEFANO GAUDIANO

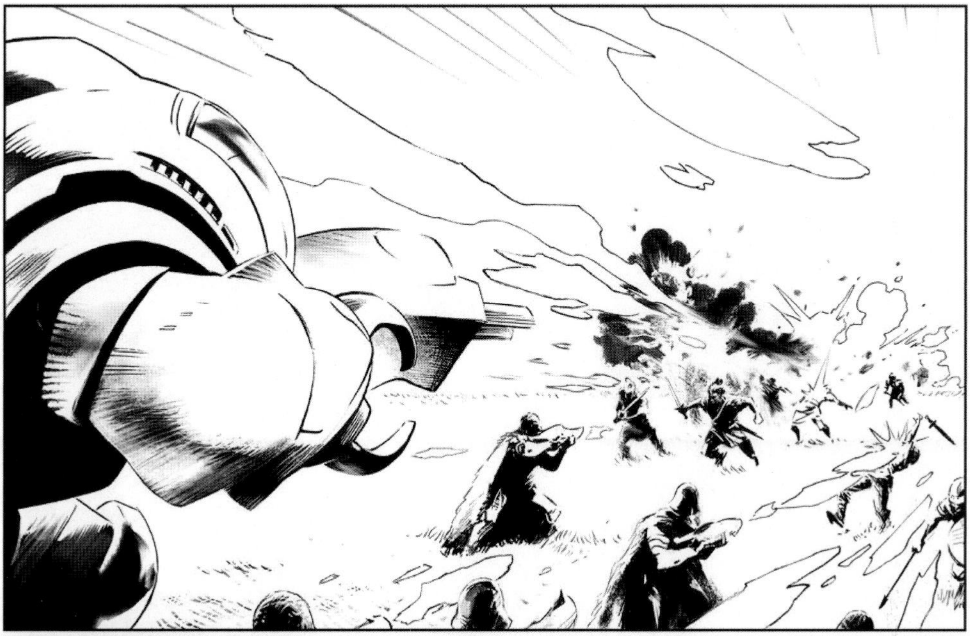
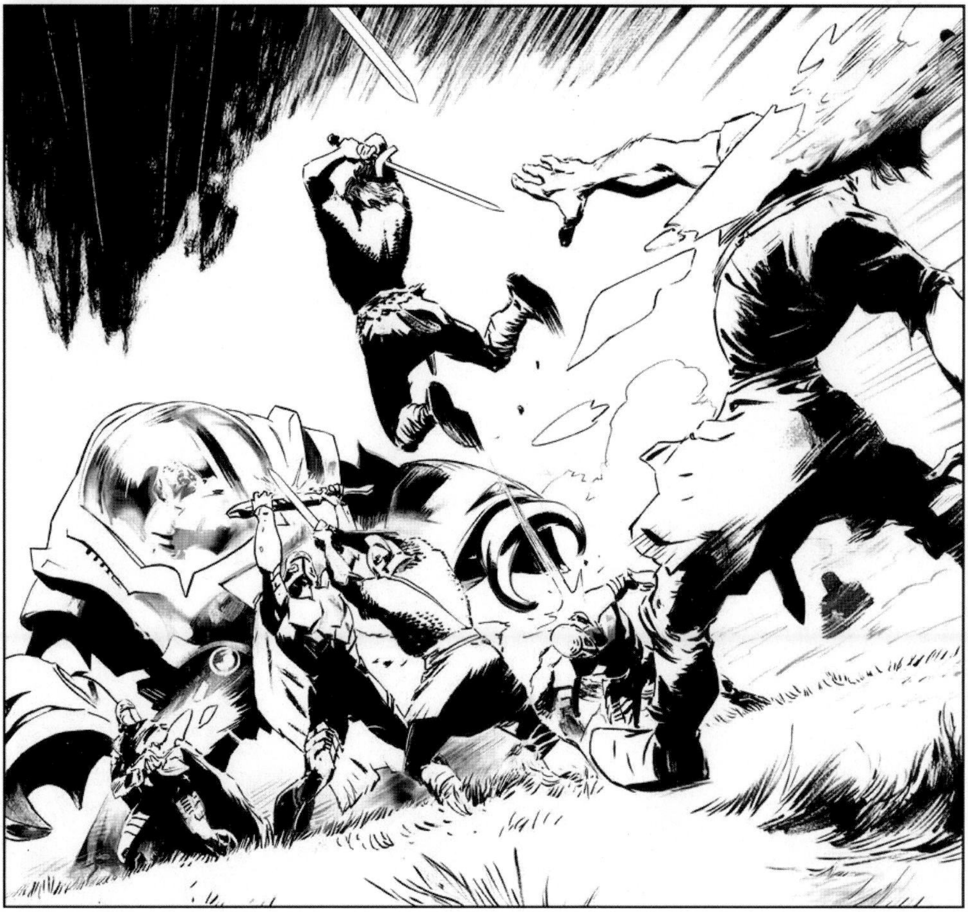

X-O MANOWAR #2, p.17
Pencils by CARY NORD
Inks by STEFANO GAUDIANO

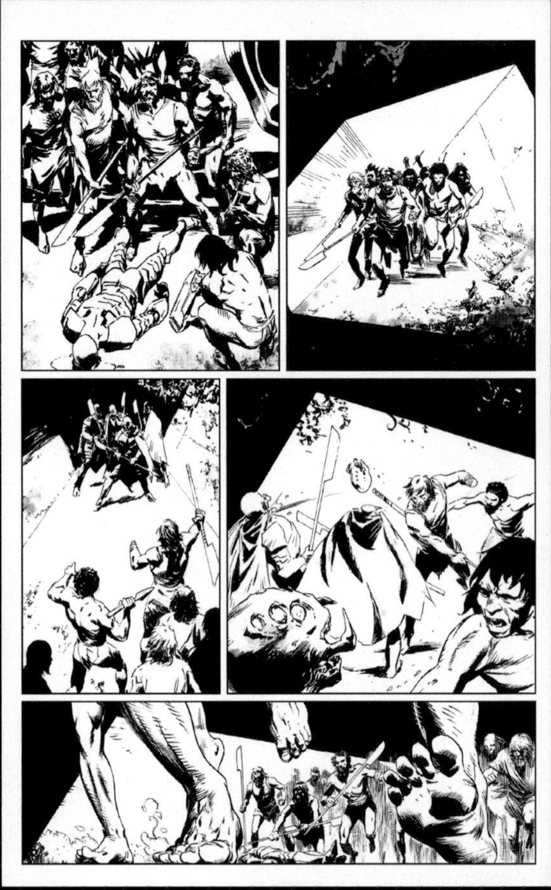

X-O MANOWAR #2, p.18
Pencils by CARY NORD
Inks by STEFANO GAUDIANO

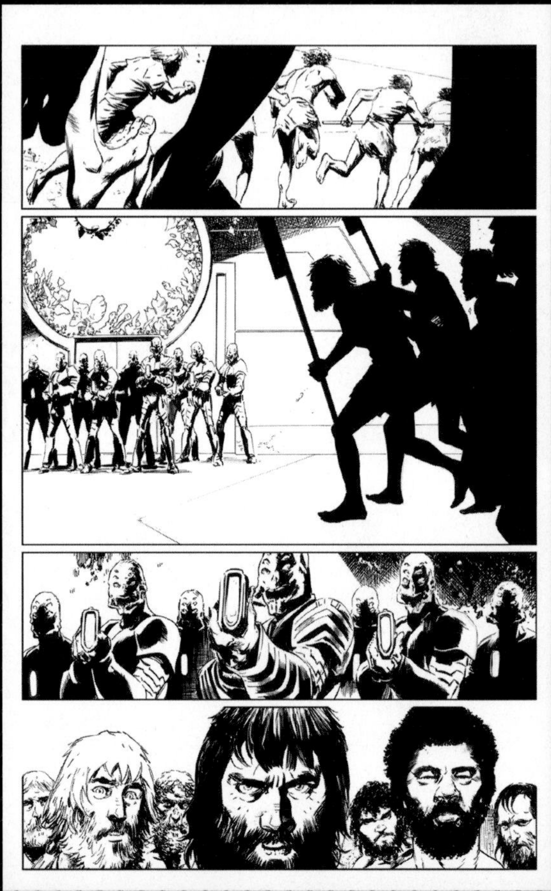

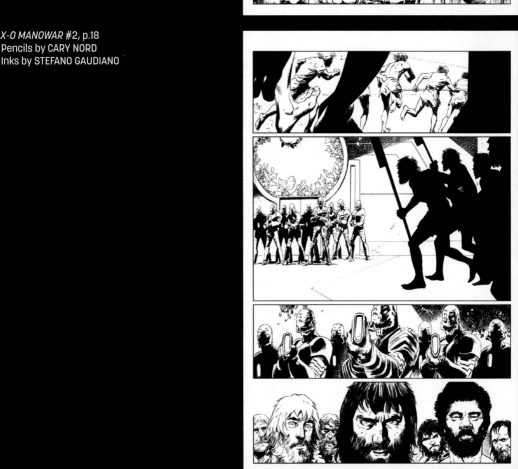

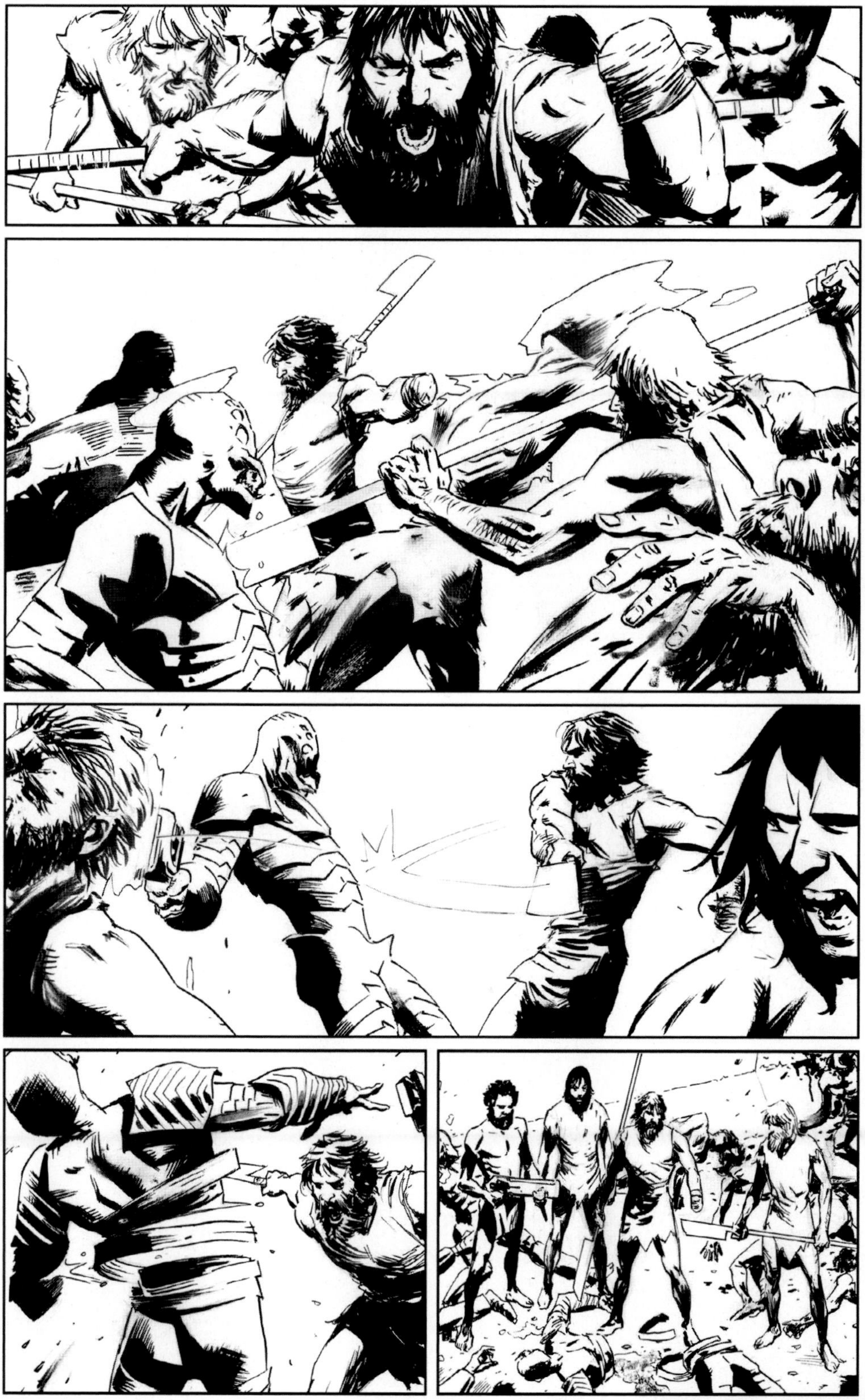

X-O MANOWAR #2, p.19
Pencils by CARY NORD
Inks by STEFANO GAUDIANO

EXPLORE THE VALIANT UNIVERSE

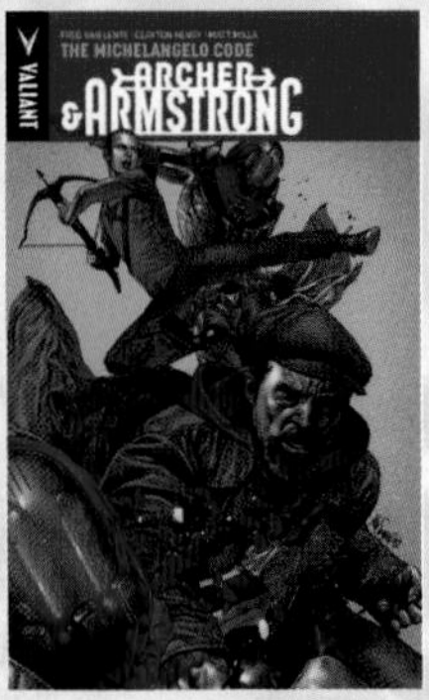
VALIANT
THE MICHELANGELO CODE
ARCHER & ARMSTRONG
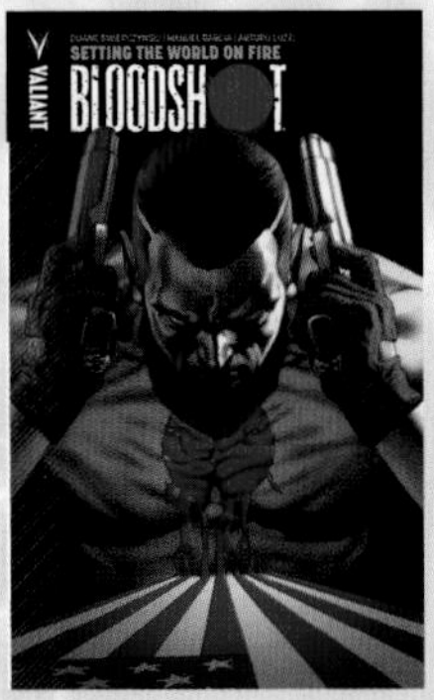
VALIANT
SETTING THE WORLD ON FIRE
BLOODSHOT
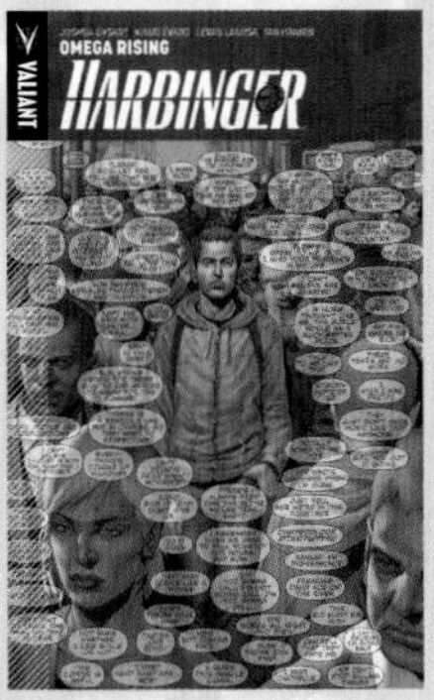
VALIANT
OMEGA RISING
HARBINGER
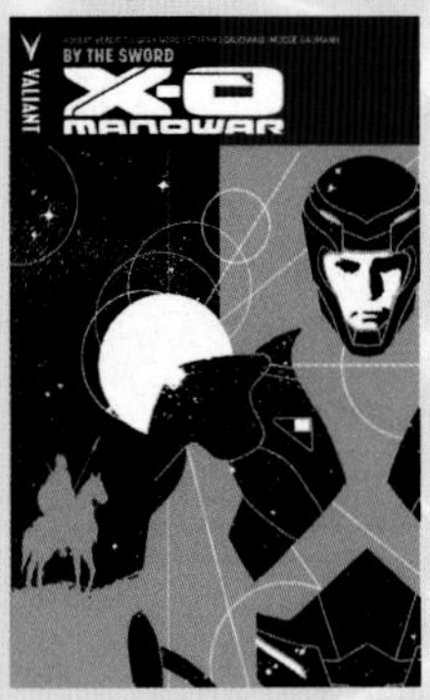
VALIANT
BY THE SWORD
X-O MANOWAR
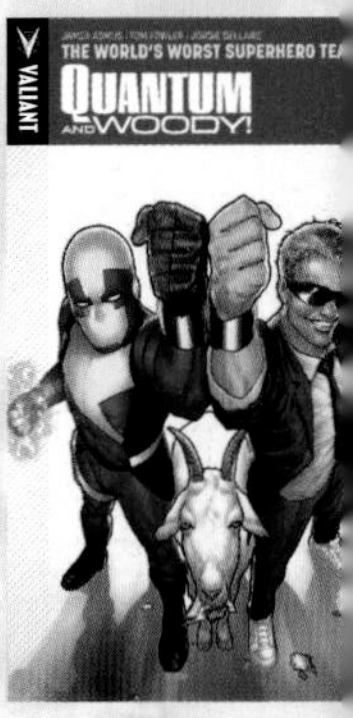
VALIANT
THE WORLD'S WORST SUPERHERO TEA
QUANTUM AND WOODY!

ARCHER & ARMSTRONG

Volume 1: The Michelangelo Code
ISBN: 9780979640988

Volume 2: Wrath of the Eternal Warrior
ISBN: 9781939346049

Volume 3: Far Faraway
ISBN: 9781939346148

Volume 4: Sect Civil War
ISBN: 9781939346254

Volume 5: Mission: Improbable
ISBN: 9781939346353

Volume 6: American Wasteland
ISBN: 9781939346421

Volume 7: The One Percent and Other Tales
ISBN: 9781939346537

ARMOR HUNTERS

Armor Hunters
ISBN: 9781939346452

Armor Hunters: Bloodshot
ISBN: 9781939346469

Armor Hunters: Harbinger
ISBN: 9781939346506

Unity Vol. 3: Armor Hunters
ISBN: 9781939346445

X-O Manowar Vol. 7: Armor Hunters
ISBN: 9781939346476

BLOODSHOT

Volume 1: Setting the World on Fire
ISBN: 9780979640964

Volume 2: The Rise and the Fall
ISBN: 9781939346032

Volume 3: Harbinger Wars
ISBN: 9781939346124

Volume 4: H.A.R.D. Corps
ISBN: 9781939346193

Volume 5: Get Some!
ISBN: 9781939346315

Volume 6: The Glitch and Other Tales
ISBN: 9781939346711

BLOODSHOT REBORN

Volume 1: Colorado
ISBN: 9781939346674

Volume 2: The Hunt
ISBN: 9781939346827

DEAD DROP

ISBN: 9781939346858

THE DEATH-DEFYING DOCTOR MIRAGE

ISBN: 9781939346490

the DELINQUENTS

ISBN: 9781939346513

DIVINITY

ISBN: 9781939346766

ETERNAL WARRIOR

Volume 1: Sword of the Wild
ISBN: 9781939346209

Volume 2: Eternal Emperor
ISBN: 9781939346292

Volume 3: Days of Steel
ISBN: 9781939346742

HARBINGER

Volume 1: Omega Rising
ISBN: 9780979640957

Volume 2: Renegades
ISBN: 9781939346025

Volume 3: Harbinger Wars
ISBN: 9781939346117

Volume 4: Perfect Day
ISBN: 9781939346155

Volume 5: Death of a Renegade
ISBN: 9781939346339

Volume 6: Omegas
ISBN: 9781939346384

HARBINGER WARS

Harbinger Wars
ISBN: 9781939346094

Bloodshot Vol. 3: Harbinger Wars
ISBN: 9781939346124

Harbinger Vol. 3: Harbinger Wars
ISBN: 9781939346117

EXPLORE THE VALIANT UNIVERSE

KICK
ME
UANTUM
WOODY
BY PRIEST & BRIGHT
1: KLANG

VALIANT
BATTLE FOR NEW JAPAN
RAI

VALIANT
THE VALIANT

VALIANT
THE DEATH-DEFYING
DOCTOR MIRAGE

VALIANT
DIVINITY

インピリアム
IPERIUM

e 1: Collecting Monsters
9781939346759

e 2: Broken Angels
9781939346896

INJAK

e 1: Weaponeer
9781939346667

e 2: The Shadow Wars
9781939346940

UANTUM WOODY!

ne 1: The World's Worst Superhero Team
9781939346186

ne 2: In Security
9781939346230

ne 3: Crooked Pasts, Present Tense
9781939346391

ne 4: Quantum and Woody Must Die!
9781939346629

UANTUM WOODY BY PRIEST & BRIGHT

e 1: Klang
9781939346780

e 2: Switch
9781939346803

e 3: And So...
9781939346865

e 4: The Return
9781682151099

RAI

Volume 1: Welcome to New Japan
ISBN: 9781939346414

Volume 2: Battle for New Japan
ISBN: 9781939346612

Volume 3: The Orphan
ISBN: 9781939346841

SHADOWMAN

Volume 1: Birth Rites
ISBN: 9781939346001

Volume 2: Darque Reckoning
ISBN: 9781939346056

Volume 3: Deadside Blues
ISBN: 9781939346162

Volume 4: Fear, Blood, And Shadows
ISBN: 9781939346278

Volume 5: End Times
ISBN: 9781939346377

Ivar, Timewalker

Volume 1: Making History
ISBN: 9781939346636

Volume 2: Breaking History
ISBN: 9781939346834

UNITY

Volume 1: To Kill a King
ISBN: 9781939346261

Volume 2: Trapped by Webnet
ISBN: 9781939346346

Volume 3: Armor Hunters
ISBN: 9781939346445

Volume 4: The United
ISBN: 9781939346544

UNITY (Continued)

Volume 5: Homefront
ISBN: 9781939346797

Volume 6: The War-Monger
ISBN: 9781939346902

THE VALIANT

ISBN: 9781939346605

VALIANT ZEROES AND ORIGINS

ISBN: 9781939346582

X-O MANOWAR

Volume 1: By the Sword
ISBN: 9780979640940

Volume 2: Enter Ninjak
ISBN: 9780979640995

Volume 3: Planet Death
ISBN: 9781939346087

Volume 4: Homecoming
ISBN: 9781939346179

Volume 5: At War With Unity
ISBN: 9781939346247

Volume 6: Prelude to Armor Hunters
ISBN: 9781939346407

Volume 7: Armor Hunters
ISBN: 9781939346476

Volume 8: Enter: Armorines
ISBN: 9781939346551

Volume 9: Dead Hand
ISBN: 9781939346650

Volume 10: Exodus
ISBN: 9781939346933

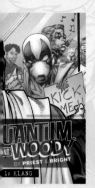

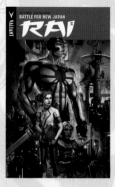

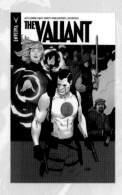

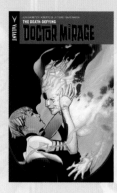

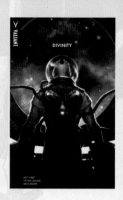

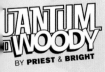

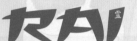

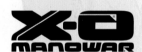

EXPLORE THE VALIANT UNIVERSE

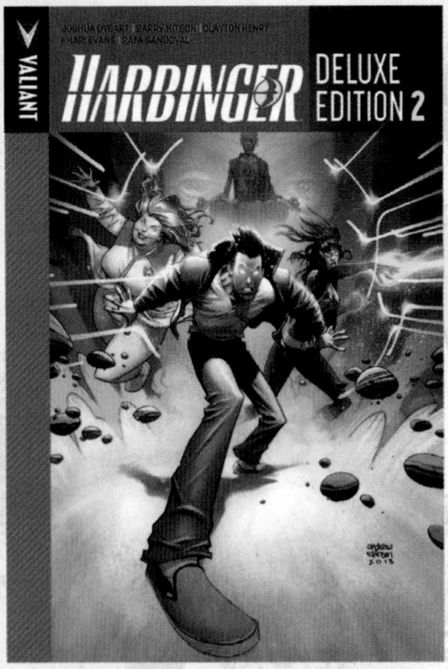
VALIANT
JOSHUA DYSART | BARRY KITSON | CLAYTON HENRY
KHARI EVANS | RAFA SANDOVAL
HARBINGER DELUXE EDITION 2

Omnibuses

Archer & Armstrong: The Complete Classic Omnibus
ISBN: 9781939346872
Collecting ARCHER & ARMSTRONG (1992) #0-26, ETERNAL WARRIOR (1992) #25 along with ARCHER & ARMSTRONG: THE FORMATION OF THE SECT.

Quantum and Woody: The Complete Classic Omnibus
ISBN: 9781939346360
Collecting QUANTUM AND WOODY (1997) #0, 1-21 and #32, THE GOAT: H.A.E.D.U.S. #1, and X-O MANOWAR (1996) #16

X-O Manowar Classic Omnibus Vol. 1
ISBN: 9781939346308
Collecting X-O MANOWAR (1992) #0-30, ARMORINES #0, X-O DATABASE #1, as well as material from SECRETS OF THE VALIANT UNIVERSE #1

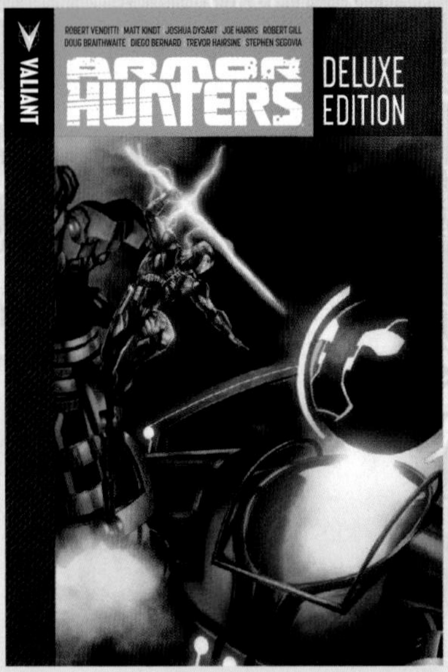
VALIANT
ROBERT VENDITTI | MATT KINDT | JOSHUA DYSART | JOE HARRIS | ROBERT GILL
DOUG BRAITHWAITE | DIEGO BERNARD | TREVOR HAIRSINE | STEPHEN SEGOVIA
ARMOR HUNTERS DELUXE EDITION

Deluxe Editions

Archer & Armstrong Deluxe Edition Book 1
ISBN: 9781939346223
Collecting ARCHER & ARMSTRONG #0-13

Archer & Armstrong Deluxe Edition Book 2
ISBN: 9781939346957
Collecting ARCHER & ARMSTRONG #14-25, ARCHER & ARMSTRONG: ARCHER #0 and BLOODSHOT AND H.A.R.D. CORPS #20-21.

Armor Hunters Deluxe Edition
ISBN: 9781939346728
Collecting Armor Hunters #1-4, Armor Hunters: Aftermath #1, Armor Hunters: Bloodshot #1-3, Armor Hunters: Harbinger #1-3, Unity #8-11, and X-O MANOWAR #23-29

Bloodshot Deluxe Edition Book 1
ISBN: 9781939346216
Collecting BLOODSHOT #1-13

Bloodshot Deluxe Edition Book 2
ISBN: 9781939346810
Collecting BLOODSHOT AND H.A.R.D. CORPS #14-23, BLOODSHOT #24-25, BLOODSHOT #0, BLOODSHOT AND H.A.R.D. CORPS: H.A.R.D. CORPS #0, along with ARCHER & ARMSTRONG #18-19

Divinity Deluxe Edition
ISBN: 97819393460993
Collecting DIVNITY #1-4

Harbinger Deluxe Edition Book 1
ISBN: 9781939346131
Collecting HARBINGER #0-14

Harbinger Deluxe Edition Book 2
SBN: 9781939346773
Collecting HARBINGER #15-25, HARBINGER: OMEGAS #1-3, and HARBINGER: BLEEDING MONK #0

Harbinger Wars Deluxe Edition
ISBN: 9781939346322
Collecting HARBINGER WARS #1-4, HARBINGER #11-14, and BLOODSHOT #10-13

Quantum and Woody Deluxe Edition Book 1
ISBN: 9781939346681
Collecting QUANTUM AND WOODY #1-12 and QUANTUM AND WOODY: THE GOAT #0

Q2: The Return of Quantum and Woody Deluxe Edition
ISBN: 9781939346568
Collecting Q2: THE RETURN OF QUANTUM AND WOODY #1-5

Shadowman Deluxe Edition Book 1
ISBN: 9781939346438
Collecting SHADOWMAN #0-10

Shadowman Deluxe Edition Book 2
ISBN: 9781682151075
Collecting SHADOWMAN #11-16, SHADOWMAN #13X, SHADOWMAN: END TIMES #1-3 and PUNK MAMBO #0

Unity Deluxe Edition Book 1
ISBN: 9781939346575
Collecting UNITY #0-14

The Valiant Deluxe Edition
ISBN: 97819393460986
Collecting THE VALIANT #1-4

X-O Manowar Deluxe Edition Book 1
ISBN: 9781939346100
Collecting X-O MANOWAR #1-14

X-O Manowar Deluxe Edition Book 2
ISBN: 9781939346520
Collecting X-O MANOWAR #15-22, and UNITY #1-4

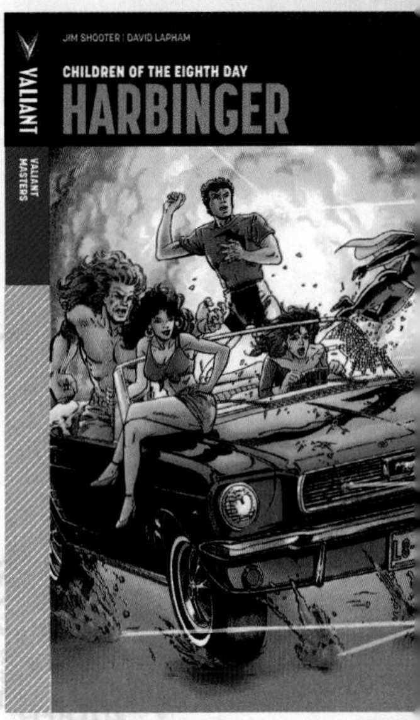
VALIANT
JIM SHOOTER | DAVID LAPHAM
CHILDREN OF THE EIGHTH DAY
HARBINGER
VALIANT MASTERS

Valiant Masters

Bloodshot Vol. 1 - Blood of the Machine
ISBN: 9780979640933

H.A.R.D. Corps Vol. 1 - Search and Destroy
ISBN: 9781939346285

Harbinger Vol. 1 - Children of the Eighth Day
ISBN: 9781939346483

Ninjak Vol. 1 - Black Water
ISBN: 9780979640971

Rai Vol. 1 - From Honor to Strength
ISBN: 9781939346070

Shadowman Vol. 1 - Spirits Within
ISBN: 9781939346018

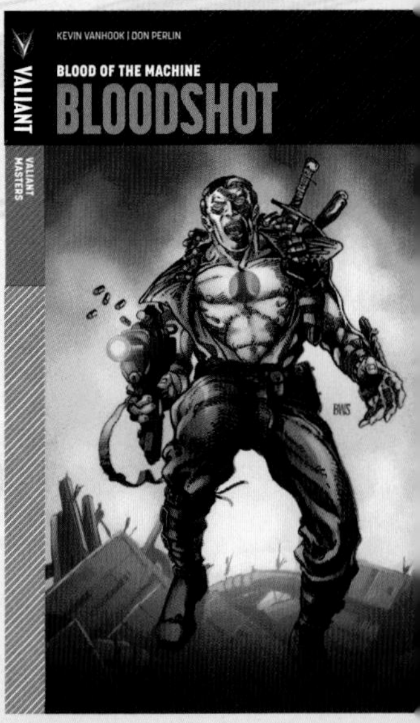
VALIANT
KEVIN VANHOOK | DON PERLIN
BLOOD OF THE MACHINE
BLOODSHOT
VALIANT MASTERS

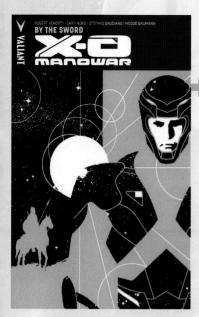

ROBERT VENDITTI | CARY NORD | STEFANO GAUDIANO | MOOSE BAUMANN
BY THE SWORD
X-O MANOWAR
VALIANT

X-O Manowar Vol. 1: By the Sword

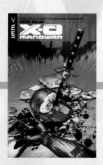

ENTER: NINJAK
X-O MANOWAR
VALIANT

X-O Manowar Vol. 2: Enter Ninjak

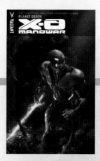

PLANET DEATH
X-O MANOWAR
VALIANT

X-O Manowar Vol. 3: Planet Death

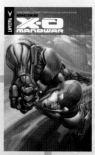

HOMECOMING
X-O MANOWAR
VALIANT

X-O Manowar Vol. 4: Homecoming

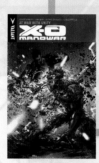

AT WAR WITH UNITY
X-O MANOWAR
VALIANT

X-O Manowar Vol. 5: At War With Unity

TO KILL A KING
UNITY
VALIANT

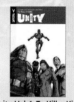

Unity Vol. 1: To Kill a King
(OPTIONAL)

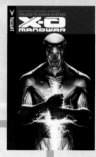

PRELUDE TO ARMOR HUNTERS
X-O MANOWAR
VALIANT

X-O Manowar Vol. 6: Prelude to Armor Hunters

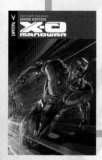

ARMOR HUNTERS
X-O MANOWAR
VALIANT

X-O Manowar Vol. 7: Armor Hunters

ARMOR HUNTERS
VALIANT

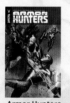

Armor Hunters
(OPTIONAL)

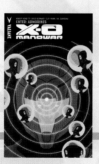

ENTER: ARMORINES
X-O MANOWAR
VALIANT

X-O Manowar Vol. 8: Enter: Armorines

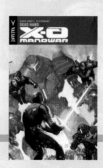

DEAD HAND
X-O MANOWAR
VALIANT

X-O Manowar Vol. 9: Dead Hand

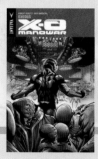

EXODUS
X-O MANOWAR
VALIANT

X-O Manowar Vol. 10: Exodus

"One of the industry's top superhero books."
-Complex

"Fantastic, action-packed storytelling that never fails to satisfy."
-IGN

Start at the beginning with the smash-hit series that relaunched the Valiant Universe!
From New York Times best-selling writer
ROBERT VENDITTI
And an all-star cast of artists including
CARY NORD, **LEE GARBETT**,
and **DIEGO BERNARD**

VALIANT

X-O MANOWAR

VOLUME TWO: **ENTER NINJAK**

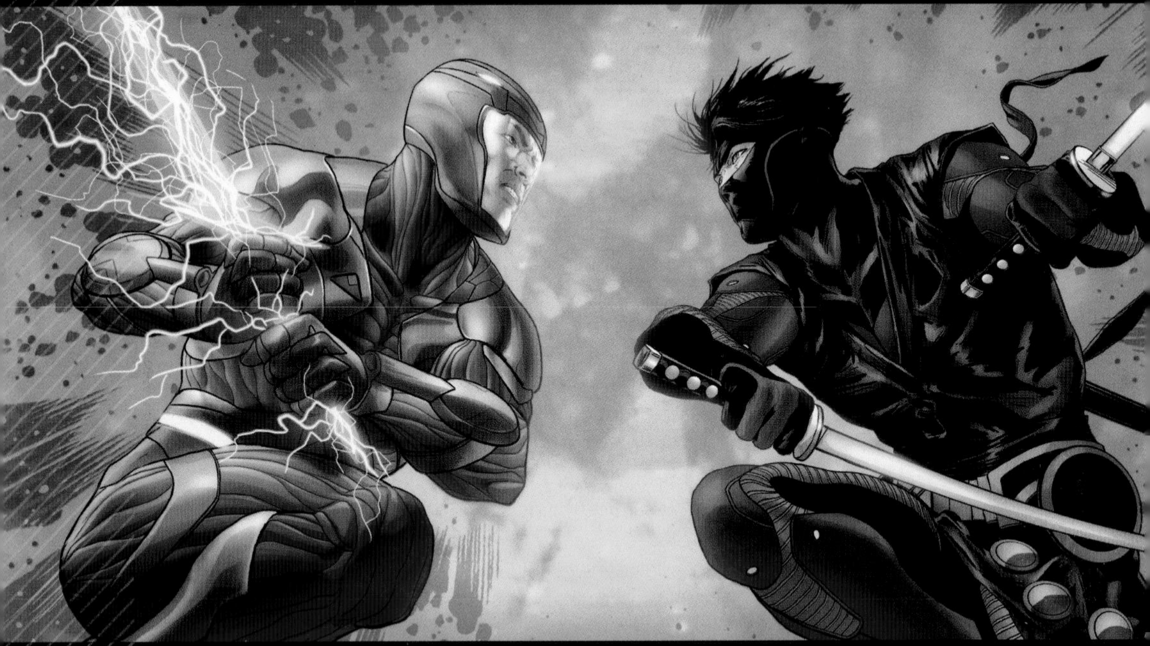

X-O MANOWAR COLLIDES WITH THE **VALIANT UNIVERSE**...
AND THE BRUTAL MI-6 OPERATIVE KNOWN ONLY AS **NINJAK**.

Aric of Dacia has landed on Earth – and now the world's most lethal intelligence agent has a new target. Hired by members of The Vine hidden deep within Earth's governments, Ninjak has been sent to bring back the Manowar armor at any cost. But what happens when the world's foremost weapons specialist engages the universe's most powerful weapon head on? And even if Ninjak can defeat the armor's defenses, does he stand a chance against the savage warrior that controls it? It's raw power versus stealth and cunning in the second thrilling volume of X-O Manowar – and the Valiant Universe will never be the same again.

X-O MANOWAR VOL. 2:
ENTER NINJAK

Collecting **X-O MANOWAR #5-8** by New York Times best-selling author Robert Venditti (*The Surrogates*) and acclaimed artist Lee Garbett (*Batman & Robin*).

TRADE PAPERBACK
ISBN: 978-0-9796409-9-5

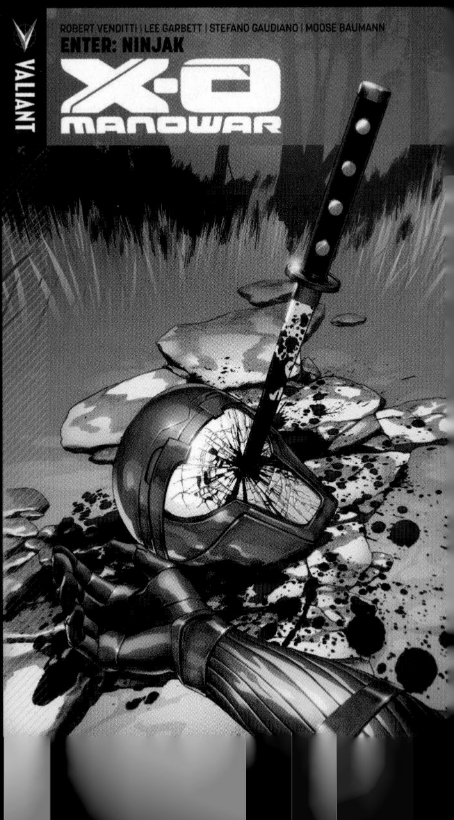
VALIANT
ROBERT VENDITTI | LEE GARBETT | STEFANO GAUDIANO | MOOSE BAUMANN
ENTER: NINJAK
X-O
MANOWAR